ANATOMY
OF DECEIT

ANATOMY OF DECEIT

An American Physician's First-hand Encounter
with the Realities of the War in Croatia

Jerry Blaskovich, M.D.

Dunhill Publishing, Co.
New York

A DUNHILL HARDCOVER EDITION
Published by:
Dunhill Publishing Company
A division of the Zinn Publishing Group
ZINN COMMUNICATIONS, INC. / NEW YORK

ISBN: 0-935016-24-4

Printed in the United States of America

Published in association with:
Atchity Entertainment International

Library of Congress Cataloging-in-Publication Data

Blaskovich, Jerry, 1934-
    Anatomy of deceit : an American physician's first-hand encounter with the
    realities if the war in Croatia / Jerry Blaskovich.
    p.   cm.
    ISBN 0-935016-24-4 (alk. paper)
    1. Blaskovich, Jerry, 1934-   . 2. Yugoslav War, 1991- —Croatia.
    2. Yugoslav War, 1991- —Atrocities. 4. Yugoslav War, 1991-
    -Personal narratives, American. 5. Physicians—United States-
    Biography.   I. Title.
DR1313.4.B57 1997
949.72—dc21   97-9433
                                               CIP

TABLE OF CONTENTS

Anatomy of Deceit is respectfully dedicated to the
countless dead and the survivors of genocide
taking place in former Yugoslavia and all victims
everywhere of misguided nationalism.

and

To the editors with the courage to publish
reporter's stories that were contrary to the State
Department's political agenda.

MY RUDE AWAKENING

My Rude Awakening: December 15, 1991

"We live in an age where people no longer produce or create their own opinions, but rather, where people reproduce opinions presented in the media."

———*Jean Baudrillard*
post modern critic, in Simulations.

On December 15, 1991, I was awakened at 5 A.M. by a phone call from the Foreign Press Bureau's chief, J.P Mackley. He was phoning from the combat zone: "I need your help there's been another massacre and we have bodies to prove it! In a place called Vocin near Podravska Slatkina. What's different is that the Cro Army is holding the terrain; the Serbs can't hide the evidence. Unfortunately the Croatian Army has started burying them."

"Stop them; dig up those already buried and put them on ice. Pressure the Croatian government to send pathologists from Zagreb's Medical School and work up each corpse as they would any murder case."

With this began my direct exposure to crimes committed by the Serbs in the name of nationalism and ethnic cleansing.

When Mackley called I was blissfully ensconced in the safe cocoon of the Lotus Land called California, though I was scheduled, on behalf of the Foreign Press Bureau, to leave for Croatia that very day to evaluate the health care conditions in Croatia and investigate allegations involving incidents of poison gas and chemical warfare. Throughout the country, the medical facilities had been devastated. Since the onset of hostilities in June, 1991, the Yugoslav Army's primary targets, aside from non-Serb civilians, had been hospitals, churches, and Croatian cultural treasures. By February 1992, 378 towns, 210 Catholic churches, and 160 historical buildings had been destroyed, 28 of which were designated by UNESCO as world cultural monuments, including the city of Dubrovnik. The loss and destruction of the large number of medical facilities seriously crimped health care delivery.

After Mackley told me about Vocin, and knowing the way other Serbian atrocities had been handled, the first thing I blurted out, after being suddenly awakened from my deep sleep, was for him to institute a forensic investigation. He confirmed my arrival time, and told me to get on it.

Going back to sleep proved impossible. My wife, already fearful for my safety on this trip, became completely unglued when I told her what had happened in Vocin. The previous evening she had discovered her growing fear was justified when she found a Kevlor bullet proof vest and helmet among my clothes, and told her the items were the required wear in the areas I would be visiting. Another suitcase brimmed with desperately needed anesthetics, antibiotics and anti-scabies medications. Mackley had previously informed me that scabies and crabs were endemic at the front lines, which was wherever Croatian civilian forces were resisting the Yugoslav Army. When the Yugoslav army began hostilities, they immediately rolled over everything in sight until the Croat civilian defenders started to resist with whatever weapons they had. These "frontlines" unexpectedly held (the Croats' motivation was, after all, to defend their families).

My wife Kathy had become painfully aware of the situation in former Yugoslavia when the island of Brac in the Adriatic Sea, where her family has its roots, had been bombed a few months earlier by the Yugoslav air force.

After Mackley's call, my wife knew she could not dissuade me. A commitment was a commitment. To the contrary, my resolve stiffened after hearing about this latest outrage. I was cognizant of the civilized world's moral inertia that followed previous Serbian atrocities.

The Croatia I would be going to would be a far cry from the Croatia where I studied medicine on the GI Bill in the 60s. During my years as a medical student in Zagreb the power of the Communist Party was at its apogee. It was a time when one had to talk in whispers about anything political to another person; if a third person was present, all political discussion stopped. You were never sure of who could be an UDBA (secret police) informant. National identity was suppressed to a point that the mere mention of the noun "Croatian" was viewed with suspicion.

The friendships made in my student days in Zagreb have persisted. It may be that true relationships, which develop in a communist society, are somehow even more endearing and enduring than those nurtured in democracies. With every new acquaintance, one always had to be on guard, both in deed, and in how one talked, because of the lurking threat that 'someone' might be working for UDBA (secret police). In my particular case, since I was a student from America, I was perceived by some as working for the CIA or on a more Machiavellian note, an agent provocateur for UDBA. But once one was trusted, the relationships grew and persisted, warts and all. One way to maintain that trust in a totalitarian society is never to volunteer information to anyone, outside your own circle, who your close friends are. Another feature of totalitarian societies is the preference not to name names of those who are present when certain events take place. Until the situation in Croatia is resolved, it is necessary that I continue to use such precaution.

In present day Croatia these fears no longer exist, nonetheless the mentality persists. Among my circle of friends the formula of compartmentalizing of friends has proven to be successful; by my definition, "successful" means that none of those friends has gone to jail or disappeared during the communist heyday. Friends from my student days have come to be judges, doctors, professors at the university—not only in medicine but in other fields, including architecture and engineering.

Since my student days, I had revisited former Yugoslavia numerous times. Although each visit had been interesting and a learning experience about new facets of life under communism, none of my visits were of any political consequence. This trip was my first in an official capacity. Yet, by coincidence, I was fortunate enough to be in Zagreb on the two most historic days in contemporary Croatian history: the Croatian Communist Party delegates walking out of the Yugoslav Communist Party Congress in Belgrade and the Croatian Sabor (Parliament) voting to secede from Yugoslavia. When I witnessed the walkout in January 1990, my parasympathetic system response went into overdrive.

I immediately realized it to be the death knell for Yugoslavia. Anything that happened after this could only be anti-climatic. When the momentous event took place in Belgrade, I was watching television in Zagreb with a number of my closest friends. It would be an understatement to say that everybody was shocked; even those who had access to the workings of the Communist Party at the highest levels were flabbergasted.

Few of my Croatian friends realized at the time the ramifications of the walkout in Belgrade. Perhaps they were too close to the forest to see the trees—possibly, if they had been vocal it might have placed them in jeopardy; they may have feared that somehow the power and wrath of the Communist Party could rain upon them.

Following the parliament vote on February 21, 1991, the euphoria on the streets of Zagreb had no bounds. My wife and I had been in Zagreb to celebrate our 25th wedding anniversary. On Zagreb's main square, Trg Ban Jelacic, everyone was embracing or extending hands in congratulations. It was akin to *Life* magazine pictures I'd seen of Times Square in New York City following V-E day. Only one thing dampened the scene for us. My wife ran into a man, an ex-army officer from her hometown, whom she had not seen in years. After warm greetings and comments about the parliament vote were exchanged, he predicted that the Serbs would not give up Croatia easily nor would they allow the Croats their self-determination without a great deal of blood being shed. How right he proved to be!

When the Croatian parliament voted to secede from the Yugoslav federation, Slovenia's parliament also voted the same way. The federal government's (read Serbian) response to Slovenia secession was a tacit "good riddance;" but the Croatian resolution was greeted in Serbia with consternation, and immediately labeled "nationalistic." The federal government's response, retrospectively, portended the Serbs' true feelings, as exemplified by what, transpired in the facts of the subsequent months.

Although I hadn't been to Croatia since the Yugoslav army unilaterally initiated their aggressive acts, I was nonetheless acutely aware of what was happening there. When I visited Croatia in February, 1991, there had been rare, isolated incidents of aggression. But within a few days after I left, incidents instigated by the Serb rebels steadily increased, and these rebels became more and more brazen when they were abetted by the Yugoslav army. The aggression reached its crescendo after the army started attacking Croatian cities. Between February and the time I received Mackley's phone call in mid-December, the city of Vukovar had fallen to the Serbs and Dubrovnik besieged for months. Vukovar's dead lay buried under heaps of rubble.

I couldn't reconcile the vast discrepancy between what I knew and what I was watching on CNN and reading in the newspapers. The large number of atrocities being committed by the Yugoslav army and Chetniks, the Serbs' paramilitary force, on civilian Croats were ill-reported. And if they were reported at all, the articles and broadcasts were loaded with half truths.

Prior to the fall of communism in former Yugoslavia, my life style could have been best described as typical for a middle American. My existence centered on my family and I was happy practicing medicine in my specialty of dermatology. Although concerned about America's growing drug problem, illiteracy, and falling educational standards, I could not have, by no stretch of imagination, been considered an activist. To the contrary, I was apolitical and content with the superficiality of the news: the visual and sound bytes from television, the *Los Angeles Times*, the local "fish wrapper" *San Pedro News Pilot*, and sporadically *US News and World Report*. Naively I believed in the sacred responsibility of the media that could be trusted to deliver the truth.

The hostage crises in Iran during President Jimmy Carter's and Secretary of State Cyrus Vance's watch, however, unequivocally changed the direction of my life. Since the media offered more confusion than explanation about what Shi'ites, Sunnis, or whatever any other sects they cited were all about, I took a course at UCLA to get a better understanding. Before I knew it, I had the tiger by the tail and couldn't let go. I was so intrigued I decided to pursue the subject further. While maintaining a full time practice and caring for my patients, I took the required classes at UCLA, as well as all the available courses in Balkan history, and ended up getting a masters degree in Islamic art history.

Since the 1960s I had been a keen student of Yugoslav affairs, but once the various republics started to make overtures toward self-determination in the late 1980s, my readings increased markedly. Aside from having a number of close friends in Croatia who kept me informed, I received faxes of a newsletter from Croatia's Ministry of Health, *Facts About Croatia*. Although issued by a government agency, this newsletter gave the most objective information about the subject. The information I had at my disposal, derived from a variety of sources, enhanced by my background in history, kept me abreast about the events occurring in Croatia.

When the situation in former Yugoslavia reached the crises stage, I knew Croatia would be in dire straits, by every standard of measurement. Croatia, aside from being ill-equipped for a war, was economically devastated; Serbia had confiscated Yugoslavia's assets, including all its foreign monetary reserves. As the Yugoslav army regiments pulled out of Croatian cites and towns, they took with them everything, even the toilets out of the barracks, or whatever wasn't nailed down. Medically speaking, too, Croatia was a disaster in the making. When the first Yugoslav shells fired in 1991, I immediately began soliciting friends and medical colleagues for contributions to help implement humanitarian aid. The Croatian ministry of health sent updated lists of desperately needed medical supplies that I undertook to send to the devastated areas.

From September to December, 1991, a number of reports had claimed that the Serbs were using poison gas in some of their air attacks on civilian targets. Even Croatia's capital, Zagreb, was not exempt from air attacks. Following ten days of air raid alerts, Yugoslav MIGs fired missiles into the very heart of the city. They hit the parliament and presidential buildings on September 7, 1991. Croatia's president Franjo Tudjman; the Yugoslav federation president

Stipe Mesic; and Yugoslavia's Prime Minister Ante Markovic, escaped injury. It seems more than coincidental that the attack came at a time when the highest ranking Croatian leaders in the Yugoslav government were attending a summit conference with Croatia's president. The air attack may have been the Serbs' way of sending a message to the Croatian parliament, for that very same morning the parliament's agenda was to vote for full independence, which didn't take effect until 4 months later.

Between the air attacks and the certain knowledge that the Serb forces were committing atrocities in the areas they had conquered, the rumor mills among the population were working overtime. The reported gas attacks had tremendous psychological ramifications on the Croatian citizenry. Each time a plane flew overhead (Croatia had no planes) it would elicit a degree of panic.

It enraged me that, though *all* Serb aggressive actions during the conflict in Croatia had so far been directed *only* at civilians, the Western media kept making it sound as though the Yugoslav Army (JNA) and the Serb paramilitary forces were facing a hostile and formidable Croatian army.

I knew very well that Croatia, for the first two years of the conflict, had neither a national army nor any organization that could, in the wildest imagination, be considered an "army." The Croatian defenders were auxiliary policemen or local civilians trying to protect their families. They were, in the strictest sense, analogous to the Minutemen who fought the British in the American Revolution. And like them, the largest weapons at their disposal were hunting rifles.

The big league world media had a long and cozy relationship with Belgrade, and seemed to relentlessly justify the JNA's actions as a effort to protect the Serb minority in Croatia. But, in carrying out this so called "defensive policy," one of the JNA's first actions was to occupy Slavonia, an eastern province in Croatia, and to expel most of the Croatians and Hungarians who made up the majority population in the villages there. Once this was accomplished, the Yugoslav army proceeded to attack the large towns: Osijek (70 % Croat, 15% Serb), Vinkovci (80% Croat, 11% Serb), and Vukovar (47% Croat, 32% Serb). The alleged "defenders" of the Serbs were, in fact, attacking Croatian towns and villages.

The relationship between the JNA and the Croatian government was difficult to understand. Nearly every town in Croatia still retained a military presence. During the very time the JNA were laying siege to Slavonian Croatian towns and cities, the JNA bases in non-combat zones in Croatia, not only were never attacked, but the Croatian government continued to supply the day-to-day needs to those JNA garrisons. The government were fueling the very tanks that were destroying Croatian cities and towns less than 100 kilometers from Zagreb. They allowed access to its ports and free movement of war material to the Yugoslav Army while it was engaged in besieging Croatian cities. The situation seemed to me baffling, to put it mildly.

As I prepared to leave, I packed literature about poison gas to read on the plane to Graz. I was landing in Austria, by way of Frankfurt. Commercial airlines quit flying into Zagreb because the Yugoslav Air Force controlled the air space. But reading proved to be difficult since I was haunted by the possibility of what Mackley described by phone had not been an exaggeration. Finally I gave up and settled back in my seat to reflect on the difference between reading about a war and actually entering a war zone. I had served in the U.S. Navy and with the Marine Corps as a Corpsman during the Korean War, but that experience was from a different time and place, from an altogether different world. Now I was heading into a situation where there were no clear battle lines and all civilians were potentially in harm's way. I didn't know that my experiences treating casualties of the Korean war and covering the emergency room at Cook County Hospital, euphemistically called the "zoo," could not have come close to prepare me for Vocin.

Mackley really opened my eyes to the true situation in Croatia. I had met him several months earlier after he gave a talk to a civic group in Los Angeles on the political situation in former Yugoslavia. His knowledge was first hand because he had recently returned from Croatia after spending a great deal of time there—from observing the front lines to the dealing with the highest echelons in the government. Since that time we had many extensive discussions centering on Yugoslavia and about the ongoing atrocities committed by the Serb forces. Although what Mackley had told me about Vocin was shocking, it was not surprising. In November, after Croatian civilians destroyed a Yugoslav tank close to the village of Skrabrnje, Serb forces retaliated by massacring 55 villagers. Autopsy reports had revealed that most of them had been executed by a bullet to the head at close range—Nazi style—though some of the victims had perished under the treads of Yugoslav tanks. Identification of the crushed remains had been almost impossible. Yet a few were identified; I recall one witness telling me he had identified his father because one quarter of the face, with one eye still in the orbit, and the surrounding skin, was relatively intact. Despite the media had received more than adequate substantiation about other Croatian slaughters, they were mostly ignored. Although what happened at Skrabrnje wasn't unique, it was the very first massacre that appeared in the American press.

Initially, in early November, the Foreign Press Bureau had invited me to Croatia to lend my expertise as a physician in investigating alleged Serbian poison gas attacks on civilian targets and evaluating the way health care was being delivered in the devastated areas. Because of my commitments to my practice and business in California, it took me a month to make preparations to leave.

The coincidental massacre in the Croatian village of Vocin now took precedence over my primary mission. Although the alleged gas attacks were the main topic of discussion in Croatia, the issue was clouded with controversy since government sources were reluctant to be interviewed and few could get a handle on the situation. The Foreign Press Bureau had contacted me to tap my experience in A.B.C. Warfare (atomic, biological, and chemical) learned in the American military; and because of my expertise as a dermatologist who understood the skin manifestations of disease (The most common sequelae of gas attacks are skin lesions).

Aside from being knowledgeable about the clinical effects of chemicals and/or gas, I knew many physicians in Croatia on a personal basis and spoke Croatian. With my access to the highest levels in the medical field, including the Chief of Medical Services of the Croatian Armed Forces and the Health Ministry, the Foreign Press Bureau felt I was ideally suited to obtain accurate medical information. Besides questioning my personal contacts, during my three weeks of investigation I interviewed physicians practicing in a number of hospitals, especially those at the front lines. As the primary treating physicians, they, more than anyone else, eventually provided me with all the information I needed. None were able to cite that they have seen or treated one clinical case of poison gas exposure.

From what I gathered and concluded from my in-depth investigation, what triggered off the poison gas scare, apparently, was that the Serbs, whether purposely or accidentally, were sporadically dropping from their planes almost microscopic sized, spider web quality filaments. These filaments were comprised of inorganic substances that "stuck to the skin." Evidently, contact with this material had no clinical significance. According to military experts these objects had something to do with anti-radar or anti-detection devices.

My investigation established that such attacks were unsubstantiated and probably a manifestation of mass hysteria—a common phenomena under the conditions the Croatians had been subjected to.

Although I'd been to Croatia less than a year earlier, nothing could have prepared me for the excess of unbridled nationalistic symbolism I witnessed when I arrived in Zagreb on my mission in December 1991. In contrast to the former Yugoslavia era, there was now an outpouring of Croatian symbolism everywhere: Croatian flags fluttered from every window; Croatian songs poured from boom boxes every few meters; and busts of the Croatian president, Franjo Tudjman, were being sold like cherished icons on every corner.

What I found most surprising, all hindrances to free speech had vanished. The plethora of political parties in Croatia are testimony to this new found freedom, belying the media's contention that Croatia is a dictatorial state.

The Western media misinterpreted Croatia's unbridled nationalism and lambasted it. Without foundation, they equated the reborn Croatian nationalistic spirit to the fascist government of World War II. To be sure, what was now going on seemed like an orgy of nationalism; but, after decades of repression under the artificially constructed Yugoslavia and its Communistic dictatorship, the new political climate was simply the spontaneous explosion of a forty- years-in- the-making, pent up identity crisis.

Thoughts of what had taken place in the previous months ran through my mind. Whenever legitimate Croatian government officials confirmed the minority Serb rebel aggressive act, the Yugoslav Army always intervened on the rebels' behalf. With each incident, the distinction between the Army and the rebels blurred. When the Slovenes and the Croats seceded in June 25, 1991, the Yugoslav army unleashed their juggernaut attacks. Since then they took 30% of Croatian territory, most of which has been only recently regained by the 1995 Croat offensive. The reason the Serbs didn't take more land was the steadfast resistance of the Croats who defended their homes with hunting rifles.

At the time of my December 1991 mission, the State Department had placed a travel advisory against travel to Yugoslavia. While planning my trip I had anticipated that I would have to be smuggled across the border close to Graz, Austria, because the borders were still controlled by Yugoslav forces. However, by the time I arrived the borders of Slovenia and Croatia were no longer in the hands of Yugoslavia. Since all flights to Zagreb were canceled because of the potential of being shot down by Yugoslav MIGs, the trip had to be made by bus from Graz. Crossing the borders into Slovenia and then into Croatia was, for me, a red letter day. Getting visas stamped in my passport from the new authorities was the first evidence of the sovereignty of these new states. For the first time in centuries, Slovenia and Croatia had their own borders, symbolizing that they were in control of their own destiny.

In contrast to my earlier visit in February of that same year, the mood on the streets was somber and subdued. A curfew and a blackout were in effect. The citizens of Zagreb were still being subjected to air alerts. The front lines were within streetcar distance away, and it was not uncommon to hear an occasional explosion.

Serbian sniper attacks from Zagreb's apartment windows, although rare enough, kept everyone on edge. Branko Zmajevic, a Croatian Supreme Court Judge and a close friend of mine, was almost hit by a sniper a few yards from his home. The bullet flew by within inches of his head. At street level, most of the windows of the buildings had sandbags in place.

This was the atmosphere in Zagreb when I arrived to investigate what happened at Vocin. The ground floor of The Hotel Intercontinental, where I was housed, and which served as headquarters for the Foreign Press Bureau, looked like a bunker because its windows were boarded up and lined with sandbags. The hotel's lobby, a favorite watering hole for Western media folk, teemed with refugees from Vukovar, the city which had been reduced to rubble by the Serbs after a siege as devastating as that of Stalingrad in World War II.

As these events were taking place in Croatia the international media, aside from misinterpreting the causes of the conflict, painted an entirely different picture. Filing their stories, they all but ignored Croatian sources, which, in any case, were inadequate to the task of setting the record straight. A group of concerned Croatian Americans established the Foreign Press Bureau to help provide objective news analysis. Originally its function was to act as translators for the growing presence of the international media in Croatia, but in a short period of time, the reporters came to rely upon the Bureau for hard and fast information and access to inside sources which heretofore had been closed to them.

When I first entered the Bureau's office, everything appeared to be in chaos. I soon learned that the apparent chaos was, in fact, orderly; and I came to respect the dedicated young men and women volunteers who ran the Bureau. Even before I had a chance to unpack and freshen up, Mackley had me roll up my sleeves to begin evaluating and verifying 43 pathology reports that were available of the 58 Vocin victims. Although I felt a sense of mission as I approached the work at hand, I learned from reading a number of related documents that many other massacres had occurred in Croatia, which had gone unreported by the press. Vocin was only the latest in a series of atrocities committed by the Serb forces in widely separated geographic locations in Croatia, which have now been well documented by teams of the European Community (EC) and of the Helsinki Watch.

A January 21, 1992, open letter from Helsinki Watch addressed to President of the Republic of Serbia Slobodan Milosevic and Acting Minister of Defense and Chief of Staff of the Yugoslav People's Army General Blagoie Adzic, focused on rampant Serbian human rights violations and accused the Yugoslav Army and Federal government of

being directly responsible for atrocities. Despite the scathing indictment the media were loath to report it.

When Mackley asked me to investigate the medical aspects of the
slaughter he told me especially to look for chicanery in the pathology
reports. In other slaughters committed by the Serbs, some of the investigating pathologists not only downplayed the Serbs' inhuman acts
in their reports, they tried to cover them up. In one example of many,
following atrocities in Sisak, an ethnic Montenegrin pathologist's protocol made no mention that a victim's throat was cut ear to ear.
Rather, his report stated that the victim had succumbed to a rico-
cheted projectile. Apparently the pathologist had forgotten Mackley
was present during the autopsy and Mackley placed his finger into
the lumen of the severed carotid arteries and jugular veins after the
pathologist pointed them out to him.

Since there were a number of pathologists who were ethnic Serbs
and Montenegrins that performed some of the autopsies on the Vocin
victims, Mackley's index of suspicion was high. In the Vocin massacre, although there were a number of reports about genital mutila-
tion—including one by an American journalist who saw the bodies in
situ—I found no mention of those findings in the reports. The pho-
tographers either selectively omitted taking photos and/or the pathologists ignored the mutilations. Was it a cover-up? At this stage, only
their consciences know the truth.

For some strange reason Mackley's attempts to get the reports and
photos from the forensic department met a stonewall. Mackley suspected this lack of cooperation was due to ethnic Serbian or
Montenegrins being in the department's leadership positions. His suspicion prompted Mackley to tell Branko Salaj, Ministry of Information, that he would use force to obtain the records. After Salaj notified
the lab that a crazy American would be coming with an intent to do
violence they suddenly cooperated.

With this information in mind I proceeded to organize my investigation systematically, beginning by correlating the pathology reports
I'd requested with the photographs (many of which are reproduced in
this book) taken prior to the autopsies. I personally interviewed some

of the eye witnesses. Bill Bass, a judge of the Texas Court of Appeals, who happened to be among the first to arrive on the scene, summarized the situation I witnessed only as a post-mortem analyst: "A mindless orgy of violence. There is no excuse on earth to justify this kind of murder and devastation."

From the time Mackley called me on the phone in Los Angeles, between the flight to Europe and transfer to Zagreb, and as I was immediately put to work on the Vocin pathology reports, I had been up for 44 hours. Despite the fatigue, sleep did not come readily that first night in Zagreb. It was an eerie feeling to hear sporadic explosions and machine gun fire in the background. Although they were supposedly a great distance away, I received little comfort from the knowledge that my room was not in the line of fire from potential Serb artillery. What was even eerier was the lack of city noises, of lights, and of any vehicular traffic whatsoever. It was a far cry from the Zagreb that I knew so well. The boarded up windows and sand bags that surrounded the hotel's ground floor provided no security for me on the tenth floor where I had a panoramic view. What disturbed my rest even more were the images of the pathology photos from Vocin that I had examined shortly before. I couldn't help imagining what the last hours and minutes had been like for the victims, and how they were tortured before they were murdered.

At first I could not understand why, despite the ample documentation, the press had either disingenuously chosen to avoid reporting about Croat victims or had chosen, with motives that seemed increasingly suspicious to me, to report them with skepticism. Yet when rumors that Croats *may have* committed war crimes circulated, the world press on the scene immediately published the stories that were verified by the JNA. And, almost invariably, later investigation would reveal that the stories describing Serb victims were fabrications.

At times the reporting has seemed almost intentionally perverse. In a number of instances, when the media reported finding Serbian victims of an atrocity, subsequent investigations revealed the victims were, in fact, Croatians. In one example of the many I had first hand knowledge of, the British media reported under banner headlines that the Croats slaughtered a large number of Serbs in Daruvar in October 1991. But European Community (EC) monitors, who were called in to investigate the alleged slaughter a month later, concluded that the victims had been Croats. United Nation Forces (usually British) often reported finding Serb victims who had been mutilated by either Croats or Muslims. Time and again, investigators were unable to provide verification. In spite of glaring evidence to the contrary, there has never been a retraction to this day. These stories were used by Belgrade to inflame the Serbs against the Croats. The pattern continues.

After the Croats retook their territory in Western Slavonia in May 1995, the U.N. and in particular the British delegation, immediately attributed "massive and inhuman" human rights violations by the Croatian forces upon the fleeing Serbs. These charges were later dispelled by independent investigating organizations. The leading human rights watchdog, the Helsinki Watch, criticized the U.N. for its false report and concluded that the U.N. misused the issue as a pressure mechanism against the Croatian government.

Reuters committed one of the most perverse examples of media abuse in November 1991, when they reported that one of their journalists had witnessed the discovery of the bodies of 41 Serbian children butchered by Croatian guardsmen. The children, between the ages of five and seven, were found in a cellar of a school in Borovo Naselje, a Croatian village near Vukovar. The bodies were so badly mutilated that the, "Serbian soldiers were weeping when the children were brought from the cellar." The Reuters journalist related that he saw the body of a young man sprawled at the top of the cellar steps with the severed head of a young woman cradled in his arms. At the foot of the steps lay a woman's corpse, and next to it a dead seven year old child.

Although what Reuters reported was horrific, it was, in actuality, a hoax. The journalist admitted it was a fabrication. Yet other newspapers picked up the story and published it without question, helping to perpetuate the notion that "all sides were guilty of atrocities." The story ran on Serbian television, and Reuters as its source gave it great credibility throughout the world. The Serbs who saw it believed it, and so did the rest of the Western media. CNN, which had ignored numerous verifiable massacres of Croatians, choose to believe the Reuters fabrication to a degree that they ran the story every hour. Reuters' story played a major role in inciting acts of revenge against Croatians by the Yugoslav military.

LEGEND-INDUCED PARANOIA
OF THE SERBS AND THE HITS AND
MYTHS OF THE CROATS

LEGEND-INDUCED PARANOIA OF THE SERBS AND THE HITS AND MYTHS OF THE CROATS

> *"Whenever one pulls a trigger in order to rectify history's mistake, one lies. For history makes no mistakes, since it has no purpose. One only pulls the trigger out of self-interest and quotes history to avoid responsibility or pangs of conscience."*
> ——*Joseph Brodsky, Nobel Prize laureate.*

From the moment the Serbs unleashed their onslaught on Croatia, pundits, reporters, and authors of numerous books and articles about the Yugoslav crisis have offered highly speculative and suspect opinions. They've persistently pontificated that regional history was the exclusive genesis of today's conflict without accurately understanding that history. So they've invariably recounted Serbian mythologies instead.

To the detriment of more important priorities, the Croats have spent a great deal of energy trying to set the record straight. In the process, they've gotten caught in the trap of quoting their own history *ad nauseam*. The Croats felt history was on their side and once the world learned the real truth, in contrast to the Serbian version, everything would miraculously fall into place for Croatia.

Instead of discussing the contemporary political situation, most Croatian government representatives spent all their time trying to deconstruct the Serbian take on Croatia's past. Croatian spokesmen didn't comprehend that the attention span of their audiences started to drift as soon as they brought up the Croats' significance during the time of Christ's birth. By the time the spokesmen reached the seventh century when the Croats finally settled in the Balkans, they had lost their audiences completely. Croatian officials never reached the point where they could articulate the real issues and Croatia's present agenda because they spent all their energy explaining history. For example, Croatia's representative to Washington, Franjo Golem, always thought the answer to any American legislator's question, "What can we or what do you want us to do for Croatia?" was *carte blanche* to deliver a lesson on Croatian history. One leading congressman told me that he dreaded having to meet with Golem, but did so because of protocol. He described the meetings as analogous to asking someone for the time and receiving a lecture on how to make a clock instead.

Every interested outside party and all the protagonists in former Yugoslavia except Slovenia have used a different version of history to embellish their own agendas. Whether that history was credible was of least importance. For a long time we were bombarded with the "Looney Toons" Serbian version because it was the only one used by Western leaders and the media. But I have no doubt that because of the decisive Croatian military victories in 1995, we'll soon be inundated with the Croatian "Merry Melodies."

Although history is always instructive, the past had little bearing on the recent debacle. The war was simply a land grab by Serbia to control the industrial and economic wealth of its neighbors. Because the Croats have buried their agenda in bombastic history lessons, they've never been able to clearly articulate that their goal is simply self-determination.

Everyone in the world watched the Berlin Wall fall, none with greater interest than the former captive nations. But Serbia was only marginally affected by the world-wide change in political climate and attitudes that followed the fall. The Belgrade government functioned as normal because it remained intact. But in order to stay in power and maintain its privileges, Milosevic's renamed Serbian Communist Party decided to reawaken a twisted version of history that would pander to Serbian nationalism and chauvinism.

The West's perception of former Yugoslavia as an amalgam should be corrected. Yugoslavia was a contrived country. Being markedly heterogeneous, multi-ethnic, multi-religious, and having four distinct languages and two alphabets, Yugoslavia possessed none of the pre-requisites for a lasting, successful union. Despite their differences, the various ethnic groups lived side-by-side in peace for 45 years after World War II, and it wasn't until Milosevic divided Yugoslavia along ethnic lines that the peace shattered. Behaving like a classic mountebank, Milosevic tried to unilaterally redefine the area's demography. He found his power base among Serbian intellectuals and Serbian Orthodox Church officials.

Milosevic raised that most visceral of appeals, nationalism, to hysterical heights. Fully realizing the power of the media, loyalists were placed in every influential positions of the Serbian press establishment. Even the bureau chief of the Associated Press in Belgrade was loyal to Milosevic. Using television, he fomented hatred by exposing the Serbs to a daily diet of wartime footage of the Ustashe, the quisling government installed in Croatia by Nazi Germany, and equated the Ustashe with Tudjman's government.

To fully understand the motives for the Serbian war, the West must fathom the Serbs' morbid fascination and obsession with darkest aspects of history. The linchpin of Serbian history, based more on legend than fact, is their defeat at Kosovo in 1389 by the Ottoman Muslims. In 1993, Serbian-American Dusko Doder wrote in *Foreign Policy*: "For centuries the myth of Kosovo has been the banner of Serb national pride and a justification for the Serbs' miserable condition. The Kosovo myth is the touchstone of the Serb national character, its disdain for compromise, its messianic bent, and its firm belief in the meaninglessness of loss and the promise of restoration of Serb glory and might." After the defeat at Kosovo in 1389, Serbia remained under Ottoman influence until 1878, when it was recognized as an independent state by the Berlin Congress. This recognition came as a result of a number of uprisings against Ottoman rule that started in 1804.

Newly independent Serbia revived the dormant Greater Serbia concept that Ilija Garasanin, the Minister of Internal Affairs in 1844, articulated in a document called *Nacertanije*. Its ramifications are fundamental to understanding all later Serbian policies.

The *Nacertanije's* primary goal was to unify all the Serbs within one empire. Serbia wasn't to remain a small country, but would have to expand outside its ethnic and historical borders by conquering its neighbors. Men of science, university professors, writers, journalists, and the Serbian Academy of Science and Arts (SANU) formulated a far-reaching and deliberate strategy to fulfill these goals. What was articulated in the *Nacertanije* was reintroduced in 1986 by Dobrica Cosic in the *SANU Memorandum*, with input from the same professional fields and Academy. Milosevic further refined the plan to include the concept that any place is considered to be Serbian soil where there's a Serbian grave.

Although Serbs thrive upon the legend that their ancestors defended Christendom at Kosovo, they never mention that an equal number of non-Serb Christians also participated in that battle. They also fail to mention that after Kosovo, the Serbs fought as loyal Ottoman-Muslim vassals for several centuries against Christian forces. The *Porte* in Istanbul maintained a special relationship with the Orthodox Church, affording it privileges denied other subjected religions. Under Ottoman rule the Serbian Orthodox were the only Christians granted autonomy to administrate and collect head taxes. The Ottomans looked upon Roman Catholics with suspicion. As Roman Catholic churches and monasteries deteriorated in Ottoman held lands, the Catholics were denied permission to repair or build new ones. Orthodox institutions, on the other hand, prospered. Yet contemporary Orthodoxy views Islam with hatred.

As members of the Eastern Rite of Christianity, the Serbs were inexorably bound to Byzantine thought and mores, which added to their paranoia about the West. Because the Serbs had been under Ottoman domination for almost 500 years they weren't exposed to and couldn't participate in the ideas that emanated from the Renaissance and the Age of Reason, the cornerstones of Western civilization. The first Serbian exposure to Western philosophical ideals came in the late 19th century.

The *SANU Memorandum*, the expression of Serbia's Academy of Sciences and Art, became the Serbian equivalent of *Mein Kampf*. The document portrayed the Serbs as victims and as the most oppressed nationality in Yugoslavia. Most importantly, it clearly espoused Serbian aspirations and raised the specter of the right of Serbs to live in a single state known as Greater Serbia.

The first real effort to implement the Greater Serbia concept occurred in 1903 when a group of Serbian army officers led by Colonel Dragutin Dimitrijevic-Apis formed the Black Hand, a secret terrorist organization. In 1911 its name was changed to Unity or Death.

The Black Hand organization had a long history of violence in the promotion of a Greater Serbia. Gavrilo Princip, who assassinated Archduke Ferdinand in Sarajevo and in so doing triggered World War I, was one of 27 Black Hand terrorists armed with bombs and guns stationed at different points along Ferdinand's processional route. Black Hand conspirators murdered the King of Serbia, Alexander Obrenovic, and his wife Draga in 1903. Exiled Alexander Karadjordjevic, who was linked to the Black Hand, returned to Serbia and was crowned. A Black Hand member in 1928 shot and mortally wounded three Croatian delegates, including Stejpan Radic, in the parliament in Belgrade. The perpetrator of the crime was confined for a short time in his home. Rather than punish the Black Hand, who were responsible for the conspiracy, King Alexander Karadjordjevic declared the Kingdom a dictatorship, renamed the country Yugoslavia, and imposed Draconian measures on all non-Serbs. To implement his mandate, King Alexander appointed Prime Minister Zivkovic. He was the individual who opened the gates for the assassins of King Alexander Obrenovic and his wife in 1903.

The *Memorandum's* main grievances were the deteriorating economic conditions of Yugoslavia, the loss of faith in socialism, and the deleterious effect these factors had on the Serbs. The document concluded that the non-Serbs, particularly the Muslims of Kosovo, victimized the Serbs perniciously. It also blamed the Croats for the deterioration of Yugoslavia.

The *Memorandum*, which was universally hailed by the entire spectrum of the Serbian intelligentsia and Serbian Orthodox Church, provided Milosevic with the ideological basis justifying his militaristic actions. Milosevic precipitated a war intended to rectify mythological grievances by resurrecting Serbian nationalism and ethnic hatred toward non-Serbs. He cast the Croats, in particular, as devils.

To understand just who these devils were that the Serbs ranted about so disparagingly, a brief background on them would be instructive. I may be criticized for giving a too superficial and simplistic view. But that's precisely the intent, because I don't mean to be comprehensive. For in depth studies, I defer to the works by a number of excellent historians including Noel Malcolm, Ivo Banac, Robert Donia, and John Fine.

Since the outbreak of hostilities, most of the media and Western pundits have ceaselessly cited Serbia's version of history, but none honestly addressed the history of the victims. Whenever the victim's history was expressed it was shallow and distorted. History didn't create the present situation, but history can help us understand the background of the people comprising the area.

The area that makes up present day Croatia and Bosnia-Herzegovina arose from the ruins of the Western Roman Empire. After Rome's disintegration in 476 A.D., the Balkan peninsula became the scene of mass movements from a variety of marauding tribes that came into Europe. One tribe, the Slavs, unlike other groups, engaged in agriculture and established settlements. The Slavs were firmly entrenched in the area by the mid-seventh century.

The Croats, a tribe of Indo-European origin, who became Slavicized in culture and language during their migrations, also arrived in the seventh century and settled in the area corresponding to modern Croatia and most of Bosnia. In tandem with the arrival of the Croats, another tribe, the Serbs, settled in the area that is modern Southwestern Serbia.

According to the Byzantine historian and Emperor Constantine Prophyrogentius, the Croats came in response to an invitation from the Byzantine Emperor Heraclius I to drive out the Avars who had allied themselves with the Slavs to usurp Byzantine rule. At that time, the area was under Byzantine dictum. Records indicate that Christian baptisms occurred among the Croats in the seventh century, and by the ninth century the Croats were almost totally Christianized. The region was governed by a number of loosely organized principalities.

In 925, at the height of Croatian power and stability, King Tomislav integrated the principalities into a unified Croatian state. After his death, dynastic power struggles threatened the survival of the state. For political stabilization, Croatian and Hungarian feudal lords signed the *Pacta Conventa* in 1102, which acknowledged the rule of the Hungarian King Koloman. Although Croatia's sovereignty was compromised at times, the state remained intact. The contractual relationship between Croatia and Hungary remained intact until 1918 despite much waxing and waning.

Soon after the *Pacta Conventa* was realized, the Mongols invaded Europe. Some of the most decisive battles against the Golden Horde were fought on Croatian soil. Those Croatian nobles who fought so well were rewarded with land; the nobles thereby created powerful dynasties that weakened and diluted the Hungarian king's ability to rule.

The Venetians, who had long coveted the Dalmatian coast, were able to wrest it easily from the enfeebled kingdom of Hungaro-Croatia in 1408 because the Croats were actively fighting in the Eastern reaches of the kingdom against the new threat to Europe, Islam.

Following the Ottoman excursions of the 15th century, the Croatian state lost much of its territory. Seemingly unending bloody battles were fought in the area because it marked the fault line between Christian Europe and Islam. But none of the battles were considered ethnic.

The battle of Mohacz had tremendous ramifications for Croatian history, despite the fact that the Christian forces were beaten decisively. The Hungarian-Croatian dynasty was almost wiped out; their king, Ludovic II, and most of the nobles were killed in the battle. To fill the vacuum, the Croatian parliament chose Ferdinand Hapsburg as king in 1527. The merger with the Hapsburg Monarchy lasted until 1918.

The Croats had hoped the alliance would support their efforts against the Muslims. Many years of battling the Ottomans resulted in numerous deaths, lowered birth rates, and a mass exodus of Croats from the battle areas. As a consequence, the demarcation line between the Muslims and Christians became sparsely settled, and that vacuum placed the European defenders at a disadvantage. The Pope bestowed the title *antemurale chrisianitatis* (the bulwark of Christianity) on Croatia for its valiant efforts and bravery against Islam.

More for its own security than Europe's, Austria encouraged Serbs to man the border areas called the Military Borderlands. Contrary to Serbian revisionism, the arrival of the Serbs in the 16th century was the first time the Orthodox religion made its appearance west of the Drina and Neretva Rivers. Austria provided all the financing and weapons. Once Muslim-held territories in Croatia were liberated in 1699, the Military Borderlands became institutionalized and expanded upon by Austria rather than reverting back to Croatia.

The Napoleonic wars brought yet another outside force that had a far-reaching political impact on the region. When the French came to rule Croatia in 1806, French inspired ideas and Italian nationalism stimulated Croatian intellectuals. The Croats came up with their own romanticized version of nationalism that was based on linguistics, but ignored the reality of diverse cultural characteristics. Nonetheless, the kernel of the idea of "Yugoslavism" took root. The so-called Illyrian movement remained limited for the most part to Croatian intellectuals and was almost totally ignored by the Serbs.

By the terms of the Congress of Vienna in 1815, after the defeat of Napoleon, Austria acquired Venice's properties in Dalmatia. The Hapsburgs saw the Military Borderland as a tool that could be used to dominate central and southeastern Europe. The Austrians enlisted the Serbs manning the Croatian frontier as regular soldiers under the command of Vienna. The communities in the Borderlands were free from feudal bonds. But all decisions regarding the areas were the responsibility of the Hapsburg military and bypassed Zagreb's authority. This situation lasted until 1881, when the Borderland was abolished and the region reverted back to Croatia.

The Military Borderland corresponds roughly to the course of the Una River and generally to the regions that the Serbs have conquered in Croatia during the present conflict.

In 1848 the Hungarians rebelled against the Hapsburg crown and declared that Croatia should be abolished. Hapsburg Emperor Franz Joseph offered unity and autonomy to Croatia if it would help him crush the Hungarians. But once achieved the emperor broke his pledge. In 1867, the *Ausgleich* (Compromise) returned Croatia to Hungary, but recognized Croatia as a nation. Hungary returned the Military Borderlands to Croatia. But Hungary always had pretensions of absorbing Croatia as its vassal state and did everything in its power to provoke incidents that would justify its rule. In a Machiavellian move, Hungary encouraged dissension between the Serbs and the Croats. The Austro-Hungarian-Croat alliance ended by the Treaty of Versailles.

In reaction to the almost dictatorial fiats imposed by Hungary, disillusion with the protection promised by the Austrian crown, and the disturbance caused by the influx of Serbs into Croatia's Military Borderlands, the Croats demanded their own national state. The movement was led by Ante Starcevic of The Party of the Right (*Stranka Prava*). The party's ideas and basic tenets are the linchpins of today's self-determination movement in Croatia. Serbia's rule by fiat in Yugoslavia eventually caused the same backlash that Hungary's dictates had caused in Croatia.

In the late 19th century, the Yugoslav idea was brought to full fruition by Josip Juraj Strossmayer from the seeds planted by the Illyrian movement. Strossmayer, a Catholic bishop, was a firm believer in ecumenicism and sincerely wanted to mend the schism between Catholic and Orthodox Christianity. He founded the Yugoslav Academy in Zagreb, an institution that had far reaching political impact. At best, the Yugoslav idea received a lukewarm reception among the Serbs.

In the mid 19th century, many of the ethnic groups under Muslim suzerainty (Serbs, Bulgarians, Greeks, and Montenegrins) established nation states while the ethnic groups in the Austro-Hungarian Empire had to wait until 1918. Out of the ashes of World War I and the break-up of the Austro-Hungarian and Ottoman Empires a number of new nations came into being.

The south Slavs (Slovenia, Croatia, Bosnia-Herzegovina, Vojvodina) joined with Serbia to establish the Kingdom of Serbia, Croatia, and Slovenia. Serbia received a significant economic gain with the merger. Although much smaller geographically and numerically, Croatia's real and net assets were several times greater than Serbia's. After Serbia's designs became clear, the Croatian Sabor (Parliament) refused to ratify the union. Nonetheless, the kingdom became a reality when Serbian troops were sent and stationed in Zagreb. The Western powers envisioned a loose confederation as one of President Woodrow Wilson's Fourteen Points. The Serbs formulated a constitution favoring themselves instead. Thereafter all political and economic infrastructure was controlled by the Serbs. Tax inequities blatantly favored the Serbs. To further enhance their control in Croatia and Slovenia they often established the jurisdiction of military code over civil cases. Adding insult to injury, an army edict viewed non-Serbian areas of the kingdom as "enemy territory." Taxes were several times higher in the non-Serbian areas for similar types of property.

The era between the World Wars was devastating for non-Serbs. Human rights were non-existent. Knowledge of the rampant abuses soon extended far beyond Yugoslavia's borders. Albert Einstein, among other prominent figures, lodged a number of protests against the Belgrade government for its violations against minorities.

Yugoslavia was ripe to implode. It was only a question of time before the non-Serbs self determination efforts would be realized, as there had been movements in that direction. Outside forces, such as Italy, infused a great deal of capital to finance the non-Serbs' activists. On the eve On the eve of World War II, Yugoslavia, as a state, was on the verge of collapse and headed for the dustpan of history. Ironically, World War II saved Yugoslavia's territorial integrity.

Milosevic and the Serbs have justified their recent actions by claiming that they must recover lost Serbian territory. But their premise has no foundation. After World War II, three men emerged as the political architects of the second Yugoslavia. Mainly formulated by Tito, a half Slovene and half Croat, but input from Aleksander Rankovic, a Serb, and Milovan Djilas, a Montenegrin, they declared

Macedonia to be a separate republic and gave the region of Vojvodina the status of an autonomous province. Kosovo, despite its preponderance of Albanians, was made an autonomous region of Serbia. The historical borders between Bosnia and Serbia, drawn during the Ottoman and Austro-Hungarian periods, were left intact. Serbia was given Srem, an eastern portion of Croatia.

Macedonia, with a non-Serbian population, had been incorporated into the Serbian kingdom after it was conquered in the Balkan War of 1912-13 (The Balkan Wars were the only European conflicts that could be considered ethnic). Vojvodina, although never bound with Serbia, was incorporated into Serbia when it became part of the Yugoslav kingdom in 1918. The only republic that lost territory in the post-World War II cartography was Croatia. Yet the Serbs were led to believe that territory had been taken from them and that they were victims of discrimination.

A favorite Serbian ploy used to cast aspersions on Croatia has been the exploitation of the Ustashe's role during World War II. Serbian propagandists were extremely successful in convincing the media that the Croats relished that role because the Croats had an inherent propensity for violence. Meanwhile, the Serbs were cast as lambs led to slaughter.

Contrary to what the media espoused, the present Croatian government is neither a reincarnation of, nor responsible for the acts of the Ustashe. Croatian President Franjo Tudjman, although he's been frequently labeled a fascist by the media, fought the Germans as a Partisan during World War II. Ironically, when the world learned that the former French President François Mitterand had been an active Nazi collaborator, the media strangely didn't pursue the issue, even after he excused his war time activities as youthful indiscretions. This double standard is typical of the media. Nonetheless, while Tudjman apologized for the Ustashe crimes on a number of occasions, Mitterand refused to apologize for the Vichy government's excesses.

The French government and its media equated the Tudjman government with Ustashe collaborators of World War II. France's holier than thou attitude blinded it to Vichy's collaboration with the Nazis. Mitterand maintained that the Vichy government didn't represent the

French republic and that Vichy's actions weren't those of the state. But Mitterand still sent a wreath, as homage, each year to the grave of Marshall Philippe Petain who headed the Vichy government.

Once Jacques Chirac was elected president, he acknowledged what a generation of French political leaders were loath to—that the French state was, in fact, an accomplice in the deportation of 75,000 Jews to Nazi concentration camps. Only 2,500 French Jews survived the Vichy regime. Chirac added that France's complicity with the Nazis was a stain on the nation. "The criminal folly of the German occupier was seconded by the French, by the French state." His statements directly contradicted Mitterand's.

Following any German conquest during World War II, the Nazis installed or kept governments that would carry out Germany's mandates. The Germans installed a puppet government in Croatia led by the formerly exiled Ustashe. Contrary to the media's take or present day rabid ultra-national Croatians' fantasies, the Ustashe government wouldn't have come into being or lasted one day if Germany hadn't supported it. The Ustashe were an extremely small group of ultra-right Croats who came together in reaction to the intolerable measures imposed on all non-Serbs in pre-World War II Yugoslavia. They lived as exiles in Italy under Mussolini's largesse. But at times they had been incarcerated in accordance with Mussolini's political agenda and whims.

Carrying out Nazi policy to the letter, the Ustashe destroyed the synagogue in Zagreb, established concentration camps, and created terror. Unlike the Vichy and Quisling governments of that time, the Ustashe never enjoyed the popular support of the Croats at large. Credible sources, such as J. Tomasevich's *The Chetniks*, indicate that the Ustashe movement numbered less than 28,500 even at its peak.

Just as the Tito regime labeled every Croatian misstep Ustashe inspired, the international media has also equated, without a scintilla of substantiation, the Croatian government under Tudjman with the Ustashe regime of 50 years ago. But the media has never informed the public about the facts that preceded the installation of the Ustashe. In the late 1930s, Yugoslavia was on the verge of collapse due to self-determination efforts by non-Serbs who were responding to the excesses of the Serbian establishment. To save the state from disintegration, Prime Minister Dragisa Cvetkovic, who represented the legitimate Yugoslav government, entered into negotiations with Vladko Macek of the Croatian Peasant Party who represented the overwhelming majority of Croats. Macek was the political successor to the assassinated Stjepan Radic, the most charismatic Croat of this century. In order to preserve Yugoslavia as an entity, the Yugoslav government compromised by giving Croatia autonomous rule over territory where Croats comprised a majority, including Herzegovina, and appointing Macek vice president. But the Cvetkovic-Macek agreement didn't sit well with the Serbian Orthodox Church or the military.

At the time Yugoslavia was negotiating with the Croats for its survival, Mussolini was competing with Hitler in Yugoslavia. Mussolini feared that the imminent breakup of Yugoslavia would favor an independent Croatia under German protection. Despite Hitler's assurances, Mussolini was primarily concerned that Germany could control the Adriatic Sea and the Dalmatian coast, which had long been coveted by Italy. Count Galeazzo Ciano, the Italian foreign minister from 1939 to 1943, wrote in his diaries that "the Croats are anti-German but ready to fall into the arms of Berlin, if only to escape from Serbian tyranny." The Italians actively courted Macek, donating vast amounts of funds toward the Croatian struggle in order to convince him to accept Italy's terms for implementing its agenda in Yugoslavia. Meanwhile, Hitler entered into an agreement with Yugoslavia in order to protect Germany's Balkan flank and avoid tying up his troops there.

Soon after the Yugoslav military, in collusion with agents from the British government, overthrew the pro-German Prince Regent's government in Belgrade and replaced him with Prince Peter, Germany declared war on Yugoslavia. The Serbian-led Yugoslav Army didn't even offer token resistance. Within days the Prince and the Serbian political elite fled to England. The German war machine's success added a new dimension to Yugoslav politics, the installation of an occupying force.

Germany successfully established quasi-states in conquered lands to help carry out its mandates. As a prerequisite these new governments had to carry out genocide on Jews and Gypsies. The Germans offered Macek the position of heading the puppet state in Croatia. Unable to agree to the German conditions or Italian terms, Macek vacillated. So Germany accepted Mussolini's suggestion that Ante Pavelic and his 250 Ustashe members rule Croatia. Pavelic, the Ustashe leader, had witnessed Stjepan Radic's assassination in Belgrade when he was a Croatian delegate in Parliament. Macek was placed in the Jasenovac concentration camp.

The international media has long ignored Macek's refusal to cooperate with the Nazis, although his attitude mirrored the sentiments of the Croatian majority. The media also hasn't acknowledged the fact that the Jasenovac camp continued to operate long after the war's end, functioning on behalf of the Communist regime as it had for the Ustashe.

The Jasenovac camp has long symbolized Ustashe genocide. Information supplied by Serbian propagandists and echoed by the Western media cited claims that over one million Serbs were slaughtered at Jasenovac. But objective scholarly sources estimate that the true figure was between 30,000 to 60,000, which included Gypsies, Jews, Serbs, and thousands of Croats. These excesses by the Ustashe regime drove many previously apolitical Croats and Bosnians to join the Partisan forces.

When the Ustashe were installed in Croatia, most of the Dalmatian coast and islands were annexed to Italy. Living under the Italian flag proved to be more intolerable for the Croats than living under Yugoslavia. General Mario Roatta's imposition of Italy's mandate and reign of tyranny also drove many Croats to join the Partisans. The Partisans later became the backbone of Tito's resistance movement.

A number of telling instances indicate the general lack of popular Croatian support for the Ustashe and their pro Nazi policies. In 1941, the Nazis asked Croatian youths to line up at the main soccer stadium. All Jews present were ordered to take one step forward. Much to the chagrin of the Nazis, *all* the youths stepped forward in a sign of solidarity. In another case of support for the Jews, the Zagreb archbishop, Cardinal Alojzije Stepinac hid the last rabbi of Zagreb, Salom Freiberger, in his residence.

In Serbia, by contrast, the Nazis installed a government headed by the former Yugoslav Minister of War General Milan Nedic. Serbia collaborated to such an extent with the Nazis that it was able to retain significant civilian authority. The Serbian Orthodox Church openly supported Nazi policy and justified the persecution of the Jews theologically. These elements, working together, caused Nazi civil administrator Harald Turner to proclaim Serbia the only country where the "Jewish Question" was solved, and Belgrade to be the first city *"judenfrei."* Phillip J. Cohen noted in a November, 1992, *Midstream* article that six months before World War II, Serbia had enacted laws prohibiting Jewish participation in the economy and the university. The Belgrade Historical Archives states that out of the 11,870 Jews living in Belgrade before 1941, only 1,115 survived.

A few days after the onset of World War II, the Yugoslav king and his entourage fled to England and the pro-Nazi, Nedic, was installed. The only viable force against the Germans were the Chetniks, a pro-royalist group under the command of former Yugoslav Army Captain Draza Mihailovic. But the Chetniks spent most of their energy continuing the royalist policy of terrorizing non-Serbs. Using the excuse of war, they massacred real and imagined Ustashe allies, mostly innocent Croatian or Muslim villagers. The Chetniks unleashed their fury most particularly on the Muslims. During World War II more Muslims perished in Yugoslavia than any other ethnic group. The media's belief in Serbian resistance during World War II is yet another example of how the media was duped. The Serbian Anti-Fascist Council was founded in the last half of 1944, later than similar councils in any of the other Yugoslav republics. Historical revisionism has created the impression that the Chetniks were somehow engaged in helping the anti-Axis powers during the war. But the June 23, 1945 final report of Arthur Cox, Chief of the Office of Strategic Service, summarized the OSS's dealings with the Chetniks as counterproductive and noted that Chetnik participation "probably decreased the amount of intelligence gathered . . .by half."

According to the *Encyclopedia of the Holocaust,* not only did Chetnik resistance against the Nazis come to a complete halt by early 1941, they initiated and maintained a pattern of collaboration with the Nedic government and with the Germans and Italians. Tito's Communist Partisans didn't participate in the war until Germany attacked Russia. In Walter Roberts' book, *Tito, Mihailovic, and the Allies,* the author states that an American officer attached to the Tito forces in 1943 said, "The Partisans placed less emphasis on the fight against the Germans than preparing for the political struggle at the end of the war." The Partisans became a force only after receiving vast supplies and air support from the allies late in the war—after the fall of Italy. Tito's Partisans were mainly Croats and Orthodox Serbs who lived in Croatia and Bosnia, and had virtually no following in Serbia proper. Tito, promising cooperation against the British and Americans, actively solicited Germany with his own peace plans. But Hitler rejected the offers, saying he would not do business with a bandit.

When the Communists took over the government after the war, all political and economic infrastructure became, once again, Serbian controlled. This reversion happened even though the Serbian Communist Party formed after the end of World War II.

The Serbian military force was vastly overrated during World War II as it has been during the present conflict. In April 1941, the Royal Yugoslav Army of one million troops, led by 161 Serb, two Croat, and two Slovene generals, surrendered to the German forces after 11 days. In his book, *Britain and the War for Yugoslavia 1940-1943*, Mark Wheeler described the Yugoslav Army and how it fought the Germans as follows: "They resisted (occasionally), dispersed or mutinied (more frequently), and surrendered (eventually on an ad hoc basis)." In an Autumn 1993 *Parameters* article, M.F. Cancian claimed that the Germans suffered only 151 killed, 392 wounded, and 15 missing during their initial campaign. Historian Norman Stone destroyed another often quoted myth that the campaign in Yugoslavia "pinned down dozens of German military divisions in World War II" when he asserted that according to the German Military Research Office, the actual number of German divisions was six, including two manned by Croats. The Germans had only one division at the front lines.

Despite historical evidence to the contrary, many contemporary opinion writers have continued to perpetuate myths about the Serbian role during World War II and Serbia's fighting ability. Contributing editor to the *Los Angeles Times* Walter Russell Mead has sustained these erroneous beliefs. In a February 2, 1994 piece, Mead implied that it would be hopeless for U.S. ground forces to intervene against the Bosnian-Serb fighters because the Serbs were the best and most determined fighters in Europe. Mead's revisionist version of history stated that there had been a national resistance when Germany attacked Yugoslavia and that Serbian fighters tied down Germany's toughest and most cruel divisions.

No one source can unequivocally state how many died in the World War II Balkan cauldron. Since victors write history, the Serbs have freely used unsubstantiated figures. They claimed, without substantiation, that over 700,000 Serbs perished in the Ustashe concentration of Jasenovac alone. Probably the most accurate numbers of deaths in Yugoslavia for the period was what the Yugoslav government furnished to Germany in 1964 in order to extract war reparations from the German government. The Yugoslav government came up with a total of 346,740 Serbs who had died throughout the *whole* territory of Yugoslavia. The number included those who had died at the hands of the Germans, Ustashe, Partisans, Luftwaffe and Allied bombings, those killed by other Serbs or Soviets for political expediency, and those who died of endemic diseases like typhus and typhoid—which was rampant. The same report stated 83,257 Croats died.

After the war, the Communist Partisans emerged triumphant in Yugoslavia. In late May, 1945, with British and American complicity, the Yugoslav Army attacked, killed, and took prisoner 20,000 Croatian soldiers and half-a-million civilian refugees who had fled the new communist regime. Minister Resident in the Mediterranean Harold Macmillan, a man with direct contact to the British Prime Minister, Cabinet, and Foreign Office, explicitly instructed Commanding Officer General Keightley to turn over all refugees, with the exception of the Chetniks, to the Yugoslav Partisan forces at Bleiburg, Austria. Macmillan ignored Intelligence Officer Nigel Nicolson's conclusions that repatriated refugees would meet "certain death at the hands of Tito," as well as General Keightley's moral repugnance at the order.

The Bleiburg slaughter became a truly black mark for England and the United States. After the British guaranteed the safety of a large group of Croatian refugees, the Croats ran up white flags in surrender. Apparently the flags signaled Yugoslav Army troops hidden in the surrounding forest. Despite having many ethnic Croats in its own ranks, the Yugoslav Partisan Army opened indiscriminate machine gunfire on the densely packed refugees. When they received no return fire, the Yugoslav Partisan Army slaughtered the survivors with truncheons and knives. The British and Americans had front row seats. Nicholai Tolstoy described the Bleiburg incident with painstaking detail in *The Minister of Massacres*.

The British returned the few survivors and other Croatian refugees who hadn't been at Bleiburg to Yugoslavia where they were forced into a death march and further mayhem.

Although the new Yugoslavia was led by a half-Croat/half-Slovene, Tito, all economic and political infrastructure returned to Serbian hands. Tito's ethnic origins were irrelevant to his policies, as he was committed to an international communist revolution. His iron fist dictatorship reined in the Serbian expansionistic aspirations somewhat, but not Serbia's power base.

In order to strengthen its position, the Yugoslav Communist Party exploited Nazi history in Yugoslavia in much the same way Russia exploited Nazi atrocities in Eastern Europe. The Serbian-led Communist Party, painting the Croats on the same canvas with the Nazis, successfully suppressed knowledge of Serbian collaboration with the Germans. The noun "Croat" became a euphemism for fascism to the people of Yugoslavia. Many young Croats came to feel ashamed of their ethnic roots. The public relations firms hired by SerbNet projected a fascistic image of Croats during the recent conflict.

Joseph Brodsky must've had the situation in former Yugoslavia in mind when he said, "Geography, history, and politics are a gold mine for pundits and bandits. Whoever pulls a trigger to rectify history's mistakes, lies." But history provides a justification rather than a reason and teaches us that wars start because of self-interest. Contrary to the smoke and mirrors that appeared in the media, Serbia didn't start its war to prevent Croatia and Slovenia from seceding. Stated purely and simply, the Serbs engaged in a land grab in order to create a Greater Serbia. In the process, their aggression has violated all rules of war.

Many have been critical of comparing Serbia's policy of ethnic cleansing (a term the Serbs themselves coined) to the Holocaust. The numbers are smaller, but the results are the same. Simon Wiesenthal, commenting on Serbian ethnic cleansing in an interview with Roy Gutman, author of *A Witness to Genocide*, said: "This is genocide, absolutely." Although comparing one horror to another is an odious exercise, the silence and inaction from governments that knew about the extermination of the Jews during World War II resembles the outside world's reaction to what has recently happened to the non-Serbs in former Yugoslavia. Inaction is in itself is an action.

Chicago's De Paul University has the largest repository of documented evidence of atrocities committed in former Yugoslavia. Although the United Nations tried to ignore irrefutable evidence of a large number of horrific, wholesale massacres, maltreatment of civilian prisoners, and the shelling of civilians, it eventually bowed to pressure from Non-Governmental Organizations(NGOs) to establish the Commission of Experts. The commission's mission was to collate information about atrocities into data banks of specific cases and then separate the verified cases from propaganda and blind allegations. Compiled under the direction of De Paul Law Professor Cherif Bassiouni, the files show that 96% of the crimes were perpetrated by Serbs. Atrocities committed by Croats or Muslims were mostly spontaneous events. In contrast, the Serbian ethnic cleansing of Muslims and Croats were a national policy coordinated by the Serbian hierarchy in Belgrade.

A U.S. senators staff members fact finding mission to Bosnia and Croatia in August, 1992, concluded that Serbia's forcible removal of a population in war was a violation of Protocol I of the 1949 Geneva Convention.

In March 1995 *The New York Times* said a leaked CIA report irrefutably concluded that Serbs had committed 90% of the ethnic cleansing and emphatically suggested that the Serbian leadership had exercised a role in destroying and dispersing the non-Serb populations. The CIA conclusions should forever lay to rest statements put forward by British, French, and American leaders calling the conflict a civil war and suggesting that the guilt should be shared equally by Serbs, Croats, and Muslims. If President Clinton and Secretary of State Warren Christopher knew about the report's findings, they chose to ignore the evidence. Perhaps they thought the report wouldn't be made public, or perhaps the CIA simply failed to share it with them.

The report couldn't have come at a worse time for the Western allies and Russia as they were in the process of lifting sanctions on Serbia, even though the Serbs were stepping up ethnic cleansing in Banja Luka and shipping new weapons into the Bihac area. The reports put on hold the whitewashing campaign to nominate Milosevic for the Nobel Peace Prize.

Serbian and Nazi perpetrators of genocide perceived their actions in markedly different ways. The Nazis tried to carry out their demonic acts in secret, while the Serbs have openly proclaimed their acts and thrived on the publicity. This seeming lack of concern about witnesses wasn't reckless. The Serbs were aware that there would be no effective tribunal to punish them. Their goal was to let the witnesses talk to their friends, neighbors, and families. Within days, every hamlet, town, and city in the country would shiver with fear.

The general population of Serbia has been kept ignorant of their leadership's activities in Bosnia and Croatia. During the first several months of Sarajevo's siege, Belgrade's television never mentioned that the Serbs were firing upon and besieging the Bosnian capital. Instead, official television reported that Muslim extremists were killing Serbs and Muslims. The Belgrade media fed its populace a steady diet of marauding Muslim fundamentalists and fascist, genocidal Croats. The only news source found on Serbian and Montenegrin television sets emanated from Belgrade. According to this source Croats and Muslims were ethnically cleansing Serbs, not vice versa. The atrocities committed by Serbian troops went unreported.

Ever quick to cast the Croats in a negative light, the international media quoted out of context, *ad infinitum*, Tudjman's comment that he was "thankful that his wife did not have Jewish blood." But the media disingenuously omitted the completion of his statement, "or else she would have died at the hands of the Fascists."

The triumph of Serbian propagandists has been the unqualified acceptance by many Jews and the government of Israel of the notion that the Serbs were anti-Nazi and saviors of Jews, while the Croats and Muslims were Nazis who exterminated the Jews. What was especially disconcerting to learn from Philip J. Cohen's *Serbia's Secret War: Propaganda and the Deceit of History*, was how easily the Israeli government was duped. Cohen pointed out a number of ironies in Israel's steadfast acceptance of the Serbian line. "In no other country has the Serbian propaganda campaign for Jewish sympathy been more successful than in Israel; a country uniquely founded on the ashes of the Holocaust, the public's outrage over Serbia's policy of frank genocide has been successfully blunted to the point of near nonexistence. It is further ironic that Serbia, which has a history of persecuting Jews, has courted the sympathy of Jews amid a genocidal war against non-Serbian nationalities and minorities." Cohen systematically refuted most of the widely accepted World War II Serbian mythology that was the linchpin for the recent bloodshed in former Yugoslavia. I wonder how many non-Serb victims could've been saved had Cohen's scholarly work been published earlier.

Igor Primorac, an associate professor of philosophy at the Hebrew University of Jerusalem, told me in a personal letter that "the situation with the Serb lobby in Israel is much worse than in the West. . .They enjoyed a monopoly on analyzing and interpreting the events in ex-Yugoslavia. . .It is still very well organized and financed, and extremely aggressive as well." In a number of his published articles Primorac articulated that the overwhelming majority of Israel's political establishment, media commentators, and ordinary citizens staunchly defended the Belgrade regime and all its actions—including ethnic cleansing. Whatever happened to the non-Serb victims was what they deserved. Moreover, the Israelis have believed that the fledging Croatian government was comprised of resurrected Ustashe.

Croatian human rights activist Dr. Slobodan Lang said that the Serbian propaganda success was due, in large measure, to the efforts of the Jewish-Serbian Friendship Society. The Serbs mobilized and encouraged the Jews in former Yugoslavia to form the Society. Instead of fostering friendship and understanding, the Society became a vehicle for justifying hatred against Croats and for extolling Serbia's agenda. The society was particularly successful in a blanket indictment of Croatia for having a natural propensity for fascism. But Cohen's work clearly established that the Ustashe were an aberration that didn't have the support of the Croatian people.

The Society intensely publicized throughout the world real and imagined Ustashe crimes during World War II. In particular, Klara Mandic, a Serbian Jew, has successfully manipulated the thinking of many Jews in the United States. She crusaded against the new Croatian government, accusing its leaders of being resurrected fascists, and espoused a belief that the Jews had a deeply ingrained historical alliance with Serbia.

Not only has Israel failed to recognize the independent states of Croatia and Bosnia-Herzegovina, Israel has morally supported the Serbian agenda and supplied Serbia with weaponry. In a July 18, 1993, *Jerusalem Post* article, Primorac wrote that "during the time the Serbs were shelling Dubrovnik and razing Vukovar, and one month after the UN Security Council passed an arms embargo on all the republics of Yugoslavia, the Israeli government entered into an arms deal with the Bosnian Serbs." Primorac was so moved after he'd reported that fragments of exploded shells found in Sarajevo were clearly Israeli in origin, he commented, "After Greater Serbia's collapse, we may yet see the official representatives of the Jewish state go down on their knees at the ruins of Vukovar and Sarajevo and beg forgiveness for the mind boggling fact that the first genocide in Europe since the Holocaust was carried out, in part, with arms made in Israel."

In a seminal paper published in *International Minds*, Dr. Lang concluded that by focusing upon the plight of the Jews and history, the Serbs used anti-Semitism to cover up Serbian aggression and genocide against the Croats and Muslims. The attempt to influence Jews in Serbia and internationally by evoking their historical sufferings was a misuse of Jewish tragedy. Lang also pointed out that anti-Semitism exists in Croatia as it does in any other country in the world.

Robert D. Kaplan was particularly vitriolic about Tudjman's alleged fascism. His review of Tudjman's book, *Wilderness of Historical Reality*, read like a personal vendetta. Kaplan, quoting out of context, inserting his own additions, and deleting critical portions of Tudjman's original sentences, did a masterful hatchet job. Kaplan's bowdlerized critique bore little resemblance to the book he was reviewing.

After the Jewish Center and cemetery in Zagreb were bombed in 1990, the Serbian propaganda apparatus characterized the destruction as consistent with Croatia's Ustashe past and another example of Croatian anti-Semitism. Following the bombings, thousands gathered in Zagreb's main square in support of their Jewish brethren. President Franjo Tudjman won approval from Zagreb's city government to rebuild the synagogue destroyed by the Ustashe on the original site. Croatian artists sponsored a concert to raise funds for this purpose.

As the result of a show trial in Belgrade, evidence surfaced that the bombing had in fact been carried out by two civilian members of the Yugoslav secret police. The former head of Yugoslav Army intelligence, General Aleksandar Vasiljevic, former Air Force intelligence officer Colonel Slobodan Rakocevic, and a host of other former top brass were indicted at the same trial. According to the *Jerusalem Post* (Feb. 3, 1993), the trial was an attempt to rid the army of pro-Communist commanders and replace them with Chetniks (Serbian nationalists). Other independent investigations unequivocally disproved Serbian allegations of Croatian complicity.

In an open letter titled "Appeal to our Jewish Brothers and Sisters" addressed to the World Jewish Congress and its affiliates the Jewish Community Congress of Croatia summed up its status in

Croatia thus: "Even though claims are made trying to show that the Republic of Croatia is anti-Semitic and neo-fascist, the Jewish community has enjoyed all rights of a religious and ethnic minority without obstruction or any kind of discrimination. Therefore, we express our full support for the declared policies of the Republic of Croatia which desires to build a new and democratic state in which human and political rights, ethnic and religious rights, for all citizens or groups, will be honored."

Jeri Laber, executive director of Helsinki Watch, stated:"The ethnic wars in the Balkans are not, as many want to believe, the results of age-old hostilities long repressed by the communists. . . they are the result of a relentless propaganda campaign, aimed at stirring up old tensions engineered by Serbia's irresponsible and power-mad leader, Milosevic."

THE ROAD TO VOCIN

THE ROAD TO VOCIN

When the Soviet Union failed to protest the fall of the Berlin Wall or the mass exodus from East Germany, which had been *the* bastion of communism, other captive nations including Croatia and Slovenia suddenly realized the impotence of Russia's monolithic power. Because these nations no longer feared the threat of Russian intervention, they stopped suppressing long-held desires for self-determination. Although European communism wasn't quite dead, it was in its last agonies. Slovene, Croatian, and other Eastern European sentiments seemed to echo Richard Nixon's proclamation that "someday historians will look back on the defeat of communism in the Cold War and recognize it for what it was, one of the most magnificent achievements of free people in the history of civilizations."

In 70 short years, communism had damaged more lives than any other philosophical force in history. But as practiced in Yugoslavia, Marxism was more along the lines of 50% Karl and 50% Groucho. Its leaders performed a never-ending comedy of corruption and mismanagement, indulging themselves in decadent extravagances financed by the West. The Western media called Yugoslavia the "America" of communist countries and treated it as their darling. Meanwhile, the Yugoslav government brutally policed its own citizens, showed no mercy to dissidents, and held more political prisoners than all the Eastern states of the Soviet Bloc combined. Helsinki

Watch and other human rights organizations branded Yugoslavia one of the worst violators of human rights in the world.

Despite Yugoslavia's abominable human rights record the United States was enamored by Tito's regime. No less an expert than America's last ambassador to Yugoslavia, Warren Zimmermann, said that this one sided love affair persuaded the U.S. to look the other way on human rights violations.

The seminal event that precipitated the conflict in former Yugoslavia occurred when the Slovene Communist Party delegation walked out of the Yugoslav Communist Party Congress in January, 1990. Apparently their sudden exit caught everyone off guard. Doctor Slobodan Lang, one of the Croatian delegates, approached the head of the Croatian delegation, Ivica Racan, grabbed him by the arm and said, "If you don't get up and leave, I'll leave on my own." So the entire Croatian delegation walked out as well.

The Communist Party was the supposed glue that bound Yugoslavia together. But instead of having the strength of Krazy Glue, the party was as weak as water-soluble paste. So the concept of Yugoslavia essentially died after the Party Congress. As a result, the first multi-party elections were held in Slovenia and Croatia. Monitored by international bodies experienced in election protocol, Croatia and Slovenia's populace voted into office parties that represented their own national interests rather than those of Belgrade. The results of the early 1990 Croatian and Slovene elections were more triumphs over Serbian hegemony than victories over communism.

The democratic movement in Yugoslavia started in Slovenia. During the early 1980s, the Yugoslav federal government steadily came to look upon Slovenia's involvement with movements such as feminism, environmentalism, anti-nuclear protests, and (that horror-of-horrors for communism) pacifism as violations of Yugoslav communist dogma. The movements coalesced in early 1988 after journalists from *Mladina*, a youth magazine, were arrested for printing documents stating that the federal military establishment had organized forces to suppress Slovenia's nationalist movement. As a direct consequence of their arrests, a call arose among Slovenes for free elections and the formation of multiple political parties, both illegal according to the Yugoslav constitution.

Nevertheless, the Slovenes voted into office essentially the same cast of characters who had ruled from the old Communist Party. But now these politicians had clearly switched allegiances. The dogmatic Communist Party itself won only 38 seats out of the 240.

Although the Croatian elections also resulted in a seemingly decisive victory over Communist Party rule, the electorate voted in mostly ex-Communists who had been purged from the party in the aftermath of the so-called Croatian Spring, Croatia's self-determination attempt of the 1970s. I should emphasize that most of the dissidents of that era came from within the Communist Party and that the average Croatian citizen didn't participate in the attempt.

In the 1970s, Croats in the Yugoslav Communist Party hierarchy had thought the time was ripe for Croatia to gain some degree of autonomy because the main enforcer of Serbian aspirations, secret police head Aleksandar Rankovic, had fallen from grace in 1967. But the Croatian Communist Party had misread Rankovic's purging. Belgrade's hard-liners still held control. As a result, the majority of Croatian dissenters, which included present Croatian President Franjo Tudjman, went to prison. The Croatian Spring turned into the Croatian Silence. For the next two decades, organized Croatian opposition collapsed, and Serbian power in Croatia became even more rampant.

The dossiers and the true numbers of dissidents who went to prison in the aftermath of the Croatian Spring are still buried deep in the archives of the secret police. After the dissidents had served their sentences, the "rehabilitated" ex-prisoners were forbidden to write, to take part in public activities, and in most cases even to work. Twenty years later, these same Croats became the main force behind a more successful self-determination movement. For example, General Janko Bobetko, Croatia's present Army Chief of Staff, had been a career military officer in the Yugoslav Army. But as punishment for his role in the Croatian Spring movement, the authorities denied Bobetko all civil rights and stripped him of his position and rank.

The Slovene and Croatian election results of early 1990 weren't well received in other parts of Yugoslavia because they carried undertones of self-determination. The Slovene Assembly's passage of a constitutional amendment transferring its defense forces from federal to local control especially aggravated those opposed to self-determination. Non-commissioned conscripts, who came from all the republics, made up the bulk of the infantry in the Yugoslav Army. Slovenia's announcement that it would no longer permit its citizens to serve outside the boundaries of their republic and would ally itself with Yugoslavia's defense only with Slovenia's unilateral consent directly challenged Yugoslavia's federal rule.

For all practical purposes, only one federal institution, the Yugoslav Army, remained intact after the elections. Tito had left the constitution of 1974 as his legacy to guide the transition from his personal rule and to maintain Yugoslavia's unity. But its precepts were a nightmare to implement. More than any other factor, the constitution directly accelerated Yugoslavia's demise. The constitution established a collective presidency with a president to be appointed yearly and rotated among each of the member republics and provincial states. Obviously, under this system no strong leader could emerge, nor could one have the time to nurture a power base. Additionally, the yearly rotation weakened the president's ability to run the country effectively. But it offered each republic, even the weaker ones, the opportunity to fill the position. This provoked animosity from Serbia, Yugoslavia's strongest state, despite the fact that the presidential seat remained in Belgrade.

In December, 1990, several months after the Slovene and Croatian elections, the renamed Communist Party captured four out of five seats in the Serbian Parliament, a victory that heightened the already rampant fear of Serbian aggression among the non-Serbs.

Most importantly, the 1990 Slovene and Croatian elections gave the republics the means to openly address their fundamental grievance with the Yugoslav federation, economics. Slovenia, with a population of two million and 10% of Yugoslavia's work force, produced one-third of all Yugoslav exports and 20% of the country's gross national product. But the Slovenes paid four-and-a-half times more in federal taxes than they received in federal benefits.

The disparity was no better in Croatia. In 1971, Croatia contributed 51% of Yugoslavia's hard-currency earnings while Serbia earned

18%. Over the next 20 years, the Croatian economy grew steadily, but Croats perceived Serbia as reaping most of the federal financial benefits. Croatia's leaders, and to a lesser extent Slovenia's, thought that the most equitable solution was to reorganize Yugoslavia into a confederation.

Before a Croatian referendum on confederation with Yugoslavia was voted upon in late 1990, the Serbs orchestrated a series of staged provocations against the Croats. Serbian political leaders in Croatia refused to participate in the new political system. Instead, they set about establishing an illegal Serbian autonomous area that comprised 2.4% of Croatia's population and 8.8% of its territory. The Serbs committed their first overt act on August 17, 1990, in the Knin area when separatists blocked the main roads and the only railline that connected the coast, particularly Split, the second largest city in Croatia, from the Croatian heartland. By cutting off the flow of goods and people, the rebel Serbs threatened the very survival of the Croatian state.

The Serbs then began a nine-month siege of an isolated town north of Split. Violence broke out on May 2, 1991, when nine Croatian policemen were ambushed and killed in a village predominantly inhabited by Serbs. The Serbian rebels launched a three-pronged attack in widely separated locations. Between March and June of 1991, the Serbs ambushed and killed 12 Croatian policemen at Pakrac, Plitvice National Park, and Borovo Selo near Vukovar. Each time the JNA intervened, but instead of backing the legitimate government, it openly allied itself with the Serbian rebels.

Belgrade ordered the JNA to prevent the referendum on confederation from taking place. Both Belgrade and the rebel Serbs preferred a centralized, Communist Party-controlled Yugoslavia that would continue to be financed largely from the wealth generated by Croatia and Slovenia. Serbian leaders and the army feared that confederation would cut their budgets and bankrupt both entities because the new union would have meant full economic sovereignty for the individual republics.

Shortly after the referendum votes and the collapse of negotiations by Slovenia and Croatia with Serbia, Serbian activities intensified. Using the pretext of protecting its "endangered" minority, Serbia tried to reestablish control over Croatia's infrastructure and natural resources. From the onset, the confederation idea had been doomed to failure. Croatia was the only republic that seriously considered it. From April, 1990, to the very eve of the conflict in June, 1991, Croatia, ever naive, expected a resolution. Slovenia, ever realistic, placed little credence in negotiating. Serbia, ever pragmatic, was totally unyielding.

Slovenia opted for independence on June 25, 1991, after it became clear that confederation was a dead issue. Not to be outdone by Slovenia, Croatia seceded from Yugoslavia earlier that same day. Two days later, after Slovenia took control of the border and custom posts with Italy and Austria, the JNA launched an attack on Slovenia. The federal army derived substantial funds from custom fees.

When the JNA tanks crossed Croatia into Slovenia without hindrance, Tudjman reneged on Croatia's mutual defense pact with Slovenia. Tudjman's decision, which overrode his chief general, Martin Spegelj, who wanted to honor the pact, produced a near rift at Croatia's command level. J.P. Mackley, an ever astute political analyst, said the decision was based on Tudjman's clinging hope for confederation. Even at that late date and after his constituency had overwhelming rejected it, confederation was still in his mind.

But it was the U.S. who really opened the door for the JNA's attack. Apparently the JNA heeded Secretary of State James Baker statement that Yugoslavia must be held together at all costs.

From the very onset, Belgrade's effort to subjugate Slovenia was doomed to failure. Slovenia had no indigenous Serbian population to assist the JNA and the Slovenian Alps' terrain were not conducive for mechanized warfare. The conscripts in JNA came from all the republics that comprised Yugoslavia. But once self determination had a chance of being realized, some republics refused to supply conscripts. Consequently, the JNA had no infantry to support an effective mechanized force. Given these factors the JNA withdrew. To pacify the chauvinists they said Slovenia wasn't in the plan for creating a

Greater Serbia. Slovenia's self-determination effort cost them nine lives, whereas the JNA lost thirty-seven.

Following the Slovene campaign, the JNA hierarchy instituted an ideological cleansing of its officer cadre. Although the Yugoslav armed forces had always been overwhelmingly Serbian, the purge effectively turned the military into an ethnically pure entity of Serbs.

The Slovene campaign may have been an effort to intimidate Croatia without resorting to a Serb-Croat war. But Croatia's self-determination efforts continued, and the JNA attacked. Regardless of how Belgrade justified its assault on Croatia, the invasion led to the deaths of over 12,000 people, most of them Croatian civilians.

When the Yugoslav Army confronted Croatian forces, they found nothing more than a bunch of auxiliary policemen. But the Croats, all volunteers indigenous to the area, exhibited remarkable resilience against a trained, technologically superior, and larger army. They were motivated by those most basic human needs—to protect their families and homes. They would rather die than allow the same horrors perpetrated by Serbian extremists on their brethren in neighboring villages to be visited upon their loved ones.

Although Zagreb's government was willing to offer plenty of political advice, at the time of the first attacks it wasn't in a position to help anyone, let alone provide meaningful military help. The high command in Zagreb was exactly what the term implied, a high command only, with neither lower echelons nor an army to command. Zagreb's government had little influence outside the buildings they were sitting in.

The concept that Croatia had a viable central government was figment of the imagination rather than a reality. Mayors of cities like Zadar or Sibenik often thumbed their noses at Zagreb's authority. General Raseta had 20,000 JNA soldiers in Zagreb walking around with fixed bayonets, one kilometer away from where the Croatian Sabor (parliament) were putting the finishing touches on the Croatian constitution.

The Zagreb government should burn candles in thanksgiving that Washington didn't have anyone on the ground in Croatia to provide hard intelligence. Washington instead relied on the hard intelligence reports that U.S. Ambassador Warren Zimmermann gathered at Belgrade's cocktail parties, where Croatia was projected, because of its "super-nationalism," as having a well armed disciplined army and a cohesive government. If the pro-Serbian cabal in the State Department knew just how vulnerable Croatia really was, I'm certain Deputy Secretary of State Lawrence Eagleburger and company would have taken measures to tilt that precarious balance.

The Croatian defenders, mostly armed with weapons no larger than hunting rifles, were loosely controlled by commanders whose communication with Zagreb was non-existent. This lack of chain of command made the defenders more effective. Their knowledge of the tactical situation enabled them to mount defenses without Zagreb's political interference, which often seemed self-serving and counter-productive. But the lack of communication also severely hindered Croatia's ability to logistically coordinate its sparse military ordnance to where it was most needed.

The overwhelming Serbian aggression wasn't simply a military operation. The Serbs systematically set about destroying Croatian communities, historical monuments, churches, and birth, death and property registers. Destroying the registers would effectively confuse property ownership issues and give the Serbs legitimacy when arguing about demographics at international tribunals. The conquerors tried to remove any trace of Croatian presence and culture in the Serbian occupied areas. Furthermore, the Serbs intimidated and coerced remaining Croats to leave. After noting the destroyed churches, hospitals, and graveyards that the Serbs had left in their path, human rights advocate Dr. Slobodan Lang aptly described the Serbian army actions as "The War Against Three Crosses."

Civilians made up 84% of the causalities in Croatia. But the Western response to attacks on mostly unarmed civilians was negligible. Following the slaughter that took place in Croatian cities like Vukovar and in the siege of Dubrovnik, the Western media finally came to question Serbian justifications for the war. Reporting became more objective. But prior to that awakening, Serbian propagandists had convinced the international media that the casualties and the destruction of churches, historically meaningful structures, and villages were appropriate responses to the Croatians' alleged propensity for violence.

When the Serbs first attacked Croatia, the defenders had to create an army from scratch. Weapons and ammunition had been almost non-existent. Despite the paucity of weapons, the Croats held their own once the shock of the initial JNA attacks wore off.

President George Bush inherited the final chapter of the fall of communism from President Reagan. Unfortunately, Bush didn't know how to react. Although some political pundits applauded Bush's foreign policy, he wasn't any better at foreign policy than he was at the domestic policy that cost him the election. A major objective of foreign policy is to prevent war, an objective Bush failed to achieve in both Iraq and Yugoslavia.

A remarkable parallel exists between the Iraqi and Yugoslav conflicts. A week before Saddam Hussein invaded Kuwait, U.S. Ambassador April Glaspie assured Hussein that "the U.S. has no opinion on the conflict regarding [Iraq's] border disagreement with Kuwait." Likewise, in June, 1990, Secretary of State Baker made a pivotal speech in Belgrade concerning Yugoslavia's territorial integrity. He stated that Yugoslavs should use "all means possible to preserve the stability of the country." Thus Baker gave the Belgrade regime carte blanche to proceed with a five year pattern of genocide.

Although Yugoslavia didn't have enough oil to interest the United States, the country's geo-strategic position was vitally important to the U.S. during the Cold War. After Yugoslavia's split with Russia in 1947, the U.S. based its Balkan policy on Tito's supposed resistance to Moscow. When the Russian military threat disappeared in 1989, the integrity of Yugoslavia was no longer strategically significant to U.S. national interests.

The fall of the Berlin Wall foreshadowed the collapse of European Communism and transformed fear of the Russian monolith into bravado. One-party rule broke down throughout Eastern Europe as long-suppressed desires for self-determination began to energize nationalistic forces. Caught up in the euphoria, Croatia and Slovenia opted to secede from Yugoslavia. Remaining tied to Serbia would've meant remaining chained to the anachronism of an ineffective Communist past because the Communist Party was reasserting itself in Serbia. But a Croatian-proposed loose confederation of former Yugoslav republics was flatly rejected by Serbian President Milosevic. Instead, Serbia advocated a strong central government with majority control of a renewed federation.

Milosevic rekindled Serbian nationalism by whipping up myths that inflamed a pathological and hysterical hatred of the Croats. This hatred was a direct result of an effective brainwashing campaign. Disinformation convinced the Serbian population that Croatia had built concentration camps where the Croats were slaughtering thousands of their Serbian minority. The Serbs claimed to have uncovered a Vatican plot against Orthodoxy and an Austrian-German-Croatian conspiracy to form a Fourth Reich. The Serbs also claimed that the Croatian government was a reincarnation of the Ustashe. By stirring up anxiety and paranoia among Balkan ethnic groups Milosevic had begun to implement the tenets of the *SANU Memorandum*.

In 1987, Milosevic denounced the leadership in the autonomous region of Kosovo and subsequently installed a Serb-led police state there. Milosevic's Kosovo speech brought him out of relative obscurity and into the limelight of Yugoslav politics. The speech also laid the groundwork for the spread of nationalistic chauvinism and the campaign to create a Greater Serbia.

During 1988 and 1989, Milosevic organized numerous nationally televised Serbian demonstrations to protest supposed Croatian fascism. The demonstrations panicked Serbs into believing that they were victims of discrimination. Conversely, the demonstrations were shrewdly designed to intimidate non-Serbs throughout Yugoslavia. Milosevic proclaimed Serbia the undisputed master of post-Tito Yugoslavia, while he and his cronies used Balkan Stalinism, deception, corruption, blackmail, demagoguery, and violence, to fulfill the slogan "All Serbs in one state."

Milosevic sabotaged the economic reforms of Yugoslav Prime Minister Ante Markovic. Markovic, a non-elected party apparatchik in whom the Bush administration had placed a great deal of trust, resigned on December 20, 1991, after rejecting a newly proposed federal budget that earmarked 75% for the Yugoslav National Army.

His resignation was a blow for those Americans who had based their approach to Yugoslav policy on Markovic. Although Markovic had no real power base nor a constituency, Zimmermann presupposed this quintessential apparatchik to be the savior of Yugoslavia. As Markovic was no longer on the scene Milosevic misappropriated billions of dollars from the individual republics' foreign reserves held in Belgrade banks, which he used to further his political ambitions.

In May 1991, after Milosevic blocked the scheduled rotation process of the presidency, Yugoslavia became a country without a legitimate president. The Serbian pretense that Yugoslavia was still a federation collapsed in October, 1990, when Serbia imposed import duties on goods from Croatia and Slovenia.

Prior to the Croatian and Slovene declarations of independence in June, 1991, the Serbian media devoted a disproportionate amount of its coverage to criticizing the secessionist republics. The Serbian press also stressed that the Serbs would be defenseless against the genocidal urges of the Croats. The Serbian government accused the leading political party in Croatia, the Croatian Democratic Union (*Hravtska Demokratska Zajednica:* HDZ), of planning to revive Ustashe terror.

The assertion that the conflict has its roots in ancient ethnic hatreds is a historical inaccuracy. Certainly the area had witnessed numerous battles as the fault line between Christian Europe and the Islamic Ottoman Empire. But contrary to media and Western politicians' allegations, prior to 1918 there had been a remarkable symbiosis between Serbs and Croats. In the Summer 1991 issue of *Foreign Affairs*, V.P. Gagon wrote: "From a historical perspective, this area experienced little ethnic violence prior to the twentieth century and never witnessed the vicious religious wars as seen in Western Europe."

Many of the myths carefully propagated by governments with a stake in the conflict break down when history is studied. The 1990-1995 fighting wasn't caused by inherently violent ethnic traits that manifest themselves every second or third generation. Rather, forces beyond the control and borders of everyday Croatian and Serbian citizens have fueled the violence. World Wars I and II can't be blamed on Balkan genetics.

Diplomats and British and American pundits added to the public's confusion by using Rebecca West's 1941 novel, *Black Lamb and Grey Falcon,* as their primary reference for understanding the causes of the conflict. The problem with West's book was that her extraordinary literary style overshadowed the historical facts. West's contemporary, John Gunther, said at the time of the book's publication: "[It's] not so much a book about Yugoslavia as a book about Rebecca West." The book was a purely subjective travelogue that romanticized the Serbs as racially superior beings.

West hated the Croats as much as she admired the Serbs. She considered the Croats pretentious for wanting to be associated with Western and not Slavic ideals. And she negated Croatian and Bosnian self-determination efforts because she felt that the Croats and Bosnians should've accepted their lot, including the murders or imprisonment of dissidents, in gratitude for having been saved from the Turks. West's pre-World War II era ideas continue to be spewed by the pundits of the 1990s. Although the book never professed to be historical, it nevertheless influenced the thinking of several generations of readers about Yugoslavia. The State Department made the book its bible for the region. Diplomats assigned to the former Yugoslavia who had been prejudiced by West's "history" severely handicapped the non-Serbian positions. Warren Zimmermann, one of the highest ranking American diplomats, acknowledged West's influence when he mentioned her a number of times in his 1996 book, *Origins of a Catastrophe.*

The republics of Croatia and Slovenia countered Serbia's chauvinism with nationalistic agendas of their own. After their first free elections the republics refused to recognize Serbia's self-proclaimed seniority status within Yugoslavia. A few days before Croatia and Slovenia formally voted for independence, Yugoslav Prime Minister Markovic, forever the naive optimist and Zimmermann's great hope, said, "The federal government will counter unilateral secession with all available means."

In the meantime, Chetnik and Belgrade-sponsored groups had infiltrated Serbian communities within Croatia and began supplying them with weapons. Violence rose exponentially in Croatian regions heavily populated by ethnic Serbs following Croatian and Slovene independence. Serbian provocations escalated into a cold and calculated ethnic cleansing program. But contrary to media reports, there were very few substantiated incidents of Serbs having fled Croatia because of terrorism.

In many instances Serbian antagonists used stratagems reminiscent of Mao Tse Tung to promote fear among the Serbs of Croatia against the legitimate government. After Serbian rebels seized the police station in Pakrac (a village in Slavonia) in Spring 1991, the Croatian government sent in reinforcements. When the Croatian police arrived, the Serbian rebels fled and found refuge in the local JNA base. Serbian provocateurs then went house to house warning the indigenous Serbs that the Croats were coming to kill them. Panicked, thousands of Serbs fled by any means available. The media then depicted those fleeing as victims and prime examples of Croatian terrorism despite the fact that none of these so-called refugees ever saw any Croat lift a finger against them. Banner headlines lamented the "Bloodbath at Dawn" and "Massacre of Innocents." Yugoslav Army tanks were called in to keep the peace.

The situation in Croatia exploded in July and August of 1991, when Serbian irregulars, aided by the JNA, initiated a series of incidents. Thousands of innocent civilians died, and entire cities and villages were wantonly destroyed. The war in Bosnia would follow a similar pattern, though on a much grander scale.

The Serbs instituted and organized a systematic policy meant to destroy the non-Serbian population, cultures, traditions, and religions. In Croatia, violence was primarily aimed at Roman Catholic churches, hospitals, and historical structures. Twenty eight of the latter were designated by UNESCO as cultural monuments. Although of no military value, medieval Dubrovnik was under siege for months.

The Serbs made a cardinal mistake when they besieged Dubrovnik in the beginning of October, 1991. The Yugoslav conflict might have remained a backwater civil disorder in the eyes of the media if the Dubrovnik attack and siege hadn't drawn international attention. For the first time the media became skeptical of Serbian justifications for their war.

Unfortunately, this change in perception didn't include the Western governments. Alone among the its allies, only Germany was outraged that an army was attacking a purely civilian target and condemned the Serbian actions. With each passing day, the siege of Dubrovnik became increasingly desperate. The city's population began to panic, especially when they saw how the civilized world ignored their plight.

For many of the inhabitants of Dubrovnik, the bombardment was their second experience living under siege. Approximately 55,000 refugees thought they had found a safe haven Dubrovnik after escaping from Serbian onslaughts in other parts of Croatia. Expensive hotels, once playgrounds for the rich and famous, where many of the refugees were housed, was within Serbian mortar range. In his pathetic attempt at shuttle diplomacy, Lord Carrington urged the citizens of Dubrovnik to surrender.

As the siege intensified press headlines read: "Shell shocked Croat soldiers abandon the last hilltop fort protecting the ancient city." The victims of the siege were in such dire straights that French Minister for Humanitarian Relief Dr. Bernard Kouchner called for surrender. Dr. Kouchner, the founder of Medecins sans Frontieres and Medecins du Monde, which are Non Governmental Organizations (NGOs) that send doctors to catastrophes throughout the world, was aware of what the Serbs were capable of doing because he had seen the aftermath of Vukovar. Kouchner naively tried to broker a unilateral ceasefire with the Serbian forces. Without Croatian consent, he offered to demilitarize Dubrovnik. The Croatian forces would surrender what arms they had and leave by sea; the EC or U.N. would monitor and guarantee the peace.

The last stage of any siege is when the defenders consider evacuating the women and children. This situation was fast approaching in Dubrovnik. The Croats knew they couldn't defend the city against a well armed, well trained army with only a few shotguns, hunting rifles, and two 1942 vintage 76 millimeter artillery pieces. After the

Serbs cut off the water supply, the reservoirs emptied, and the situation appeared desperate. Miraculously, though, it rained. Not only did the rain water replenish the bodily needs of the besieged, the rain also gave the city's defenders a tremendous psychological boost. Even one particularly terrible six hour period on Saint Nicholas Day, December 6, 1991, when 600 Serbian artillery shells exploded in the old historic district, couldn't deter the steadfast resolve of Dubrovnik's citizens.

The West assumed Dubrovnik's fall was imminent. The Serbs allowed humanitarian organizations to send three ships to evacuate 1,700 women with their children. Once accomplished, the next step would've been for the Serbs to take the city. Instead, the women refused to leave their sons, husbands, and fathers. The women of Dubrovnik evoked what Lang called the Masada strategy. The citizens of Dubrovnik felt that the only way to confront the Serbian strategy of generating refugees as tools of genocide was for every member of society to refuse surrender. The Dubrovnik crisis dissipated after the Croat forces mounted a counter-offensive, and the Serb forces retreated from the high ground.

In a January 14, 1992 full-page ad in the New York Times, as the mayhem increased in Croatia, 104 Nobel Prize winners spurred by Linus Pauling called upon world governments to stop the wanton destruction by the Yugoslav Army and save the Croatian people from extinction. Never before had so many awardees concurred on a common cause. But even this gesture didn't affect the Western governments' policy of appeasing the Serbs.

The Serbs were undeviating in their military campaigns. Prior to any offensive maneuver they forewarned the indigenous Serbian population. Once those people not having a death wish were safely removed, incessant, coordinated tank and artillery bombardment followed. Most of the terrified non-Serbian population fled and in marched the Serbian irregulars. Those remaining non-Serbs were beaten, murdered and raped, only to wish they had fled with the first wave.

Before overt hostilities erupted, the outside world found it difficult to see that a bloody conflict was brewing. President Bush ignored highly credible CIA warnings in 1990 that Yugoslavia would break up spontaneously within 18 months, with a strong likelihood that this process would be accompanied by acts of violence and civil war. European diplomats were also unconvinced. During the Slovene war the foreign ministers of the European Community supported diplomatic negotiations that, in their view, had already sorted out the entire problem. The West either didn't understand the nature of the conflict or it didn't care to understand.

Bush abandoned what had been the linchpin of U.S. policy, the destabilization of communism, because of an inordinate devotion to geo-political stability. Bush ironically first abandoned these tenets in Russia, the country that originated the need for this policy in the first place. Enamored with Communist leaders Mikhail Gorbachev in Russia and Ante Markovic in Yugoslavia, Bush was unable to comprehend realpolitik and continued supporting the status quo and survival of the Soviet Union. Bush listened enthusiastically to Gorbachev's persistent warnings about an impending catastrophe if the Soviet Union broke up. Gorbachev had a fear of new leadership, and his distrust of emerging, freely elected parties apparently influenced the American president. Instead of promoting democracy, free elections, and respect for human rights, Bush chose to maintain the existing state of affairs. The U.S. and Western European nations looked at Yugoslavia through the prism of the Soviet Union. As armed conflicts commenced support was given to the political anachronism prevailing in Serbia for fear that an outbreak of secessionist movements among constituent republics would provoke similar outbreaks in the Soviet Union and have a destabilizing effect there too.

The Western right of self-determination seemed only to apply to the Eastern European countries that wished to leave the Soviet bloc. In December 1991 Bush reiterated his policy that states should neither be created nor destroyed. Condemning "suicidal nationalism," he begged the Ukrainians to remain in the Soviet Union and stick with reliable Gorbachev. Reinforced by the advice of Ambassador Zimmermann, Secretary of State Baker notified Croatia and Slovenia that they shouldn't expect U.S. recognition. The democratic aspirations of Croatia and Slovenia were vilified in some Western political circles as the real cause of the war.

Zimmermann also actively spread disinformation about Croatia. In early 1991, in an interview in the Serbian periodical *NIN*, Zimmermann stated that America was concerned about dangers Serbs and Jews were facing in Croatia, despite a lack of any verifiable instances of Jews or Serbs perceiving themselves in jeopardy. By raising the suspicion, he created an issue out of a non-issue and aided and abetted the Serbian propagandists.

Zimmermann influenced policy makers when he articulated the pro-Serbian cabal's agenda in the State Department before the Yugoslav Economic Council meeting on September 19, 1991 in Washington D.C. He characterized the events in Yugoslavia as merely a conflict between two narrow-minded nationalisms. The only difference between the Serbs and the Croats was that the Croats weren't expansionistic. Because the Croats forced Serbs living in Croatia to take loyalty oaths, fired them en masse from their jobs, and burned and looted their homes, he said the Serbs had justifiable reasons to be angry with the Croats. Furthermore, although Serbs comprised a sizable percentage of the population in Croatia, the Serbs didn't have the power that their numbers dictated. Zimmermann's half-truths and lies might as well have been written by Serbian propagandists.

The Balkan policies of the United States, Britain, and France were based on outmoded balance-of-power politics. These self-appointed Western godfathers had an almost pathological attachment to their hybrid, Yugoslavia, an entity they had created after World War I. They looked upon their noble experiment, with its imbedded Serbian ethnic and civic nationalism hegemony, as sacrosanct—but never considered the non-Serbs' civil rights. After the eruption of the conflict, these countries tried to appease radical Serbian chauvinism because they saw that policy as the best way to keep Yugoslavia intact. History has shown that appeasing aggression only encourages a conflict to continue. So when countless Western negotiated cease-fires were disregarded by the Serbs, the only response the Western powers could come up with was to wring their hands and make statements of protest.

After a number of governments encouraged Croatia and Slovenia's self-determination aspirations, Secretary of State Lawrence Eagleburger did everything in his power to sabotage those efforts. Old wounds reopened and continue to fester amongst the allies. Following the reunification of Germany, European states took sides on the Balkan issue exactly as they had in 1914. In a *Los Angeles Times* editorial, the self-styled pundit Martin Walker presumptuously branded the German reunification as the "Fourth Reich" and claimed that Germany's breaking ranks over the Balkan issue "provoked the first European war since it plunged us into the last one." Undaunted by criticism, Germany decided to play a more forceful role in European affairs. But the German Constitution forbids deployment of its military other than in defense of German territory or outside of NATO's jurisdiction. So a military response to the crisis in former Yugoslavia was precluded.

Germany officially recognized Croatia and Slovenia in January 1991, despite almost hysterical posturing by France and England, strong U.S. objections, and a vigorous campaign by Eagleburger. U.N. peace negotiators Cyrus Vance and Lord Peter Carrington argued that recognition would only escalate the war. But diplomatic recognition brought with it the first lasting cease-fire in Croatia, after 58 previous peace agreements had been broken by the Serbs. Germany's decision was its first unilateral pronouncement since World War II. Despite having the world's third largest economy and being the second largest exporter, Germany's external political voice has been muted by its competitors because of Germany's role in World War II. But Germany's economic dominance in Central and Eastern Europe has led to political influence in the region.

Germany's moral stand on the conflict in former Yugoslavia didn't sit well with its NATO allies, particularly the Bush administration. American officials forecast that this "new German assertiveness" would be "difficult to stomach" because it thrusts Germany back into a leadership role and condemns the United States to secondary status in Europe. Germany bluntly criticized the refugee policies of its Western neighbors who were far less generous in offering asylum. As of August 1992, Germany had accepted 240,000 refugees from former Yugoslavia, while France and England together had taken less then 2,000.

Looking for a convenient scapegoat for their inertia, the other Western governments chastised Germany for prematurely recognizing Croatia and Bosnia-Herzegovina. Yet Britain and France, who had been the loudest critics of Germany, voted in the affirmative in the European Community's (EC) unanimous decision to support recognition. Germany, was the only Western country to take a moral stand when they protested the barbaric atrocities, indiscriminate shelling of non-combatant civilians in cities like Dubrovnik, and the leveling of Vukovar. Ignoring Germany's position, the United States continued to support an indivisible Yugoslavia, a policy that encouraged and contributed to the aggressiveness of the Serbian-led JNA.

The schism between the Western allies over the Balkan issue has been blamed for slowing down European integration by some pundits. But the main rationale for integration had been the threat of the Soviet Union's monolithic Communism. As a result of its disintegration, European integration has slowed to a snail's pace. Political lines have emerged based on economic spheres of influence. Germany is the prevailing economic influence in most Eastern European countries. Its economic power blocked France and Britain from competing in those new markets. France and Britain's only partners in the old Eastern bloc are Romania and Serbia. Perhaps one of the reasons for the delay until April 27, 1993, of economic sanctions on Yugoslavia was that France and Britain didn't want to jeopardize their future economic relationships with Serbia. And England's complicity with Yugoslavia has recently started to pay off. A March 1996, article in the Greek weekly *Ependitis*, titled "The Secret Major-Milosevic Agreement," claimed that British Foreign Minister Malcolm Rifkind had entered into a gentlemen's agreement with Milosevic to advance credits of five billion dollars for the purchase of British weapons. In addition to a number of high ranking British officials, several representatives of British companies and banks, including Midlands and Barclays, participated in the negotiations. As a reward, British interests will apparently control Yugoslavia's banking system and markets.

The British justified their deal with Milosevic as an effort to combat Germany's ever-widening influence in the Balkans.

Another reason for the British government's obvious complicity with Serbia may have resulted from successful influence peddling by the Serbs. According to *The Guardian* (December 23, 1996), shortly before the 1992 general election in England, the Tory Party, with John Major's full knowledge, received an enormous amount of funds from Serbian sources. As witnessed by the Clinton administration, apparently accepting campaign funds from foreign sources is common practice among Western democracies. The only harm caused by Indonesia and China funding Clinton was to the opposition party. But the harm caused by the Serb funds to the Tories added to the death and destruction of non-Serbs. The Labour Party questioned the ethics of the Tory party accepting funds from forces that had placed British subjects in harms way while serving in the armed forces in former Yugoslavia.

After the disintegration of the Soviet Union, European governments deluded themselves into believing that their new trading bloc would be endowed with political unity and power. The EC still reflects the objective economic and social interests of its members. Yet the EC's decision-making procedure allows only the lowest common denominator to work. Greece's implacable opposition to Mac–edonian recognition has caused severe embarrassment to EC members. Greece's intense lobbying on Serbia's behalf made a coherent EC approach to the Balkan crisis very difficult.

President François Mitterand of France made an unannounced visit to Sarajevo on June 28, 1992, to show solidarity with the besieged city. Although his trip was a minor gesture, it met with a great deal of criticism from European leaders. His visit particularly piqued the British because the French president had grabbed the limelight on the eve of the British takeover of the EC presidency. Clearly the EC is composed of members with independent agendas. Military involvement in the Balkans by EC members was highly unlikely because a consensus on the make-up of the intervening force would be politically contentious and ultimately an unsolvable issue.

The EC erroneously embarked on a policy of localized solutions to the war that neither stopped the violence nor resolved any of its underlying causes. Milosevic, whose regime was responsible for supplying the Serbian insurgents with weapons and other support, disappeared into the background during the seemingly endless peace discussions that had taken place in such varied spots as London, Paris, Geneva, and Greece.

The West struggled to find a solution to the crisis in former Yugoslavia and was stymied for many valid reasons. The collapse of the Soviet Union and the Gulf War absorbed considerable Western attention, so other hot-bed regions paled in strategic significance. Because Serbia posed no military threat outside of former Yugoslavia, the West found the Balkans uninteresting. But the West's assertion that military involvement would've immersed its forces in a quagmire with no discernible enemy was nothing more than a weak excuse.

Those who feared that United States or NATO air-strikes against Serbian positions or commitment of ground troops would result in a deeper Western involvement in the war were wrong. After the conflict had already caused 250,000 deaths, NATO finally employed air strikes. Although those first attacks were anemic, they did get the Serbs' attention.

WHAT HAPPENED IN VOCIN

WHAT HAPPENED IN VOCIN

When the Croat forces retook the territory the Serbs had occupied
and entered the Croatian village of Vocin on December 14, 1991, at
10:50 AM., they found bodies in the streets, in their burned houses
and in yards. With one exception, all the victims were Roman Catholic Croatian villagers who were massacred in ways that defy imagination. Half the victims were over 62; the eldest was 84. Most of the
young people, especially the males of the village had fled; or were
rounded up by the Serb invaders and shipped to parts unknown. Two
of the victims, a husband and wife, were found bound with chains
and burned. Subsequent chemical tissue analysis performed at the
University of Zagreb Medical School laboratories revealed that they
were burned alive. Others had their skulls split open by axes or chain
sawed in half while still alive. Those shot or stabbed were the lucky
ones.

One of the victims, Marijia Majdandzic, was an American citizen.
Her citizenship was verified after the Governor of Pennsylvania pressured the Bureau of Statistics to open their office on a Sunday to
investigate their files. Born in Erie, Pennsylvania, nee Skender, as a
young girl she moved to the what has turned out to be for her god's
forsaken valley in Croatia. Her life was snuffed out like a candle after
being trapped in her house when the Serbs torched it. Surprising,
Majdandzic was the only Vocin victim that didn't show signs of torture before death. The autopsy photographs depict her as a big boned

woman; her roundish figure and lack of worry lines indicate to me that she enjoyed good eating and had a zest for life. Although the pathology report said the cause of death was heart failure, even a cursory examination of the pathologist write up, lab analysis, and photos clearly indicated carbon monoxide poisoning. She was probably the first American causality of the conflict. Had she been an oil company employee, maybe the American government would have been stirred to action.

The Vocin massacre, forensically, is the most extensively documented war atrocity of the conflict. United States Congressman McCloskey and Pat Mackley had been on a fact finding mission in the vicinity when they received reports about what had taken place in Vocin. Mackley immediately made arrangements to take them to the site. While the bodies were still warm, they were among the first to arrive on the scene. A number of witnesses gave them telling testimony within hours of the event. Some of the perpetrators, who had been captured, were also interrogated.

One of perpetrators was captured through a number of remarkable circumstances. Most of the Chetniks, either before or after slaughtering, looted. One of the head Chetnik's locked a Croatian couple in a pigsty prior to ransacking their home. The only reason he didn't kill them then and there, if he wasn't satisfied with what he found, he could always go back and force them to tell where they had hidden other valuables. The couple truly had God on their side that day. The Chetnik had found some good sljivovica, got drunk, and passed out. As luck would have it, the couple's son had been one of the Croatian national guardsmen who liberated the village. He went home not knowing what he would find. To his dismay he found the passed out Chetnik; a further search found his parents in the pigsty. Surprising, rather then seeking revenge, he turned the Chetnik over to his officers for interrogation.

After witnessing the ghastly aftermath of the slaughter, Mackley made arrangements to schedule a news conference for the next morning. Unable to sleep because of what he had witnessed, McCloskey woke Mackley, after midnight. As the Washington Post reported, he told Mackley he was so shaken up he didn't wish to speak to the media. This just wasn't an issue he wanted to be involved in. Mackley said, "okay" and went back to sleep—only to be awakened three more times by the distraught McCloskey.

He said, "I don't want to talk about it, but I just can't get those faces out of my mind," recalls Mackley. "I watched him wrestle with the politics of it all that night. Ultimately, he decided he didn't care what the political implications were—for him or anybody. His sense of humanity took over."

Interestingly, Mark Dalmish, the CNN reporter in Zagreb refused to attend McCloskey's press conference because he didn't want to give the Congressman a "soapbox."

As a result of his Vocin experience, Congressman McCloskey became the first person in American government circles to articulate the situation in former Yugoslavia objectively. Although a Democrat, he became the voice of conscience in Congress where his humanistic stance embarrassed the liberal wing of his party and finally stirred it into action. Mackley subsequently became McCloskey's congressional aide and valued foreign affairs advisor. McCloskey's moral stand may have been the trigger mechanism that caused President Clinton to violate the U.N. arms embargo to former Yugoslavia.

One witness, Vera Doric, who escaped and hid in a nearby corn-field with her two-year -old granddaughter said: "I saw them set a house on fire, and they wouldn't let the people out. There were local Serbs going with them, showing them to the houses. They had a list."

In his attempt to carry out my recommendation to document the slaughter at Vocin with forensic protocols, Mackley met, not surprisingly, with a great deal of obstinacy from the Croatian authorities. Despite the body of hard evidence, the Croatian attitude was blasé. They viewed the Vocin episode as just another routine Serbian operation. The Croatians, to their loss, have never believed in public relations. Submitting proof to the world was deemed unimportant. Besides being unorganized, the government forces saw no intrinsic value in it, particularly when they pointed how the media and the world had ignored previous slaughters of Croatian civilians. Basically they looked upon the European observers as a bunch of ghoulish voyeurs.

Although Mackley had documents issued from the highest offices in Zagreb, the local police at Podravska Slatina, where the Vocin victims were brought for burial, told him Zagreb had no authority and to get lost. Mackley was caught in the middle of a turf war between Zagreb and local authorities. The latter wanted to keep the matter local since they had no faith in Zagreb's government and wanted to extract its own form of justice. Not deterred, Mackley realized the importance of documenting the latest Serbian atrocity would have for Croatia, he phoned Gojko Susak, Minister of Defense. Even Susak's direct orders had no effect on the local police commanders. Eventually special units from the Ministry of Interior were called. Their arrival almost induced a fire fight with local police over jurisdiction. After the crises was resolved the Health Minister's team of forensic pathologists from Zagreb's medical school performed some of the autopsies there and some in Zagreb. In any case, each Vocin corpse was worked up as they would a murder case.

In an all too familiar scenario that was being played out daily in other parts of Croatia, terrorist acts on the Croats in Slavonia, in western Croatia, started on August 14, 1991, when masked Serbian military forces shelled a number of villages, including Vocin. Communication and freedom of movement to the outside world then stopped when the Serbs set up barricades to isolate the local population. At 6:55, shortly after sunrise, on August 19th, almost every Croatian home in Vocin was targeted and hit by Serb artillery, as though for target practice at a carnival.

After the shelling, the terrified Croatian survivors were gathered together at 9:00 and informed by two local Serb villagers, Boro Lukic and Drago Dobrojevic—who were now wearing JNA officer uniforms—that the Serbs were in command. As a show of force two columns of local Serbs, some wearing army uniforms, some in civilian garb, marched by carrying Kalashnikovs. A few days earlier these same Serbs had worked together with the Croats as friends and colleagues in the forestry industry (a major local industry), in shops and factories; attended the same schools, drank with, and chased the same girls.

The eighty surviving Croats, from the prewar population of four hundred twenty six, were forbidden to leave their homes to go work or tend their fields and livestock. They were denied access to physicians to care for their health needs. Since most of the Croatian homes were badly damaged, the surviving Croats found shelter in the basements. During the four months the Serbs occupied Vocin the, non-Serb population had been inhumanely abused and harassed, which culminated in the December massacre. The day of the massacre, December 13, eight individuals managed to escape from the village. The testimony of a woman, R.O. (initials used to protect her identity because of fear of reprisals), recorded in Milos Judas and Ivica Kostovic's seminal work about the atrocities in Croatia, *Mass Killing and Genocide*, and verified by Helsinki Watch, best summarizes what transpired in Vocin and shows the manner in which Serbian psychological warfare was carried out—and the effectiveness of Serbian disinformation.

"The Croats in Vocin were regarded as slaves. The men were forced to work very hard in the forest and in the fields, and received only a scarce amount of food and several cigarettes from local Serbs who ran the village. When one of them was killed by Serbs, the rest of us had to say again and again that he deserved it and therefore it was normal that he had been killed. So, for example, Chetniks (Serb paramilitary) first forced four Croats to bring their ammunition to the hills around Balinci, and after that killed one of them—Drago Ivankovic. After hearing the death of her husband, his wife Fatima moved to my house—she almost went crazy and every day she had to say that it was really all right that they killed her husband. Namely, she was extremely afraid for her life and the life of her five old year old son. Some of our neighbors of Serbian nationality told us constantly that it had to be so, because Ustashe in Podravska Slatina (a large town close to Vocin) had shot 120 Serbs in the market place and that each day in Slatina 15 Serbs were shot."

"They also told us that Kurds who fought for the Ustashe would kill us, too. We were so brain-washed by their propaganda that even two days after we succeeded in escaping from our village (on December 15, 1991) we were afraid to contact members of the Croatian National Guard although we observed them from the forest. Fortunately, Pero Carevic from our group recognized some of those guardsmen and brought help to us in this way."

"While we lived in Vocin, we lived mostly in basements and in the evening we lit hand-made candles. We met each other in complete secrecy and then mostly discussed our bad fortune and how to survive. We were not afraid so much of rifles and bullets, but we were extremely afraid that our throats would be cut with knives, because Serbian Chetniks like to execute people in this way. Furthermore, although we were not in a real prison, we were in fact hostages in our own homes. So we were never able to predict whether one day we would be released or whether they would just kill us. On Friday, December 13, 1991, a friend arrived in our basement and said that Chetniks had started to slaughter villagers in the other part of the village called Busija. Therefore we decided to run away immediately and, thank God, we succeeded in doing so."

Even before the actual massacre, the manner in which Franjo and Kresimir Doric were maltreated, two cases I personally verified from a number of EC and Croatian government documents, typified the Serbs' behavior during their four month "occupation." The Dorics were beaten with wooden rods, stomped by Serbs wearing boots, then tied to a tree for five days without food. A number of times they were blindfolded, and had the barrel of a gun placed in their mouths—which was fired repeatedly on empty chambers.

Evil incarnate descended on that cold Friday the 13th day of December 1991. After the Serb forces received orders to retreat, following a Croatian offensive to regain some of their lost territory, they ordered the local Serbs to go with them. While they were withdrawing, a group of Serb forces called the "White Eagles" stayed behind—and went on a killing spree. Most of the Croat homes were then torched, or were hit by mortars, grenades, and shoulder held anti-tank rockets.

The destruction acted as a catalyst for a killing orgy. Soon the town was filled with screams of the dying. Inasmuch as the victims were geographically concentrated around the Roman Catholic church the Serb murderers decided to blow it up, thinking the devastation would cover up the massacre. They didn't take into account the church's 6 foot thick walls. The church's basement was loaded with munitions of almost every description since it had been used as a central ammunition depot by the Serb occupiers. Despite the massive destruction, 58 bodies were eventually found; a great number of others, including children, disappeared without a trace.

The historic, Our Lady of Vocin, a Catholic church built only 25 years after the Gutenberg Bible was printed, was destroyed in seconds. Standing among the rubble like a sentinel stood a stump of masonry wall—all that remained of the 750 year old church (see photograph).

The Serbs, in their haste to retreat, left behind a number of credible witnesses. Their accounts agree on the essential details of the slaughter. Most of the surviving Croatians lived because their Serbian neighbors warned them about what the Serbian forces had planned for them. Thirteen found refugee in a small basement in the remains of what was once called a house; a number of others hid in cornfields, or in a pigsty.

Probably the Serbs' most grotesque act was when they handcuffed a 23 year old Croatian and hung him by his arms high on a tree limb across the road from the Catholic church. According to witnessess, the Serbs toyed with him by lightly cutting his face with a chain-saw several times. They then proceeded to amputate his lower limbs. While still alive they chain-sawed him in half. His body parts were doused with gasoline and set afire.

The Croatian was a soldier who came home on leave, but wasn't aware that the Serbs had occupied his village. He was captured and stripped naked. His actual torture began when the Serbs chained him to a tractor and dragged through the village before stringing him up on the tree.

The witnesses were questioned, along with several captured Serb soldiers who had been in Vocin during the slaughter. Congressman McCloskey was present at the interrogation of the soldiers. Aside from giving details about the slaughter, the Serb soldiers admitted to being members of Vojislav Seselj's infamous "White Eagles" and that they had been acting under direct orders from Belgrade.

Once the conflict extended into Bosnia-Herzegovina the White Eagles were linked to all the major atrocities there.

The White Eagles are only one of many Serbian paramilitary organizations whose objective is to terrorize non-Serbs. In the global context of Yugoslavia, Serbian paramilitary units, regardless of what subtitle they may carry, are called Chetniks. They are the enforcers of Serbian policy, at its most base. Most Westerners erroneously associate the Chetniks with the guerrilla fighters of World War II, but their main activities were terrorizing the non-Serb populations. At that time the Chetniks were carrying out the Yugoslav royalist government policies. Today they are carrying out the policies of Milosevic's Serbia.

Atrocities have always been part and parcel of Serbian policy. The link between the Serbian leadership and the ethnic cleansing programs has been established by a variety of sources. In 1995, a leaked CIA report and a high ranking Serbian defector with documentary evidence clearly shows the link. Information in the data banks at DePaul University, where the evidence for the war crimes trial is being compiled under the auspices of the U.N. Commission of Experts provide verification. According to Helsinki Watch, as early as 1992 evidence existed that was sufficient to indict the top officials in the Serbian forces for grave breaches of the Geneva Conventions.

The paramilitary group's agenda is to "ethnically cleanse" an assigned area and it works in conjunction with the Yugoslav army. Their *modus operandi* follow a clearly defined pattern of massacres, sexual torture, torture of elderly and children, looting, burning, and destruction. It is truly mind boggling for me to learn that this is happening in the latter part of the twentieth century.

Yet despite McCloskey's presence and trustworthy documentation furnished by European Community monitors and Helsinki Watch, some media accounts implied the massacre never happened; or that it was an act of disinformation planted by the Croats. For example, *The New York Times*, two days after the event, said the Croats have "alleged" that a massacre may have occurred in a village near

Podravska Slatina. Perhaps the photographs printed in this book will allow the truth to be known.

Mackley, a media animal, had gotten me involved in the Vocin aftermath for several reasons. He knew I was, coincidentally, heading for Croatia to investigate the poison gas stories. Also, as an American physician and, although I was by no means representing the University of Southern California, an Associate Clinical Professor at the USC-LA County Hospital Medical Center, I would, he felt lend credibility to the incident.

Which, in retrospect, I indeed did. CNN had been extremely skeptical about Vocin, not reporting it all until ten days after it occurred and then only when the rest of the media slowly started to believe it really happened. But after Mackley told the CNN staff in Zagreb that an American doctor possessing good credentials was involved and presently in Zagreb, they begged for an interview. The interview, conducted at the Intercontinental Hotel in Zagreb, lasted a half hour, but aired less than a minute. My bite of fame lasted a few seconds; yet it was enough to get the salient feature of the atrocities across.

The filmclip started with the tolling of church bells, panning the huge crowd moving in procession attending the mass funeral of the victims of Vocin. Then, the film switched to close-ups showing caskets draped with Croatian flags, crowds weeping, relatives and children filled with grief, and finally the caskets being placed in hearses and trucks departing for the cemetery. The commentary overlay: "Croatian officials said Monday that an elderly American was among the victims of a massacre at the village of Vocin ten days ago. At least 43 people were killed as Serbian-led Yugoslav federal forces withdrew from Vocin. The American was identified as seventy-two year old Marija Majdandzic of Pennsylvania. Born in the U.S., she had lived most of her life in Croatia."

The film then switched to me in a conversation, but without the sound on. The commentator's overlay: "Doctor Jerry Blaskovich of the University of Southern California told CNN he had examined the autopsy reports of half the victims. And has no doubt that a massacre took place." While the commentator continued, footage slow zoomed in on two of the victims lying on the ground: then the film again switched to me but this time the microphones were on as I was saying, "The way the wounds were inflicted, most of the people were lying on the ground when shot. It was done by groups of people— uniformed soldiers apparently." The camera then switched to the commentator, holding a microphone: "Croatian officials said the death toll at Vocin could go higher as more bodies are being discovered every day. Mark Dalmish, CNN, Zagreb." CNN's presentation of the events at Vocin, with me as testimonial to their reality, was, at least, finally seen worldwide. According to Mackley my interview with them was the only reason CNN reported the Vocin incident.

Post Mortems of Slaughter:
The Autopsies

Post Mortems of Slaughter:
The Autopsies

I'd been so upset that the world turned a blind eye to the realities of this war that I felt compelled to relate, in some detail, the details of my observations—and to provide photographic evidence to accompany it. The presented pathology reports are summaries and only represent what was most typical for the victims of the slaughter. I will limit myself only to the most salient features of the pathology. Other incidental pathological findings, such as associated heart disease or ovarian cystic tumor, which one patient had, will not be commented upon.

I didn't know what I was looking at in the first photos handed to me. I stared at them for several minutes until it dawned on me that the amorphous mass, with a pair of legs protruding from it, were the charred remains of what was once a human being. The legs were festooned with heavy linked chain that tied around to what appeared to be a finely carved table or chair leg.

From the deep recesses of my mind I recalled what a professor said during a lecture in forensic pathology class from my medical school days—and what I gleaned from past discussions with pathologists about burn cases. "Even the most jaded pathologist cringe when they have to work on burn victims." The mass of carbon bears no resemblance to human beings as it brings into question the examiner's entire value system and morality. What had been a living being, with hopes and dreams of a future, was now reduced to chunks of carbon. Correlating the photos with the chemical analyses from what tissue was left, revealed the victims were indeed alive, and therefore aware that they were being burned. Usually burn victims die of smoke inhalation long before the body actually starts to burn. But these human beings continued to live and breathe as the temperatures destroyed them.

I tried to imagine the agony they went thorough while they were still conscious and when they started to smell the odors as their own flesh was being barbecued. These particular victims were chained to chairs, and if the other bodies found in Vocin is any indication, they were probably tortured before being killed. They were apparently burned in increments, since the lung tissue was devoid of smoke particles.

Tomislav Martinkovic (#28)

The pathological examination revealed a carbonized torso lacking arms and the head. All that remained of Tomislav Martinkovic were the left pretibia and the lower part of the right pretibia (shin.) A large linked heavy chain was wrapped loosely over the right thigh and a wooden leg of a table or similar type of object. The thighs were totally carbonized but some muscle and bones were preserved. In examining the thorax and abdomen the left side of the heart were conserved and sent for analysis. Because of the amount of carbonization it was impossible to establish if any wounds occurred during life. Spectrophotometric qualitative method of the presented sample of heart muscle proved the presence of carboxyl myoglobin. This result established that Mr. Martinkovic was alive when the flames enveloped him.

Katica Martinovic (# 29)

All that was left of her remains, that could be identified as something human, was a part of one shin and foot. Tied around the shin was a large linked chain loosely tied to a wooden leg of a table or some similar object. The head and torso were completely carbonized. Both arms were missing. The only tissue that was found intact in the carbonized mass during the examination of the thorax and abdomen was a sliver of the left side of the heart. Everything else was totally carbonized. That tiny piece of heart muscle was analyzed. Spectrophotometric examination found the presence of carboxyl myoglobin, which established that Mrs. Martinovic was still alive at the time of contact with the fire.

Marija Simic (#22) 57 years old.
Four, almost identical appearing lesions were found on the scalp—all were straight, with extremely sharp regular borders. The apex of the wounds penetrated the skull bones and extended deeply into the brain tissue; all the underlying bones in their pathways were fractured. They were located on the crown (on top of the parietal region) in a transversal pattern. Immediately below those wounds was another similar appearing lesion, nine centimeters in length. Inferior, but closer to the temporal region, a 3.5 cm. wound was found. The fourth lesion, in the right temporal-parietal area, was 9.5 cm. in length. When the skin of the calvarium was removed, multiple fractures of the bones on the vault of the skull were found. The fragments extended deep in the brain cavity. Subsequent removal of the bony fragments left a defect approximately the size of a man's fist. Without going into details, the brain tissue findings were compatible with extravasation of blood (hemorrhages) and destroyed tissue. I agreed with the pathologist's conclusion that each wound by itself could have resulted in death. Clearly the wounds were inflicted by an ax.

Ivan Simic (# 21), born 12/21/32
The victim was bound with doubled knotted loops of linen cloth on the left wrist and left ankle. There also was a linen cloth noose wrapped twice around his neck that was cinched with a single knot. When the noose was removed during the autopsy, the skin and tissues of the neck showed a deep furrowed impression. Since no information was available of the circumstances in which the body was found, we can only surmise that he was tied. But the cause of death was two small stab wounds at the height of the left nipple, close to the sternum. The wounds, although deadly, had little external bleeding.

The autopsy findings showed one of stab wounds perforated the lung with resultant massive bleeding of right lung into the left pleural space. The other, parallel, stab wound penetrated the third intercostal space, pericardium, heart and finished in the left ventricle. He bled internally into the pericardial sac. Since there was minimal external bleeding, the perpetrators apparently were not sure if he was dead—and proceeded to tighten and garroted him with a cloth around his neck.

Post mortem examination revealed the larynx was crushed, but all pathological evidence was consistent that the damage to the throat tissues occurred after death. The dead person was one of the few that showed no apparent evidence of torture before death. Why he was spared is unknown. Perhaps he was forced to witness the tormentors inflicting torture on others, which is a common phenomena that I found in other documents—perhaps witnessing torture of loved ones is the greatest torture.

The remains of a married couple, Maria and Franjo Matancic were found in the front yard of their house. They were the bodies seen lying on the ground that CNN showed during my interview. The couple were summarily executed with one bullet below each of their eyes. At first glance the entry wounds seems minor, but the bullets in their pathways turned the brains to mush and exited in the back of the head as a gaping cavern filled with clots of blood, bone, and brain tissue. There can be no doubt this was murder in an execution style—and by no means an "accidental by-product of war."

Marija and Franjo Matancic (# 15 &16)

She was 64 years old when someone held an AK-47 close to her right lower eyelid and fired. The seemingly small entrance wound went upwards and backwards, taking off almost the entire right side of the back of the head. (see photographs) The exit wound measured 10 x 15 cm.

Her husband Franjo (# 15) met with a somewhat similar fate, except the entrance wound was the lower left eyelid. The bullet's direction went upward and toward the right. Once it penetrated the skull everything in its pathway was destroyed. It exited in the right parieto-temporeal area. The large gaping wound was the twin of his wife's.

Stojan Nenadovic (# 27)

The lone Serbian victim of Vocin, seventy-seven year old, Stojan Nenadovic, was mercilessly tortured by Yugoslav Army soldiers after having dared to intervene on behalf of his Croatian neighbors. Nenadovic had attempted to stop Serb soldiers who were harassing and torturing his Croatian neighbors. When he persisted, the soldiers proceeded to brand Nenadovic on at least 100 places. The uniformity of his lesions and their pattern indicated that lighted cigarettes or a heated metal chain were used to torture Nenadovic. The soldiers also filleted the skin of his lower extremities. Filleting is not a simple procedure, and requires practiced expertise. The skin is cut in a horizontal slit. The blade is then placed tangential into the subcutaneous tissues. In a feathering motion, the blade cuts through the collagen which binds the epidermis and the dermis to the subcutaneous fat. Then the fingers grasp the edge and the outer skin is tugged. The procedure is similar to pelting an animal.

Aside from these injuries, Nenadovic face, as I examined the evidence, showed multiple bruises, which clearly indicated to me that he was beaten by fists of a blunt object before dying. Nenadovic ultimately died of cardiovascular shock.

After examining the autopsies, objective laboratory analysis, and eyewitness accounts, even the blind could see or the most naive would have to agree, that what happened at Vocin weren't byproducts of war but concerted, deliberate murders. The only redeeming feature about Vocin is that it was the first Croatian slaughter which caught the media's attention after 50 previous slaughters had been ignored. A cursory review of the journalistic output regarding atrocities, prior to Vocin, reveals the media were either too jaded to report about them or couldn't or didn't want to believe the Serbs were capable of such acts. But in incidents where the evidence was irrefutable that the Serbs indeed perpetrated human mayhem, the media's take was that the acts were justified. They had completely bought into the notion that present day Croats are to be equated with Nazi beastiality.

In the global context, Vocin may seem insignificant, but the gallons of blood shed there have became part of a ocean of blood the Serbs caused to be shed in former Yugoslavia. The knowledge of what happened at Vocin is important because it transcended previous injustices and international lies about other atrocities. If the world had paid attention and reacted to the Serbs' wanton acts in Croatia the way it did to Sarajevo's breadline and marketplace slaughters the growth of the horrendous number of deaths and devastation that followed in Bosnia would not have been as great. I'd like to think the victims of Vocin didn't die in vain.

Zagreb's Hotel Inter-Continental. Favorite watering-hole for the international media and headquarters to the Foreign Press Bureau.

ŽUPNA CRKVA U VOČINU

Vocin's 750 year old Roman Catholic Parish Church, Visitation of St. Mary. Artist rendering by Branko Senoa (1912). Copy furnished by Republicki zavod za zastitu spomenika kultura (The Republic's Institute for Preservation of Cultural Monuments) Zagreb.

Bosanski Brod, Bosnia-Herzegovina. Caravan of cars and tractors waiting in a six and half mile long line seeking refuge in Croatia.

Refugees at Gasinci, former Yugoslavia army base, outside of Djakovo.

Bishop Ciril Kos, Archbishop of Djakovo in a jocular moment with the author.

The author in conversation with Dr. Vesna Bosanac, "Angel of the Killing Field of Slavonia," shortly after she was freed from a Serbian concentration camp.

Mostar's Muslim quarter. Once filled with thriving shops, now only ghosts shopping.

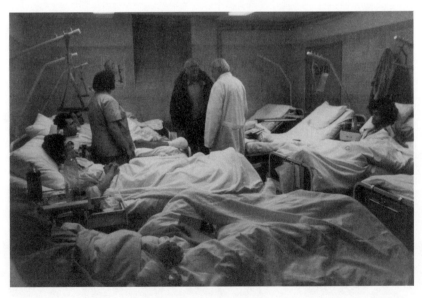

Osijek General Hospital. Wall to wall patients in the bowels of the hospital. The author with Dr. Kresimir Glavina.

The city of Split's basketball arena. Once the scene for international tournaments, now home to refugees.

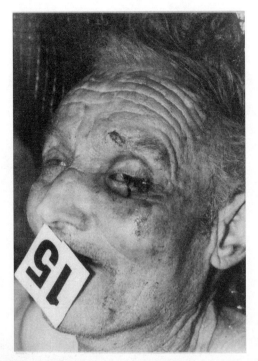

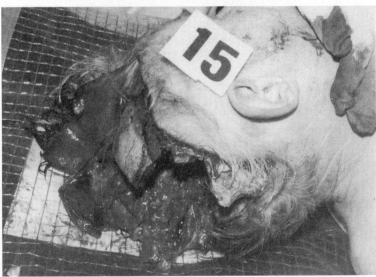

Franjo Matancic – civilian. Note the 9 mm entrance wound on the lower eyelid margin and gapping exit wound the back of the skull.

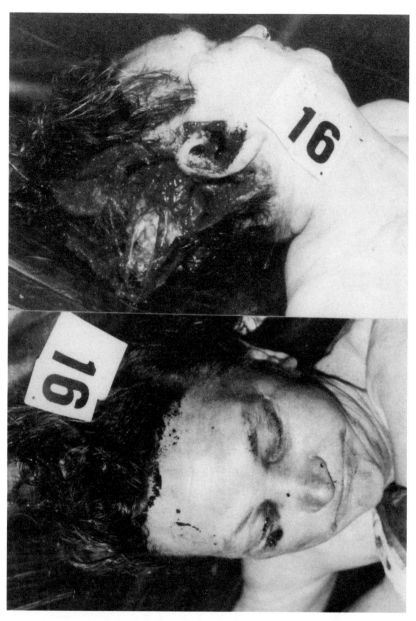

Marija Matancic – civilian. Note the 9 mm entrance wound on the lower eyelid margin and gapping exit wound the back of the skull.

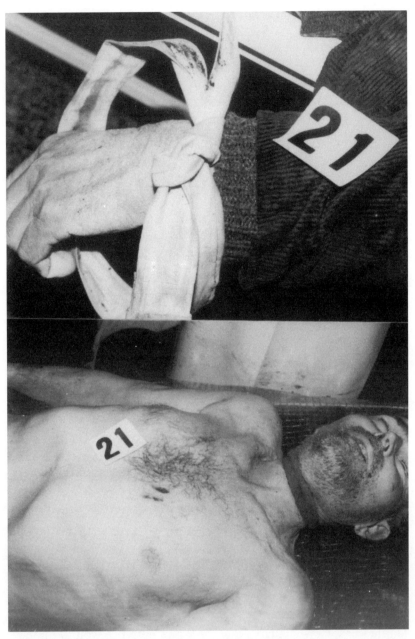

Ivan Simic – civilian. Bound, garroted and stabbed.

Marija Simic – civilian. Death caused by ax blows to the head.

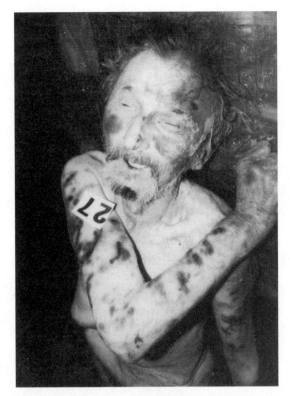

Stojan Nenadovic – civilian.

Stojan Nenadovic – Filleted skin.

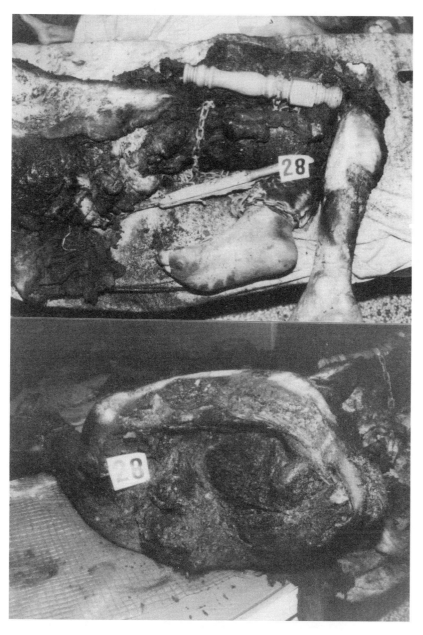

Charred remains of Tomislav Martinkovic – civilian.

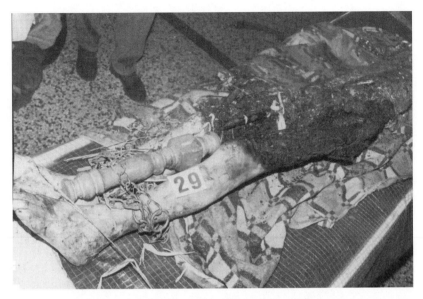

Charred remains of Tomislav Martinkovic – civilian.

Mostar July '92

The author among the smoldering ruins.

City park, Mostar 1992. Instead of being filled with children's laughter, it is now a cemetery filled with Muslims & Roman Catholics buried side by side. Rest in Peace.

THE DEVASTATION OF
OSIJEK AND THE
SMOLDERING ASHES OF VUKOVAR

THE DEVASTATION OF OSIJEK AND THE SMOLDERING ASHES OF VUKOVAR

Although I continued to participate in the aftermath of the Vocin slaughter, I still had to complete my investigation of the alleged poison gas attacks and evaluate Croatia's medical facilities for the Foreign Press Bureau. To this end, I went to the Western Slavonian city of Osijek. Because Osijek was in the very heart of the war zone I had to receive permission to travel there from the highest levels of Croatia's military authorities. General Ivan Prodan, Chief of Medical Services of the Croatian Armed Forces, personally gave me the green light and a carte blanche pass at his headquarters located in the bowels of Zagreb's main soccer stadium. During our meeting I took advantage of General Prodan and had a dialogue with him about the goals of my mission.

A great deal of territory that encompassed the main highway linking Zagreb to Osijek was in Serbian forces hands. To avoid the battle lines while crossing the scant 110 miles that separated the cities, we drove circuitously for six hours, skirting the Hungarian border and military barricades, passing through checkpoints and villages reduced to little more than rubble. When we finally arrived, the city was under heavy artillery and air attack. Serbian forces occupied all the land and towns immediately east, north, and south of Osijek.

From the very onset of hostilities in June, 1991, the city had been subjected to almost incessant artillery and air attacks. Just as everybody thought things couldn't get worse, the attacks markedly intensified after the nearby city of Vukovar fell on November 20. One international news source said the shells rained on the town's center one-per-minute. The citizens of Osijek huddled together in air raid shelters and basements under what had once been a charming, bustling city of 120,000 inhabitants, with a distinctly Austrian architectural influence. The incessant shelling of apartments, schools, hospitals, and churches appeared systematic and planned because Osijek had no military targets. The theater, a typical example of the Viennese ornate period, was destroyed; the multistoried Hotel Osijek by the Drava River had become a burnt out hulk.

When I'd visited Osijek in mid-1992 on another mission, I was among the first guests in that same hotel. The management had repaired the first four floors to make the hotel habitable and was in the process of repairing the upper stories. In June, 1995, when I was once again in Osijek, the hotel repairs had been completed without a trace of the previous destruction. But the drapes had to remain drawn since the hotel was still within sniper range of the Serbian positions across the river. The theater had been totally restored to its former grandeur. After the Croats were able to secure the northern banks of the Drava, they rebuilt the destroyed bridge that spanned the river. Rather than bemoaning the massive destruction and their plight, the citizens of Osijek remained optimistic for the future of Croatia. Despite having found themselves at the vanguard of the battle lines, they undertook a rehabilitation and rebuilding campaign that has set an example throughout war- ravaged areas of Croatia.

Osijek's General Hospital, the largest hospital close to the battle lines, was 80% destroyed. Although almost completely gutted by rockets and heavy artillery blasts, it continued to function. From the very first days of the conflict, all medical and surgical care was conducted in a maze of tunnels beneath the hospital that doubled as an air raid shelter. The situation was similar in hospitals of Vukovar, Vinkovci, and other Croatian towns and cities near the front lines. The occupied hospital beds were jammed together like sardines and filled all available space. Despite the overcrowded conditions, the patients received exemplary care. Quality was never comprised. The physicians managed to keep the postoperative mortality rate at

2.95%. They achieved a phenomenally low rate of 1.7% wound infections.

In addition to caring for patients with so-called mundane diseases like heart attacks, ulcers, or diabetes, Osijek Hospital admitted and treated 4,545 war victims between May 2, 1991, and November 1, 1992. According to Jonos and Lovric in a *Croatian Medical Journal* report, 56% were injured by shells or mines. After heavy bombardments bloodied and wounded patients lined the dimly lit hospital corridors waiting to be treated. The hallways filled with moans of agony from patients lying head to toe. Some of the patients had open, gaping wounds, and others had lost limbs; most were swathed with bandages caked with dried blood. The underground, makeshift operating theater worked to full capacity. Statistics aren't available on the numbers that were treated in the emergency room and released, but they were enormous.

Before the war Osijek's hospital, as all hospitals in Croatia, had a great number of ethnic Serbs staff members. Given their political clout, most of the department heads were Serb. But after Croatia declared independence, despite reassurances, many Serb physicians left their positions and joined the rebel forces. But those Serbs that remained continued to practice their art as usual, saving a great number of Croatian lives in the process. There were, however, some glaring exceptions.

Reliable sources told a story that shamed me as a physician after hearing how some of my colleagues had trampled the sacredness of the Hippocratic Oath and most importantly—humanity. Often working around the clock, the care that two physicians, a Serbian married couple, extended to the Croatian wounded at Osijek's hospital was looked upon by their colleagues as exemplary. The staff were surprised when the couple failed to show up at the hospital one morning. But they were numbed with shock when they learned that while the Serbian couple were acting as angels of mercy in Osijek's causality wards, during their "cigarette breaks" they went on the roof of the hospital, uncovered hidden weapons, and proceeded to snipe at Croat civilians. The angels of death were lauded as heroes in Serbia and resettled in a small town. Apparently they rapidly became bored with living in Serbia. They had the temerity to ask Osijek Hospital if they could return to practice there.

When the Serbs attacked hospitals or medical facilities as primary targets they violated all rules of war. A striking example of typical violations occurred during a three day period in September, 1991. Osijek's General Hospital was hit 94 times by mortars, howitzers, rockets, and countless times by small weapons. The barrage originated from the JNA garrison situated 50 meters from the hospital precluding the possibility the barrage was an accident or a tragic mistake.

Cyrus Vance, Secretary of State under President Jimmy Carter and official U.N. peace negotiator, visited Osijek in early December, 1991. After inspecting the damage caused by Serbian artillery on the hospital, he said, either naively or as diplomatic double-talk: "The evidence did not tally with what I had been told by army and Serbian leaders in Belgrade. The damage to the hospital is appalling. . . Observing this will affect the discussions I will have with others who have told me different stories." Although his words were comforting to those present, his pledge proved to be just empty rhetoric. At the same time Vance made his statements in Osijek, a leaked EC confidential report from the monitoring mission in Zagreb accused the Yugoslav Army of waging a cowardly campaign of shelling civilian targets in Croatia, most notably schools and hospitals. Herein lies the crux of the way the media handled the conflict: Reports that depicted the Serbs in a bad light were only made public surreptitiously.

I had a number of discussions with members of the medical staff including the director of the hospital, Dr. Kresimir Glavina, and chief of urology Dr. Antun Tucak. Because I was particularly interested in how the population and treating physicians were coping in this modern Dante's *Inferno*, I also talked to Nikola Mandic, a psychiatrist who has written extensively on the subject. Mandic was in the forefront of the battle lines from the very first day.

His primary concern was what the future would hold for the children of Croatia who had seen their homes destroyed and now were forced to live like moles deep in the bowels of shelters because of the persistent Serbian shelling. Difficult as their situation was, they adapted. But what would become of those children who had witnessed maimed or dead playmates and neighbors, and those who had lost their parents?

In a November 22, 1991 *European* article, Dusko Doder noted that several Serbian psychologists, most notably Zarko Korac of Belgrade University, were concerned that narrow nationalism was influencing Serbian children. Many Serbian schools had instituted three basic teaching objectives. Starting with the most important they were: developing national consciousness, love of motherland, and lastly, general education. Korac was most disturbed by the militarism and the hatred being drummed into young minds. "Ours is a Homeric society in many ways," he wrote. "Stories are passed from generation to generation. The hatred of Serb for Croat, of Croat for Serb, the militarism and glorification of war heroes is taking our society backwards, to a tribal level."

I'll be interested to see what attitudes evolve among Croatian and Bosnian children who've experienced and survived the grimiest realities of war and then compare their attitudes to those of Serbian children who were taught and nurtured on hatred toward Croats and Muslims from imagined wrongs. Their conflicting experiences will impact their relations for generations.

Deep in the basement of Osijek Hospital Mandic offered valuable insight into this aspect of war in between the explosions of a Serbian artillery attack. Because the dull rumble of guns was audible even in the depths of the basement, I found it hard to concentrate. I winced at every explosion, but the others in the area continued going about their business without missing a beat. They unsuccessfully tried to reassure me that the blasts you don't hear are the ones you should worry about, they kill.

A modern shopping center lies under the city's main square. But during the ceaseless bombardment and shelling of the city the mall had become a bomb shelter. In the course of the Blitz of World War II, Londoners found temporary havens in subway tunnels during the sporadic air attacks. But the citizens of Osijek had to make the shelters permanent residences. The children were most affected by this lifestyle. Even during rare, prolonged lulls in the bombardment, children refused to go out and play.

A year later I recalled the children who had to live under the terror of Serbian bombardment when I gave a talk to the first and second graders at Holy Trinity School in California. The students had "adopted" an orphan through the Save the Children of Croatia, an NGO program I was affiliated with. The program was an American sponsored organization that was a liaison between donors who contributed a monthly sum, for one year, to children who had lost one or both parents during the conflict in Croatia. Until the organization was taken over by the Croatian government, all children that fitted the criteria were eligible, regardless of ethnicity, religious, or parental party affiliation. I spotted comments by the students on the school's bulletin board based on the theme "Why I like Holy Trinity." Two particularly caught my eye: "The school is nice because we play for fun" and "Holy Trinity is small but a safe place for kids." Situations so unlike what their contemporaries in Osijek were subjected to.

While I was in Osijek I looked up my old medical colleague Ivica Ambros who, along with his wife, had practiced there for at least 25 years. They invited me for dinner. As we approached their apartment house I noticed that within the entire facade of their building, which faced the river, as well as in the other buildings in the complex, not one pane of glass was left intact; the superstructure of the entire wall was pockmarked with various-sized indentations and gaping holes. The size of the holes and indentations indicated the caliber of weapons fired by the Serbs from across the river.

The Ambroses lived on the top floor of a 12 story apartment house. I learned that they were the only tenants in the building because the rest of the occupants had moved away in fear. In response to my question about why they hadn't moved also, Ivica said, "Where else can we go? This is our home. If we move what will happen to our patients? Under no circumstances would we abandon them." The elevators weren't running because there was no electricity, so we had to walk up the 12 stories to their apartment. While we were finishing our dinner, several Serbian artillery shells hit the building next door and shook the foundation of the Ambroses' building. "Ivica," I commented, "I don't think I'll have dessert."

I recall one particular scene that I observed while returning to Zagreb from Osijek. For the first time since World War II, the Croats were overtly celebrating Christmas, something they weren't encouraged to do under the old, atheistic regime. Frost covered the road; the trees looked like skeletons, and a thick fog hung over the ground. All of the sudden, through the fog, I saw a lone house decorated with a Christmas tree and multicolored lights. To me it looked like a beacon of hope.

Upon my return to Zagreb, the Foreign Press Bureau asked if I'd chair and moderate a press conference at the Hotel Intercontinental that would center around the atrocities being committed. The FPB also asked me to introduce a number of Croatian civilians from Vukovar who were recently freed in a prisoner of war exchange. The prisoners included Doctors Vesna Bosanac (who was known as the angel of the killing fields of Slavonia) and Mladen Loncar. Although the press conference was well attended by members of the international media, the moving testimony of the former prisoners or discussion about the atrocities apparently didn't move many, since very little was reported. That evening I took most of the former prisoners out for their first real meal in months.

Dr. Mladen Loncar, the other physician released with Dr. Bosanac, had been arrested four times on unspecified charges despite the fact that he was a Serbian citizen. Apparently his only crime had been his Croatian ethnicity. Dr. Loncar was working at the Novi Sad hospital in the Serbian province of Vojvodina when he was arrested by Serbian police for carrying a package of medicine intended for his parents in Ilok, Croatia. They beat him severely during his 30 hours of captivity. Once free, he was arrested several times thereafter before ending up in Begejci camp near Zrenjanin, Vojvodina.

Out of the rubble of Vukovar a true heroine of the conflict emerged: Dr. Vesna Bosanac. Ever armed with a lighted cigarette, resembling a librarian more than a dynamo, she realized the full gravity of the Serbian onslaught from its onset. Lacking military experience, she instinctively prepared and energetically mobilized the medical staff of Vukovar's hospital into a wartime footing. Anticipating the casualties sure to come, she had the basement cleared up, placed sand bags at the windows, and opened the never used atomic bomb shelter. Her foresight saved countless lives, for these sites later provided the only protection for the patients and medical staff. Because she led with an iron will and discipline but never raised her voice, the medical staff spontaneously followed the example of this diminutive, 4 foot 9 inches tall, heroine.

The Serbs, in their aggressive efforts to create a Greater Serbia in Croatia and Bosnia-Herzegovina, weren't engaged in what could be called normal military operations. All their vaunted campaigns utilized siege tactics. Aside from inflicting psychological pressure, the besiegers have no causalities since there is no frontal attack. Yet both the Bush and Clinton administrations had characterized the aggressors and victims alike as "warring sides" and declared that only "when they get tired of killing each other" would peace be accomplished.

Vukovar was a prime example of Serbian military tactics, but the siege ultimately cost the Serbs the war. The Vukovar operation was one of the rare instances in which most of the casualties ended up being Serbs. For 89 days, approximately 4,000 ill-equipped, untrained, ragtag Croatian defenders, spread across a 100 kilometer long front were able to hold off a quarter of the third biggest army in Europe equipped with tanks, artillery and aircraft. Only after the Croats ran out of ammunition did Vukovar fall. But the Serbian victors found no spoils because there was little left of Vukovar. Almost all structures had been leveled. Buildings had been hit so many times by heavy artillery and bombs that they were no longer recognizable.

The Serbian attacks came sporadically at first, then, with an increasing crescendo, became constant. A whole spectrum of weaponry was used: mortars, large caliber artillery, and airplanes dropping 250 kilogram bombs. One bomb penetrated through the six stories of the hospital and landed, miraculously without exploding, between the legs of a surprised, bedridden patient. After the dust cleared, a nurse, thinking the bomb was an oxygen tank that had gone to the wrong patient, ordered its removal. A disaster was barely averted.

As the casualties mounted, the blood that sometimes flooded the emergency room floor had to be swept out with a broom. Blood and plasma couldn't be stored because there was no electricity, so the physicians were forced to rely on direct donors. These were plentiful, but most had to be rejected because of anemia that developed secondary to rampant malnutrition.

Apparently the only function of the huge Red Cross painted on the hospital's roof was to help the Serbs coordinate and target their artillery barrage on the hospital. "As more of the hospital was demolished, we retreated a floor lower finally we ended up in the basement, where we had three operating theaters in constant use," Dr. Bosanac told me. Since the makeshift operating theaters lacked heat, the medical staff used a hair dryer to warm the air. Sometimes physicians worked by the light of candles or oil lamps.

Of the total wounds to patients, 80% resulted from explosions. Only 10% were from small arms. Many patients suffered from multiple wounds caused by fragmenting shells and projectiles, despite such weapons being forbidden by international law. High speed projectiles characteristically have small entrance wounds but exit as huge gaping caverns that reduce the tissues in their pathways to jelly. Surgeons worked 20 hours at a stretch on the seemingly ceaseless stream of wounded. During October, 1991, the surgeons performed 939 surgeries.

Sterilization of instruments became a major problem. Because of the water shortage, the medical staff had to resort to dry methods. The sterilization units were attacked several times by Serbian artillery. Following each attack the units were repaired and relocated but no sooner would a new site become workable than it would be targeted by Serbian shelling. Clearly inside information was being passed on to the Serbian forces. Whenever the Croats transferred material, equipment, or patients to a new site, artillery was aimed in that direction.

Dr. Bosanac galvanized the staff to Herculean efforts. Respecting the Hippocratic oath, they treated everyone who crossed the hospital's threshold. Of the casualties, 70% were civilians and the remainder were Croatian combatants.

As the siege intensified, the badly damaged hospital continued functioning by "improvising in everything and solving problems as they appeared." When the utilities were cut off, Dr. Bosanac's husband, Lavoslav, devised unusual ways to get electricity into the facility. Water, that most precious commodity, came from the hospital's heating system, rain, underground wells, or even a destroyed brandy distillery. Firefighters had to stop bringing water in cistern trucks because the trucks were targeted and destroyed.

People had to get water at night because of the danger from artillery. During the rare lulls in the shelling, everyone made a mad dash to go above ground to collect water from wells. Hygienic standards were somehow maintained despite the averse conditions. But toward the end of the siege, the previously low infection morbidity rate rose dramatically, and the bane of all physicians, gas gangrene, appeared.

Despite around-the-clock exposure to death, pain, and suffering, the physicians never lost compassion for their patients. They suppressed normal human emotions in order to maintain some of their sanity and continue functioning as physicians. But all the tribulations they had suffered were forgotten when news would spread about the delivery of a newborn. Each birth was cause for celebration.

In addition to all the problems of caring for the living, problems arose with the disposal of the dead. Transporting bodies to the cemetery became impossible because the Serbs targeted the vehicles. So after being tagged for identification purposes, the bodies were placed in dark nylon sacks and stacked in a yard across from the hospital.

Most of the citizens of Vukovar had been reduced to a mole-like existence. Many didn't see the light of day for months. Children were pale, debilitated, and malnourished. Before its destruction, Vukovar had one of the highest standards of living in former Yugoslavia and had been a major manufacturing center of tires, shoes, and textiles. The latter were largely exported to the United States. The area around the city had abundant natural resources, extremely rich farmlands, and even oil. Only Belgrade surpassed Vukovar in having more telephones and autos per capita. But as a result of the siege, prosperous Vukovar had been reduced to a surreal landscape of rubble.

After the city's fall, Dr. Bosanac and other survivors were arrested and sent to Serbian concentration camps. Before Dr. Bosanac's arrest she'd been given a guarantee by Yugoslav officers that the patients would be protected according to the rules laid down by the Geneva Conventions.

Despite her abused state when she was freed in the prisoner exchange, Dr. Bosanac's first and foremost concern was her patients— she lost all clinical detachment and wept when told that JNA soldiers had forcibly evacuated and summarily executed the 259 prisoners she'd left behind in Vukovar's hospital. I can only imagine how she would've reacted if she'd known what her patients were subjected to before they were killed.

Zarko Kojic, a Serbian witness testifying before The International Criminal Tribunal for the Former Yugoslavia in the Hague in April, 1996, described how Serbian paramilitary personnel and army officers tortured the Croatian patient-prisoners with metal pipes, chains, and ax handles, bludgeoning some of them to death.

Dr. Loncar's testimony upon his release was typical for most released prisoners, but it was more interesting to me since he gave it from a physician's perspective.

All inmates slept on bare stone floors in sub zero temperatures; the only redeeming feature of being packed together like sardines with other inmates was the warmth it provided. The prisoners ranged in age from 16 to 82 years old. Since many of the inmates were old and infirm they suffered from a variety of chronic heart, lung, or diabetic medical problems. Any medications they had with them when they were captured were immediately confiscated. Despite pleas from physician inmates to the Serbian prison doctors, all humanitarian aid was withheld.

A number of inmates with obvious war or traumatic injuries, and many with open, suppurating wounds, were incarcerated with the general prison population. They were denied medical attention except the aid provided by inmate doctors who had nothing concrete to offer. Fresh orthopedic cases appeared daily. The inmate doctors did the best they could to immobilize fractures suffered by prisoners who had received injuries inflicted by the guards. At least 95% of the inmates had upper respiratory symptoms. Diarrhea outbreaks were prevalent, yet the Serbs denied prisoners access to toilets.

Horrible beatings were reported by survivors of all the camps. The infirm, aged, or even the wounded weren't exempt. Local Serbian civilians reportedly participated in the beatings of the inmates. A 60 year-old inmate with heart problems was so severely beaten that Dr. Loncar somehow prevailed upon the Serb camp doctor to examine the patient. The doctor downgraded the inmate's injuries to "not severe enough to treat." The next day the victim died. Dr. Loncar also witnessed the arrival of prisoners from Vukovar—all were civilians.

Another survivor of Serbian concentration camps said he was beaten daily until he pretended to be infested with lice. Thereafter, his tormentors gave him a wide berth.

The Serbian devastation of Vukovar saved Croatia. Vukovar became the symbol of resistance, a contemporary Stalingrad, and a rallying cry akin to "Remember the Alamo!" After losing far too tanks and airplanes, the Yugoslav army thereafter was unable to mount any meaningful attacks in Croatia. Most war colleges are now studying the methods of defense and the heroic efforts of Vukovar's defenders, which are destined to become military classics.

The selfless heroism displayed by Dr. Bosanac and the other physicians during the siege of Vukovar is unique in the annals of medicine.

On October 28, 1992, American forensic anthropologist Dr. Clyde Snow confirmed eyewitness reports regarding the whereabouts of the missing Vukovar hospital patients. His investigation concluded that a mass grave in a field at Ovcara, a small village close to Vukovar, contained their remains. According to eyewitnesses, following Vukovar's fall, lightly wounded civilian and military males were forcibly separated from the rest of the hospital patients and placed on JNA buses. They were first taken to the JNA barracks, then transported to Ovcara. The prisoners were put in a large storehouse and beaten for several hours. They were then divided into groups of twenty. Soon a truck arrived and one group was loaded. Every 15 or 20 minutes the truck would return empty and reload with a new group of prisoners. Dr. Snow said that a reconstruction of the truck's route led to the site of the mass grave.

An investigation on December 17, 1992, revealed more. A *Daily Telegraph* article titled, "Must They Get Away With It" (May 25, 1993), said that the Serbs bowed to pressure from the Physicians for Human Rights and allowed a team of experts led by Dr. Snow to dig one test trench. After checking the area for land mines, the team found human bones breaking thorough the heavy scars of soil laid bare by a bulldozer. Using classical archaeological methodology, the team carefully cataloged artifacts and body parts they found to the depths where they were discovered. Aside from the body parts, the inventory included paraphernalia normally found in association with human being—shoes, socks, pants shirts, and the like. The team estimated that it had found the remains of at least nine bodies in the 10 meter test site. Based on its observations of the surrounding soil patterns the team estimated that there could be at least 200 more bodies.

A preliminary forensic investigation of the body parts from the test site clearly indicated that at least two of the victims had been shot through the head. One skull bore evidence that a single bullet entered the right side of the head and exited through the left in three fragments; the other showed destruction of the mid-facial section consistent with a high velocity gunshot. Serbian authorities stopped further investigation and refused to allow removal of the specimens. The team placed identifiable evidence in separate bags, then sealed and replaced them. Finally, they shoveled fresh earth back in.

Just how long future forensic studies will be fruitful and worthwhile is questionable. The area's environmental factors are conducive to rapid deterioration. The area's high water table contributes to the accumulation of mud and pools of water, and the field has been heavily fertilized for farming. The Serbs recently denied site access to U.S. Ambassador to Croatia Peter Galbraith.

After Vukovar fell, a number of humanitarian groups, including the International Committee for the Red Cross (ICRC), tried to enter the city to assist in the evacuation of the civilians and hospital patients. But the Serbian forces denied access. As documented by a October 29, 1992 Foreign Press Bureau press release, when the ICRC protested, the Serbs told the ICRC "this was war" and if they didn't like it, they could leave. Approximately 3,000 civilians disappeared from Vukovar. They undoubtedly likely met the same fate as the hospital patients. Their remains may be found in other mass grave sites. However, no one, including the U.S. State Department and the Croatian government seems interested in discovering their whereabouts.

A little over year after the horrific events at Vukovar and Vocin took place, Dr. Snow, testifying before the House Foreign Relations Committee about the atrocities, brought tears to the usually jaded Washington audience. Congress members and the State Department reacted to his shocking testimony as if was a new revelation. Although these bodies long ago had detailed information about atrocities, this was the first time they publicly noticed. Apparently Under Secretary of State Lawrence Eagleburger had completely forgotten that immediately upon Congressman McCloskey's return to Washington from Vocin, McCloskey went directly to Eagleburger and briefed him in great detail. Since then atrocities continued unabated despite a number of Congressional fact finding teams who had been on the ground and provided unbiased reports and verification. Although the reports were public record, the media didn't consider them newsworthy enough to print.

Nothing stirs Congress or the executive branch as public opinion. Had the public been made aware of the true state of affairs, there may have been an outcry much earlier and many lives would have been saved. Instead, the media fed a steady diet of the Serbs' propagandist spin to the public. By their failure to report accurately, using unreliable sources, and in many cases telling deliberate lies, the media bears a great deal of responsibility for the deaths and destruction.

THE MEDIA DECEPTION

THE MEDIA DECEPTION

*"All successful newspapers are ceaselessly querulous and belli-
cose. They never defend anyone of anything if they can help it;
if the job is forced upon them, they tackle it by denouncing
someone else."—H. L. Mencken*

On the third anniversary of Vukovar's fall, a spate of articles lamented
the dreadful living conditions that the Serbian conquerors had to
endure in the rubble of a once vibrant Croatian city and praised the
Serbs' courageous efforts to rebuild and adjust. The articles never
mentioned that the destruction of Vukovar had resulted from Serbian
military tactics. Rather than inquiring about the surviving Croatian
victims who were forced to live in refugee camps and desired to
return to their confiscated homes, the media's maudlin reports wor-
ried about how the Serbs would be especially inconvenienced if the
Croats attempted to take back their territory.

   While the conflict was limited to Croatia, a majority of journalists received their briefings in Belgrade, so their reports reflected the
Serbian agenda. The media almost invariably stated that all sides were
guilty and excused the conflict as just another episode in a long history of atrocities committed among the Serbs, Croats, and Muslims.
The press made it clear that outside intervention couldn't mitigate
such ancient ethnic rivalries.

The media inaccurately characterized the conflict as a civil war. Journalists cited the nefarious deeds of the Ustashe, a German puppet state in Croatia during World War II, as justification for the Serbian actions of the 1990s, yet failed to mention the Serbian government's collaboration with the Nazis or Chetnik crimes during the same period.

The British press was guilty of blindly quoting Serbian sources without regard to accuracy. One such example appeared in a November 22, 1992, *Daily Telegraph* article. The article accused Croatian gangs of plundering supplies and money and, most severely, of maltreating defenseless Muslim refugees. The Croats supposedly said that racial superiority excused their mistreatment of the Muslims. Yet after a long diatribe about Croatian improprieties, the article finally made it clear that no evidence had been found to substantiate the allegations. The article also failed to cite the source of the racial slur. In essence, *The Daily Telegraph* reported a non-event.

Former President Richard Nixon said, "The judgment of history depends on who wrote it." As victors in the Balkan conflict, Serbian revisionists were able to write a version history that the media accepted without challenge. The Serbs had 70 years to practice their propaganda skills while they ruled and exploited Yugoslavia's entire political and economic infrastructure. They eventually became better at manipulating facts and history than even the ominous Soviet regimes.

Astutely aware of the value of public relations, the Serbian leadership nurtured an extremely effective propaganda apparatus. The predominantly Serbian diplomatic corps of Yugoslavia had been the voices of Serbia's agenda in the international community. Their seeds of disinformation eventually reaped a bountiful harvest when the international media reacted to the present conflict.

Following the Watergate debacle, the media in the U.S. skeptically scrutinized every Republican Party pronouncement. Yet American journalists blindly accepted the Bush administration characterizations of the Balkan crisis as an insoluble ancient ethnic conflict in which all sides were equally guilty. Although the Clinton administration made every effort to distinguish its domestic agenda from the previous administration's, Clinton wasted no time maintaining Bush's ill-conceived Balkan policy. Both presidents successfully articulated the futility of involvement, and by doing so also achieved their goal of limiting debate.

The American public received background information from news programs such as the McNeil-Lehrer Newshour and Nightline, but always from the perspectives of guests like Lawrence Eagleburger, Lord David Owen, and Cyrus Vance. Because these experts were intimately involved with the crisis and part of the problem, their assessments were couched in the official language of double-speak and self-service. None spoke frankly or gave honest analyses. The interviewers allowed their guests to pontificate without scrutiny. So these news programs became pulpits for the status quo rather than forums for the truth.

For example, on March 25, 1993, the McNeil-Lehrer Newshour devoted an extremely long segment to Lord David Owen. Instead of answering questions, Lord Owen delivered a contrived monologue strewn with disinformation. Owen's interviewer accepted his pronouncements as gospel.

News programs are commercial. Powerful newsmakers bring higher ratings. So if interviewers probe too deeply, they risk losing the newsmakers as future guests. Because programs like the McNeil-Lehrer Newshour avoided analysis and contrary views, they were, in fact, propagators of the Bush administration's agenda. President Bush's policy concerning Croatia had been to publicly ignore it. News coverage reflected his policy.

When the JNA attacked Slovenia in July, 1991, the McNeil-Lehrer Newshour reported the assault twice. While the JNA laid waste to Croatia for six months, an attack that resulted in a massive flight of refugees, the slaughter of defenseless civilians, and the destruction of cultural monuments including much of the city of Dubrovnik, the Newshour broadcast only eight segments about these events. Without exposure to accurate information, the media's passive audience readily accepted persuasively reported misconceptions about history, ethnic rivalries, and blame for the atrocities.

President Clinton based his policy on Robert D. Kaplan's book, *The Balkan Ghosts* rather than hard intelligence reports. Although publishers produced many books about the crisis, no book was as influential as Kaplan's. Kaplan's reportage was excellent, but whenever he wandered away from straight observation and into analysis and history, which was often the case, his book lost all credibility. Kaplan's well written half-truths soon became accepted as dogma by the uninformed. Echoing Rebecca West, Kaplan's theses were based on generalities about national character. He pontificated that primordial forces kept the conflict beyond anyone's control. *The Balkan Ghosts* offered Croatia no sympathy for its self-determination efforts and greeted atrocities committed against the non-Serb population with nonchalance. In a McNeil-Lehrer Newshour interview, Professor Fouad Ajami of Johns Hopkins explained that Clinton reneged on his campaign promises and stopped criticizing Bush's policy in Yugoslavia because he believed Kaplan's half-truths and myths about Serbian military prowess.

The Bush and Clinton administrations were successful in manipulating the media and keeping the Croatian situation off the front pages. The British and French governments found evasiveness more difficult to sustain because the crisis was occurring in their backyards. So in order for the British and French to maintain the status quo, they had to more blatantly propagate Serbian myths. British journalist Nora Beloff remained loyal to her government's agenda when she cleverly duped the public by juxtaposing certain facts about the Balkan crisis and selectively omitting others.

In democratic and open societies journalists should be the first to question governmental pronouncements. The more emphatic the pronouncements, the louder the questions should be asked. For most of us, the media is our primary source of information about governmental shenanigans. Yet during the crisis in former Yugoslavia, editors and news directors blindly perpetuated Serbian-generated disinformation while ignoring a spate of evidence that unequivocally refuted the myths. Hypocrisy has pervaded this conflict; the messenger failed to examine the message and therefore became part of the problem. News coverage reflected the conscious or unconscious agenda of the reporters and editors rather than accurately portraying important events.

Whenever journalists claimed that the causes of the conflict were too complicated to explain, the reporters were confessing their own failures. Many journalists deviated from the tenets of classic reportage by resorting to analysis and editorializing when they were unable to get hard facts. Lacking any valuable insight, the reporters were clearly working out of their depth.

Between 1990 and 1995, over 180 books and countless monographs and articles were published about the conflict. The tragedy is that most of the authors were enamored with former Yugoslavia and what it stood for—especially its politics. Many were products of an era that denied the realities and excesses of any communist regime. They did little more than project the sentiments of policy makers like Lawrence Eagleburger, Brent Scowcroft, and John Scalon. While mourning the demise of Yugoslavia, these authors conveniently forgot that the glue that once held Yugoslavia together was Tito's totalitarianism. Professor Thomas Fleiner, Chairman of the CSCE Human Rights Commission, who has studied the media's responses to the Balkan crisis in depth, concluded: "The more power the media obtain and are able to influence, through public opinion, political decision-making on important foreign policy matters, the greater is their responsibility. As far as the war in Croatia and Bosnia is concerned, it is suspected [the] local [and] international media helped the division of peoples and incitement of hatred."

Whether knowingly or not, Senator John Warner participated in spreading disinformation when he said, "*My own* research. . .indicates that. . .these people have fought each other for not hundreds of years, but thousands of years for religious, ethnic, cultural differences. . . There is certainly a history, going back, at least into *my study* of the problem, as far back as the 13th century, of constant ethnic and religious fighting among and between these groups (my emphases added)." Americans should pity their country and those who voted for Senator Warner if he researches the problems facing the U.S. in the same way he researched the background of the Yugoslav crisis. Learning Senator Warner's sources would prove illuminating.

This conflict doesn't fit Webster's definition of war: "A state of usually open and declared armed hostile conflict between states or nations." In this case, an army possessing weapons of modern warfare—tanks, planes, artillery, cluster bombs—attacked people who lacked those weapons and had no intention of fighting except to defend their homes. Contrary to the rhetoric, the Serbian invasions of Slovenia, Croatia, and Bosnia can't be considered battles in a civil war. Slovenia, Croatia, and Bosnia had declared independence in accordance with the Yugoslav constitution before the invasions.

Ethnic rivalries between Serbs and Croats aren't ancient. The Croats and Serbs had a remarkable symbiosis until they were cobbled together with other Balkan peoples into a kingdom in 1918. Animosity ignited when the Serbs commandeered all the political, military, and economic infrastructure of the country and imposed draconian measures on non-Serbs. The first armed ethnic conflict between Croats and Serbs occurred during World War II. But pundits such as Robert W. Tucker (contributing editor of *The National Interest*) and David C. Hendrickson (associate professor of political science at Colorado College), in their article "America and Bosnia" in *National Review* (Fall 1993), helped perpetuate the myth that the ethnic feuding was ancient. Without citing evidence, they ascribed the war to "notorious tribal hatreds and the violent propensities of the Balkan peoples."

The Balkans have been the scene of numerous bloody battles because the area was the fault line between Christian Europe and the Islamic Asia. But none of the battles were between the indigenous groups. Anti-interventionists cleverly limited the options for peace by implying that the problem found its genesis in the violent tendencies of the Balkan people. The usually astute former and present editors of *Foreign Affairs*, William Hyland and James Hogue, nonetheless trumpeted this erroneous message.

The JNA attack on Slovenia in June, 1991, caught the international media off-guard. Because few reporters covering Yugoslavia had been briefed by anyone, most had to resort to their own devices and inherent skills. As a consequence, that initial battle produced some of the most objective reporting of the conflict. Yet between July, 1991, when the JNA invaded Croatia, and March 2, 1992, before Serbian paramilitary forces set up barricades in Sarajevo, the majority of the international media avoided the action and descended on Belgrade instead. Reports from the Serbian capital were invariably distorted. Although skilled articulators, most journalists aren't exceptionally bright. With few exceptions, those reporting from the Balkans were ignorant of the region's history and sheepishly bought into the notion that the Croats deserved the carnage.

A study of British editorials of the period is instructive. Most condemned the Croats for daring to defend themselves against the right and might of the Yugoslav forces. Only after the JNA besieged Dubrovnik and Vukovar was there any semblance of objectivity.

While the majority of the British press was vitriolic toward Croatia, the American media remained largely ambivalent. But some U.S.-based opinion writers such as Peter Brock, Alexander Cockburn, and A.M. Rosenthal filled their commentaries with factual errors, half-truths, and historical revisions. Their articles were simply thinly disguised attempts to support the Serbian agenda. Brock's lack of objectivity is not surprising since he is a member of the Serbian Unity Party.

Besides using their own propaganda apparatus, the Serbs contracted a number of independent firms. In Britain the Serbs hired Saatchi and Saatchi, the world's largest public relations firm. SerbNet, an official Serbian lobbying group in the United States, retained Manatos & Manatos for its Washington, D.C. operation. McDermott/O'Neill & Associates, the largest American public and government affairs strategic advisory firm, created a joint venture with David A. Keene & Associates to further enhance the Serbian image in the United States. The team that worked on the SerbNet account was headed by Thomas P. O'Neill III. O'Neill is a former Lieutenant Governor of Massachusetts, former head of the Office of Federal-State Relations, and a member of the U.S. State Department Ambassadorial Selection Committee. He is the eldest son of former Speaker of the House of Representatives, Thomas "Tip" P. O'Neill.

Roy Gutman of *Newsday* reported that General Lewis Mackenzie, who had been the highest ranking U.N. officer in former Yugoslavia, was paid $15,000 by SerbNet at the time he testified before the U.S. Armed Service Committee, met with congressional representatives, and spoke before the influential think tank, the Heritage Foundation. But Mackenzie disingenuously failed to mentioned his financial ties to the Serbian apparatus during these engagements.

The worldwide public relations campaign helped blunt the facts about Serbian atrocities, created the impression that the conflict was nothing more than an insoluble ethnic battle, and equated Croatian morality with Serbia's. Although the Serbs never presented themselves as innocents, they portrayed the Croats and Muslims as their moral equals. The more complicated the Serbs made the crisis seem, the less likely the West was to intervene. Serb propaganda successfully clouded every issue related to former Yugoslavia.

Some Western media overtly helped Serbian propaganda. Reuters made world headlines after one of its reporters said he had seen 41 Serbian children slaughtered by Croats. He reiterated the gory details on Belgrade television. The next day the reporter admitted the story was a lie, but his retraction never appeared in Serbia. His false testimony continues to foment hatred of Croats among Serbs.

In another case, the press reported that Croatian forces had slaughtered a number of innocent Serbian civilians around the Croatian town of Pakrac. The reports described the condition of the mutilated bodies and listed the names and ages of the victims. The international media described the incident as typical of the bloodthirsty Croatian character. But an investigation soon revealed that the incident was a hoax perpetrated by Serbia's state-run media. The fact that the international press was duped wasn't too surprising. After all, the press' function is to report. But what made the reporters culpable in this case was their failure to investigate the story's source or print a retraction.

After the Serbs had blocked the major highway linking Croatia and Serbia in May, 1995, Croatian forces broke the blockade and went on an offensive that resulted in the retrieval of approximately 10% of Croatia's lost territory. The State Department chastised Croatia's counter-offensive as "threatening a key objective" of Clinton's policy in the Balkans. Until 1995 the Clinton administration had never articulated an objective. The U.N. shrilly blamed the Croatian action for ruining a chance for a negotiated settlement despite the fact that the U.N. had failed to successfully negotiate with the Serbs for five years. U.S. Ambassador to Croatia Peter Galbraith warned that the Croatian offensive in Western Slavonia would rekindle another war and would have "all the civility of Bosnia and ten times the firepower." His projections, like so many others by Western diplomats, proved to be entirely unfounded.

The U.N. Security Council was angered by Croatia's retrieval of territory that could not be returned through inept negotiations. Without substantiating his charge, the British delegate to the Security Council accused Croatia of widespread inhumane treatment of Serbian civilians and prisoners taken in the Pakrac offensive. But in this case the media actually contradicted a U.N. official's pronouncement. An overwhelming majority of the reporters, particularly those on the scene, stated that the conduct of the Croatian troops toward the vanquished Serbs had been exemplary. European Union observers agreed with the media's assessment. Contrary to the U.N.'s public accusations that the Croats had forcibly expelled the Serbs, a June 9, 1995, internal U.N. report (s/1995/467) from the Secretary General of the Security Council stated that the Serbian leadership had encouraged the exodus of Serbs from Western Slavonia.

In retaliation for Croatia's counter-offensive, the Serbs fired a series of missiles containing anti-personnel cluster bombs at a number of Croatian cities, including downtown Zagreb. Although cluster bombs are banned by international law, no British, French, or American official government communiqués condemned the attacks. For unknown reasons, the media remained focused on the status and treatment of the Serbs who had remained in the recaptured territory of Slavonia.

In the May 1, 1994, issue of the Catholic newspaper *The Tidings*, a front page article about Professor Daniel Smith-Christopher opinions reiterated all the favorite Serbian theses and excuses for their aggressions. Clearly Smith-Christopher's field of expertise wasn't Balkan history because his statements were loaded with errors. Moreover, he chastised Catholics for their lack of involvement in former Yugoslavia. Apparently he wasn't aware that Catholics have been involved in the events in Croatia from the onset. Catholic humanitarian organization Caritas was one of the first to supply aid and comfort to victims. The Vatican was one of the first states to officially recognize Croatia. In January, 1994, Pope John Paul II, alone among world leaders, castigated the international community for acting in a criminally negligent manner. Because Smith-Christopher's article was one-sided and loaded with half-truths, it provoked a number of letters to the editor in rebuttal; but none was published. Unfortunately, *The Tidings'* readership was indelibly etched with the impression that the Serbs were victims.

Terms that were bandied about in media and government pronouncements about the Balkan crisis like "quagmire," "civil war," and "ancient ethnic rivalry" immediately clouded the facts and warned outsiders to keep out, while terms like "war of aggression" or "genocide" encouraged outsiders to act. By the time the latter terms became popular, the conflict had already caused the deaths of at least 250,000, the wounding of untold numbers, the rape of at least 25,000, and the flight or displacement of over three million people. The former terms, "quagmire," "civil war," and "ancient ethnic rivalry," have proven to be seeds planted in the vocabulary of the international media and diplomatic corps by Serbia's propaganda machine.

The long list of inaccurate media buzz-phrases includes "ethnic blood feud" and "rebel" or "secessionist republics." Despite the existence of experts in the field (none of them in government circles) and accessible information about the background and history of the conflict, the international media elected to ignore those sources and, instead, stick to the text the Serbs provided.

The press consistently justified the Serbian invasion of Croatia as a heroic attempt to keep Yugoslavia intact. The 1990-1991 Yugoslav census revealed that the percentage of citizens who acknowledged being Yugoslav was formidable in Croatia, Bosnia-Herzegovina, and Slovenia. But no one from Serbia proper elected to call himself a Yugoslav.

The press also claimed that the Serbs were trying protect the minority Serbs of Croatia. But the majority of Serbs in Croatia were urbanized and had been integrated into Croatian society. If Serbia had annexed the Croatian land they occupied in 1991, 70% of the Serbs who had lived in Croatia would still have remained outside Greater Serbia.

Soon after Croatian independence, the international media began lamenting that Serbs had been unmercifully purged from Croatia's police force and state administrative posts. The new government did purge many from its ranks. One of the government's first acts was to dismiss Communist functionaries, regardless of ethnicity. Because government appointments had previously required Communist Party affiliation, and 40% of the party members in Croatia were Serbian, a disproportionately high number of government bureaucrats had been Serbs. For example, in 1980, 75% of Yugoslav federal bureaucrats were Serbs, while 8.6% were Croats. Ljubjana's *Daily Delo* reported, in 1987, that out of 2,900 foreign ministry employees only 120 were Slovene or Croatian. Although the Serbs dominated in raw numbers, their percentages in the upper echelons of the party, secret police, and administration were even greater. The 1980 Yugoslav census revealed that Serbs made up 11.5% of the population in Croatia, but held more than half of all key administrative positions, and that 56.5% of the uniformed policemen in Zagreb were Serbs. The significant number of Serbian dismissals by the new Croatian government wasn't especially surprising because many Serbs refused to swear allegiance to the new state. But reports of large scale discrimination and sacking of the Serbian minority workforce were unsubstantiated.

Serbian propagandists claimed that the Cyrillic script used by some Serbs, as opposed to the Roman script used by the Croats, was banned by the new government in Croatia. The charge was untrue. The Serbs were led to believe that they had lost the right to publish newspapers and magazines. But the only hindrance to publication was financial; the choice of script wasn't the problem. A perverse patronage system ruled every aspect of the economy under the old regime. Every enterprise of any consequence was subsidized by the state. The press was no exception. Because the new Croatian government was committed to free enterprise, government patronage and subsidies were slowly phased out. The Serbs had been the primary beneficiaries of the old system, so they had difficulty relating to the new ways of doing business. They felt threatened when money stopped flowing from Zagreb because the idea of raising capital privately to set up publishing houses was foreign.

When the theater of war shifted to Bosnia-Herzegovina, the reporting was mostly fair and accurate. Those reporters who went to Bosnia often risked their lives to get the true story. After an ABC Television News reporter was mortally wounded while riding in a vehicle near Sarajevo's airport, ABC News committed to objective in-depth reporting. But generally, the media continued to describe conditions and events in Croatia as if they were taking place on another planet. The press arbitrarily proclaimed that the war in Croatia was over and all but ignored the almost daily shelling of Croatian cities and towns from Serbian positions behind the U.N. peacekeeping curtain. Although there were a few reporters who got the Croatian story right, the bulk of stories that came out of Croatia after the war shifted to Bosnia tended to dwell upon the alleged reemergence of Ustashe symbols. More editorials were directed toward these symbols than toward the very real Serbian crimes against humanity.

A favorite story bandied about in the media regarded the similarities between the Croatian and Ustashe flags. Both flags were decorated with a checkerboard shield. But the press failed to note that the centuries-old Croatian national flag had also been decorated with a checkerboard. And in Zagreb, the tiled roof of an intact medieval church bears the same coat of arms. The Ustashe flag also differed from the present and medieval flags because it was emblazoned with a large letter "U."

Whenever the Croatian government announced the renaming of streets or city squares the announcement provoked a media outcry. But most of the changes applied to streets named by the Communist regime. Names such as "Lenin" or "Socialistic Revolution Street" sounded repugnant to the new order. Most often streets simply reverted to pre-World War II names that were many centuries old. Yet the media shrilly denounced the new names as proof that the Croatian government was a reincarnation of the Ustashe.

The press also complained when Croatia converted its currency from the dinar to the kuna. The controversy revolved around the fact that the kuna was the name of the monetary unit under the Ustashe regime. The worthless dinar had been associated with Yugoslav economic inequity for seventy years, and Croatia wanted to distance itself as much as possible from the Belgrade regime. The kuna is named after an animal similar to a marten whose pelt had been used for centuries in Croatia and Russia as means of exchange. The Italian lira and the German mark were currencies of fascist regimes, yet they continue to be used today without criticism. Why then should the kuna be associated with the Ustashe?

Slavenka Drakulic, a Yugoslav writer championed by Western literary circles, has been especially aghast over the new Croatian regime's renaming of streets and its destruction of the Communist symbols and monuments that she held sacred. A thinly disguised nostalgia for the good old days of Communist privileges permeates Drakulic's writings. Her background makes her nostalgia understandable. Her father was a Yugoslav military officer and political commissar. Under the Communists, commissars were the enforcers of the party line. Party members received privileges normally denied to the general population, but the perks that the super elite, like commissars, received were even more special.

A few streets didn't revert to their pre-Communist names. Andrija Hebrang Street was one that kept its more recent name. Andrija Hebrang was a founding member of Croatia's Communist Party who was murdered by the same people Drakulic's father helped keep in power.

The outside world seemed unmoved by the destruction and bloodshed in former Yugoslavia until the media began reporting mass rapes. Suddenly feminist groups rushed to do something. Afternoon television talk shows buzzed with worry and concern. But the frenzy died as suddenly as it started. The public's attention was diverted to another circus elsewhere.

Rape occurs and will continue to occur as a by-product of war. But the Serbs instituted a rape policy in Croatia and Bosnia that is unprecedented in the history of war crimes. The Catholic charity Caritas and The World Council of Churches concluded independently that the Serbs were using rape as a weapon of war. The United Nations High Commissioner for Refugees reported that one-third of 300 refugee women interviewed mentioned rape. Detailed documents available in Sarajevo in November, 1992, revealed that 1,000 rape victims were between the ages of 7 and 18, 8,000 between 18 and 35, 3,000 between 35 and 50, and 1,000 over 50. In the village of Kozarac, 2,000 women were raped out of a population of 12,400.

Rape camps aren't a new phenomenon; they have been used by conquerors throughout history. But the Serbs used the camps to humiliate and destroy an entire culture's values. In July, 1992, international authorities verified the existence of 17 Serbian rape camps. By April, 1993, 43 camps had been identified.

Typically victims were raped repeatedly until they showed overt signs of pregnancy. Those not killed were expelled and told to return to their Muslim communities so they could bear Serbian children. Rape has been perceived by many as the most humiliating form of genocide. These stigmatized women were reluctant to return to their families and communities because the difficulties inherent in reintegration compounded their humiliation. The cultural obstacles present in Muslim culture made their situations even more difficult. Many rape victims claimed to envy the dead.

According to articles in the *Croatian Medical Journal*, all the pregnant rape victims referred to the University of Zagreb's Psychiatry Department showed signs of post-traumatic stress disorder. Symptoms included attempted suicide and depression. Usually the victims would come with a female member of the family who knew her "secret." None of the married patients wanted her husband informed. They all negated their physical condition of pregnancy and considered the fetus an alien or unnatural body that they wanted to abort. Not one rape victim accepted her infant upon delivery.

Most of the stories are too shocking, too clinical, and too painfully graphic to be restated openly. Many of the victims showed extraordinary signs of trauma in the genital, anal, throat, and mouth areas. Most of these women refused to talk about the terrible ordeal they had suffered, but readily talked about different forms of physical maltreatment and abuses they had witnessed happening to other women.

One story told by a witness vividly sticks in my mind. After four Serbian soldiers gang-raped a woman, she begged to breast feed her crying infant. One of the soldiers cut off the infant's head and brought it to the mother's breast. After a hysterical outburst precluded her use as an instrument of rape, she was taken out and executed.

The archbishop of Zagreb, Cardinal Franjo Kuharic, proclaimed, "Raped women have not lost their dignity. . .They are worthy of our deepest admiration and must be treated with respect by the family, society, and the Church." These are words the world should heed.

Proponents for the Serbian cause downplayed the rape issue. But what made the victims' stories credible, objective clinical findings and pregnancies, can't be faked and few women have any motive to make up stories that are so stigmatizing.

Despite the powerful influence of Western and Serbian political disinformation, the web of deception finally began to unravel. Reports and editorials became more objective after July, 1995. Stephen Kinzer may have been the first journalist to acknowledge Serbia's decisive role in disinformation when he wrote in a July 10, 1995, *International Herald Tribune* article: "The pro-government Serbian press played a crucial role in whipping up nationalist fervor and hatred of non-Serbs.

"Newspapers were full of vivid stories, many of them exaggerated and others completely false, recounting gruesome atrocities committed against Serbs in Bosnia and Croatia," Kinzer continued. "Television news programs broadcast propaganda daily, never missing a chance to show a destroyed village, a sobbing widow or a distraught refugee."

Kinzer concluded that after the press stopped serving Serbia's political goals, President Milosevic was forced to reverse his political course. Whipping up pan-Serbian fervor no longer served Milosevic's interests and he abandoned all talk of a Greater Serbia.

The Serb's manipulative role of the media was understood by serious students of the region as early as 1991. What they couldn't understand was why the media took so long to reach the same conclusion. There were, however, some exceptional reporters who were not misled and got the story right. Egon Scotland of Sueddeutshoe Zeitung died in the attempt. But the overwhelming majority were either too lazy to investigate the true facts or followed the Janet Cooke tradition of journalism. Far fewer innocents would have died had the media heeded journalist emeritus Walter Cronkite's advice: "Journalists must ultimately have a peripheral role because their job is not to educate but to convey facts, not to proselytize, but be objective brokers of information."

INTO THE MAELSTROM

INTO THE MAELSTROM

Little did I realize that participating in the Vocin medical investigation, observing my colleagues' medical heroics at the front lines, and talking to the survivors of Vukovar would trigger my personal odyssey to attempt to rectify media distortions. Over time I began questioning who was committing the greater crime, the perpetrators of terror or those who ignored it? Because no forum existed to rebut unsubstantiated statements by media pundits, I used the only method available to an individual, the media itself. My letters to editors and Op-Ed pieces as well as my direct letters to politicians have been moderately successful because they were acknowledged and/or published.

In an attempt to set the record straight I became a frequently called upon commentator about the atrocities for various civic clubs, including the Kiwanis and Lions. I presented my paper, *The Hits and Myths of Croatia and Bosnia-Herzegovina*, at the plenary session of the XVth International Humanitas Congress of the World Federation of Humanists held at Arizona State University (Tempe). I gave one of the keynote addresses and chaired a forum on the subject sponsored by the Rosen Holocaust Center at the University of California at Irvine.

Acutely aware of the ramifications of disinformation, the Croatian Physicians For Human Rights and Professor Matko Marusic, Associate Dean of the University of Zagreb Medical School, urged me to expand upon my essays and other writings and publish them before the revisionists take over.

My desire to uncover the truth prompted me to return to the devastated areas in former Yugoslavia seven times. During each trip, while visiting the front lines, inspecting refugee camps, medical facilities, and interviewing rape victims, I witnessed the human misery increasing exponentially. There were no shortage of statistics to support my subjective observations. But for me, when the statistics took on human faces and dimensions, the conflict became personal. While interviewing victims I was often moved to tears by the victims' appalling stories. In order to separate my professionalism from sympathy, I'd excuse myself and leave for a few moments. I'd take a deep breath, occasionally mutter a silent prayer, then return to my task.

One such later mission started on July 13, 1992, in Zagreb, when I escorted Assistant Director of the Massachusetts General Hospital Dr. Thomas Durant and Attending Physician at John Hopkins Hospital Dr. David A. Bradt, both acknowledged experts in evaluating refugee problems, to former Yugoslavia. Their primary mission was to evaluate the health needs in the region. We excluded Serbia and Montenegro because both regions were undamaged, and nobody had been wounded or lost a life due to war in those republics.

We met our Croatian counterparts at the Institute for Mother and Child Health. The Institute served as the main children's hospital for the Republic of Croatia and the final triage point in the referral chain. Hospital chief Dr. Ivan Fattorini and his staff eagerly provided us with information about the medical ramifications pertinent to our mission.

The Serbs destroyed or damaged a large number of medical facilities in Croatia. Besides causing a large number of casualties, the Serbian ethnic cleansing program resulted in hundreds of thousands of displaced persons who severely strained the remaining medical facilities. But after the Serbian forces unleashed their attack on Bosnia, Croatia became inundated with an enormous influx of refugees, many suffering from major physical and mental trauma, further jeopardizing an already fragile health care system. Ironically, due to the nature of their Serbian weaponry, one-third of the treated war injured children were Croatian Serbs.

War injuries, amputations and burns, which aren't common in urban hospitals, require intensive nursing care and prolonged, costly rehabilitation. Besides the war trauma cases, the hospital was morally and ethically bound to treat Bosnian children for "normal" illnesses. Sophisticated treatments such as chemotherapy were prohibitively expensive. So since Croatia's economic status was precarious, allotments to treat these patients were given low priority. At the same time American physicians were agonizing over what creature comforts Clinton's health plan would allow for their patients, such as the size of TV screens, or whether one or two patients would be comfortable in a hospital room, Croatian physicians were agonizing over the morality of withholding certain medications from leukemic patients in order to treat patients who were considered more salvageable. Traffic accidents further strained the medical system; one-half of all traffic accidents in Zagreb involved refugees, mostly Bosnian children.

On our fact-finding mission we visited a broad spectrum of medical facilities, from comparatively tranquil Zagreb and Split to war-ravaged Osijek, Slavonski Brod, Karlovac, and Mostar. We saw facilities with sophisticated, first class equipment, and facilities where bandages were removed from the dead, washed and then reused on the living. We went to "new" medical centers in basements, bunkers, and warrens created from destroyed buildings that had forced physicians and patients underground. Major trauma was managed under unimaginable conditions, occasionally without anesthesia, but always with caring, skilled hands. Disposable items, which we in more comfortable situations take for granted, were reused ad infinitum. Despite their frustrations, the physicians never seemed to lose their compassion and respect for human life.

Although practicing medicine under often extremely adverse conditions, the heroics and expertise of the physicians and treatment protocols remained outstanding. Medically, Croatia was a first world country whose crude mortality rate was on a par with the United States.

Operations in the remaining 20% of Osijek's hospital functioned with an optimism that belies the destruction. Chief of Urology Dr. Antun Tucak graciously escorted our team around his surreal domain. The American medical team duly noted that the hospital had few buildings that were salvageable and would have to be totally rebuilt.

In the Slavonian city of Djakovo we had an audience with Bishop Cyril Kos. His briefing impressed us more than any other individual's on our odyssey. He viewed the world's reaction to the Serbian atrocities and the flood of refugees like cries in the wilderness. The bishop said Croatia was caring for 350,000 Muslim and 270,000 Catholic refugees from Bosnia and appealed to the world for assistance.

The tent and barrack city of Gasinci lay just outside Djakovo. Once a JNA base, at the time of our visit Gasinci housed approximately 3,000 Muslim refugees, mostly women and children. Those billeted in barracks were going to be the fortunate ones when winter came. One pediatrician and a couple of paramedical assistants had the responsibility of caring for all the inmates' medical and social needs. The clinic had no set closing time; it stayed open as there were people seeking help. Physicians volunteered from the Institute in Zagreb and rotated approximately every three weeks.

The high caliber of medicine practiced in Croatia and the physicians' selfless heroics had thus far kept morbidity from infectious diseases in check. Upon arrival at the camps, refugees were immediately immunized. Of course, those who brought current immunization records with them were exempt. Despite the fact that these refugees came from supposedly primitive areas, most were found to have been previously immunized. In contrast, Los Angeles County public health records show that only one-third of the county's children have received their necessary vaccinations.

We drove to Slavonski Brod whose 40,000 population had been burdened with 60,000 refugees. The hospital, geared for attack, was surrounded by sandbags. Every day approximately 100 patients were admitted, 95% of whom had shrapnel wounds. Chairman of Internal Medicine Dr. Dragica Bistrovic oversaw a hospital whose primary function was caring for the refugees in the Brod area. Her dynamic enthusiasm touched everyone with whom she came into contact.

The Sava River separates the Croatian city of Slavonski Brod from Bosnia's Bosanski Brod. In order to reach Bosanski Brod we had to be escorted by Croatian militia over a bridge that had been bombed numerous times by Serbian aircraft. Iron plates covered the partially destroyed areas so the bridge was still usable. The military personnel were lightly armed. Most of the houses around the bridge had been destroyed and all the extant buildings were pockmarked from projectile hits. So we were surprised to see that the mosque had escaped damage. Standing like a beacon, it offered a ray of hope for the Muslims. But a death pall still hung over the city.

We witnessed incalculable material destruction in all the locales of our tour, but that destruction was nothing compared to the human toll. A stream of refugees trying to cross the bridge into Croatia appeared desperate and haggard. The roads were dense with people fleeing, many packed together in the backs of trucks, or clinging to the roofs of tractors.

At the refugee center in Bosanski Brod we learned that the refugees' stories were documented carefully. Many knew the names of those who had committed atrocities in their villages, information that could prove helpful to eventual war crimes commissions.

Feeling it was physically and economically unable to cope with more refugees, Croatia began putting newly arrived refugees on trains and buses and dispatched them to the nearest borders. Slovenia, Hungary, Italy and Austria reacted by closing their borders and shifted the refugees to and from countries that didn't want them. For humanitarian reasons the Croatian government rescinded their order.

Coincidentally, about 6,000 men who had been labeled deserters by the Bosnian government fled across the Sava River to the salvation and safety of Slavonski Brod, Croatia in July 1992. Sherry Ricchiardi, an American reporter who'd been to Croatia a number of times, interviewed a great number of them. The troops had fled their posts when their field commanders read a communiqué to them that was supposed to have come from central headquarters. It read: "It has become obvious that the Serbs and Croatians will divide Bosnia . . .For all practical purposes, Bosnia is nonexistent and there is no reason for us (them) to die for a nonexistent state. . .We are not deserters, we are not refugees, we are expelled, there is nothing left to fight for." But evidence subsequently revealed that the communiqué was disinformation that had emanated from Serbia. These refugees were simply victims of JNA psychological warfare.

Croatia was faced with a dilemma since these Bosnians refused to lay down their arms; but Croatia granted them asylum in Slavonski Brod anyway. The next day the sports stadium, where the refugees were billeted, was hit by Serbian 155 mm artillery rounds, leaving many of the refugees dead and an extremely large number of them wounded. Undoubtedly they had been targeted because a Yugoslav airplane had flown over the area a number of times that day.

Split, an ancient Roman city on Croatia's Adriatic coast, had become a magnet for refugees. All the former resort hotels were jammed with Bosnians. These refugees were fortunate because many others were housed in the sports complexes, basketball stadiums, and gymnasiums; and were forced to sleep on mats. A lack of bathrooms made the overwhelming fumes that engulfed these facilities even worse.

We then drove to Mostar via Imotski. Mackley showed us the city's massive destruction and explained the military aspects. The area around the old bridge and the Muslim quarter resembled what I imagined Dresden must have looked like following the allied bombing. Only the facades of the Catholic church and the bishop's palace still stood. The destruction was so devastating that the heat had melted most of the church's marble altar. The peaceful, arbor-like city park had become a graveyard because sniper fire wouldn't allow Mostar's inhabitants to bury their dead in the town's true cemetery. The first body buried in the park was a Croatian soldier who was buried by his bride-to-be. The park is where they had walked and spent time as lovers. She was later killed. Fresh graves bearing crescents or crosses and dates that all ended in 1992 never failed to move even the most hard nosed observer.

On the outskirts of Karlovac lay the suburb of Turinj, which had been an ethnically mixed community of 5,000 people before the war. By the time we arrived, all that was left was rubble; not one building was salvageable. Only ghosts of the former residents and a handful of patrolling soldiers remained. Looking toward the Serbian neighborhood, 50 yards away, we saw, as we had in all the villages we visited, that their houses had suffered almost no destruction.

Serbian military offensives inexorably followed the same pattern. They first pressured the local Serbian population to evacuate. Once that was accomplished, JNA armored rifle regiments attack, supported by artillery and MIGs. As the defenders abandoned their positions, Chetniks moved in and cleansed the town. The Chetniks didn't discriminate. They cleansed the town of any Muslims, Croats or even Serbs who refused to cooperate.

The Serbian ethnic cleansing program struck terror among Muslims and Croats of Bosnia-Herzegovina. They were well aware of the concerted policy to carry out systematic killing and mayhem. None of the killings were "clean"; victims were repeatedly found with their throats cut, eyes gouged out, decapitated and dismembered.

The Bosnians rightly had reason to fear. For example, America Cares, a nongovernmental organization, representatives Andrew Hannah and Jonathan Bush, nephew of President Bush, listened to ham operators from Gorazde say that many inhabitants were committing suicide rather than fall into Serbian hands. Bodies were strewn all over the streets; nobody could bury them because the starving survivors had no strength left. The remaining had taken to eating roots and grass. The only human sounds the survivors heard were children crying from hunger. Absolutely no medicine could be found. This scene took place in 1992, when all of the seven major cities in Bosnia, excluding Sarajevo, were under siege and reported widespread starvation.

Although Doctors Durant and Bradt had worked in refugee areas all over the world, they said that the high caliber and sophistication of the medical community in Croatia left them with an indelible impression. Durant and Bradt were especially impressed by how the physicians were able to keep morbidity and mortality rates at tolerable levels despite the inordinate number of refugees and adverse conditions under which they worked. The Americans commended the generosity of the Croatian people and noted that they found Croatia's ability to absorb so many refugees to be without parallel in their team's previous experiences.

One lesson I learned from my missions to Croatia and Bosnia was that although every story told by refugees and survivors of ethic cleansing was unique, in the aggregate, their stories shared a common theme: terror. The story of one such survivor, Fadila Zecic, started when Serbian forces instituted genocide in the northern Bosnian town of Brcko. Even in the relative security of Paris where I spoke with Fadila and where she found refuge after being exchanged as a prisoner of war she continued to be tormented by nightmares and flashbacks of the demonic acts she had witnessed.

At precisely 5 A.M. on April 30, 1992, after the Serbs deliberately disabled a vehicle on Savski Most, one of two bridges over the Sava River that connected Bosnia with Croatia, the resultant bottleneck of vehicles, including busses loaded with at least 150 commuters, were blown to smithereens. Following the explosions that destroyed both bridges, the Serbs placed barricades at strategic locations and systematically set out to destroy the 100 or so houses around the bridges.

For the next three days and nights the Serbs committed an orgy of looting in non-Serb homes. A continuous stream of trucks and cars, predominantly with Belgrade registrations, returned to Serbia to sell their booty on Belgrade's thriving black market. Following every typical Serbian offensive campaign, Serbs from Serbia would come to the conquered Bosnian or Croatian areas by the busloads and ransack houses as if on a shopping spree.

On the fourth day, the Serbs placed a large poster of Tito sporting a hand drawn beard on a warehouse door in the port area called Lucko. The warehouse became one of the Serbs' most lethal slaughter houses. The Serbs rounded up all the intellectuals: physicians, lawyers, teachers, or anyone with organizational skills. Once accomplished, the Serbs started their systematic murdering frenzy. Thousands of Croats and Muslims were killed in two days in Brcko. Only women and pensioners survived; all youths and able bodied males ultimately disappeared.

An ancient Roman settlement situated on the Sava River with a picturesque blend of Turkish and Austrian architectural styles, the pre-war town of Brcko was a microcosm of ethnicity in Bosnia. Brcko and the surrounding area, comprised of 75,000 Muslims and Croats, and 13,000 Serbs, had three mosques, a Roman Catholic, an Orthodox and a Seventh Day Adventist church. Despite hearing reports that

Serbs were committing atrocities in other parts of Bosnia and the fact that the town was teeming with thousands of refugees that had fled from ethnic cleansing at Foca, the citizens of Brcko naively clung to the belief that they would be spared. Most of the Muslims in Bosnia believed in the concept of Yugoslavia. Brcko's mayor ironically called the town an oasis of peace. It became host to the seven furies instead.

Fadila had been a designer and dressmaker of renown. Her creations were often used in the movie industry in former Yugoslavia. She felt that she was spared the tribulations other Muslim women were subjected to because the Chetniks feared reprisals from her husband and brother, both well known to the Chetnik forces. Before the war her husband was a policeman, but later he became a commandant in the Bosnian Army. Even after she was evacuated to Paris, he remained to defend what was left of Bosnian territory. Her brother was a commandant in the 108th Brigade of the Bosnian Army who, along with 319 children in his charge, were killed during a Serbian tank attack. Throughout my interviews with her she reiterated that what she agonized over most was not knowing the whereabouts of her son's remains; he was killed by a grenade but never buried.

Fadila's house was strategically located in the area called Srbski Varos of Lucko. From her window she was able to look down on the warehouse and yard where prisoners were housed and slaughtered nightly.

Isak Gasi, one of the rare survivors of Brcko's slaughter house, in testifying to war crimes investigators from Washington, confirmed many of Fadila's statements. Fadila had witnessed the atrocities almost nightly.

Like clock work, the killings started at 11 P.M. and finished at 3 A.M. The main supervisor was Monika Simonovic, a prostitute turned Chetnik. Her favorite method of torture was to break the necks of glass bottles and then gouge the genitals and abdomens of her prisoners. She also burned them. Fadila recognized most of the perpetrators as local Serbs. A preamble to the slaughter would begin with three Serbian songs the prisoners were forced to sing. After "*Tko kaze da je Srbija malo, Tri puta rata, tri puta pobednik*" ("Who said

Serbia is small, three times war, three times victors"), then a shout "*Tisina*" (silence), the killings commenced. In the mornings, Fadila saw trucks leave the camps, their beds bulging with body parts.

The rapes and killings Fadila witnessed were under the direction of Zoran Pejic, the head Chetnik in Lucko. All the perpetrators were in uniform, displaying the Red Star of the Yugoslav Army on their hats. The Chetnik headquarters was the Serbian Orthodox Church. The *glavna rijec* (main orders) came from Pop (Father) Slavko. On August 3, all the mosques were mined and destroyed. Although the Catholic church was mined, it wasn't destroyed because it was located too close to the Skladiste, a military storage facility. All Catholic, Jewish, and Muslim cemeteries were bulldozed. The destruction of religious structures and graves was nothing more than a barbaric attempt to erase evidence of a culture and a people.

In her darkest hour, after learning about the deaths of her son and brother and witnessing the human mayhem being committed under her very nose, Fadila turned toward God. But she was shocked to learn that she didn't know how to pray. The most often heard expression in Bosnia, "Thank God," is usually uttered by those who are irreligious. Although Fadila professed to be a Muslim, she typified the attitude of the overwhelming majority of the Muslims in Bosnia: she identified with Turkish customs but was ignorant about Muslim theology. The Muslims' attitude toward their religion contradicts the Serbian assertion that the threat of Islamic fundamentalism justified the war.

As a product of communist secularism, Fadila's only exposure to religion had come from her Catholic friends. She said she sought and got religious instruction from a Catholic friend who had some knowledge of Islam. In what was probably an admixture of Catholicism and Islamic mysticism, using 110 peas as beads, Fadila recited over and over "God watch over me." On Tuesdays, she fasted, and meditated on a picture of St. Anthony donated by a Catholic friend. The prayers pulled her out of her depths of despair and she began to feel invincible. She felt as if a glass dome enveloped and protected her and her home.

A married couple took Fadila in for 20 days; the husband, a Croat, eventually had to witness the gang rape of his wife, a Muslim, before he was hanged. Fadila had to move 15 times to keep one step ahead of the terrorism inflicted by her previous neighbors. Once, when she was hiding, her Serbian neighbors opened the gas jet on her stove. On her return they assumed she would light a match because there was no electricity and cause a massive explosion (gas in that area is odorless). Only her strong sense of survival averted disaster.

Fadila noticed numerous vehicles with Belgrade registrations bringing people who moved into homes whose previous inhabitants had disappeared without a trace. She said most of the events she cited occurred in the presence of UNPROFOR forces. According to Fadila, UNPROFOR's only functions were carousing, womanizing, and drinking. The Hotel Golub, where they were billeted, maintained a holiday like atmosphere.

When Fadila received word that she was to be exchanged as a prisoner of war, she was given an hour's notice. In probable deference to her status, she was allowed the luxury of one small sack. She took some jewelry with her, and miraculously it escaped notice though prisoners were normally stripped and given tattered rags to wear. Aside from humiliating the prisoners, the process enabled the Serb guards to ransack the clothing for valuables that may have been sewed into the lining. The only satisfaction Fadila had during her captivity was knowing that information that she had relayed to her brother, such as minefield locations, saved many Bosnian lives.

Would she and other refugees return to their homes if a guaranteed peace were declared? All the refugees I interviewed answered, "Yes!" They all felt they could forgive, but never, never forget. As to living next to their known tormentors, they all responded, "No." But surprisingly few said they would seek revenge.

THE INFANT DEMOCRACY'S
FIRST STEPS

THE INFANT DEMOCRACY'S FIRST STEPS

During the years of Yugoslav Communism the Serbs kept tight reins on the development of non-Serbian politics and public relations. It's not surprising that newly independent Croatia made a number of cardinal mistakes in these sectors. Croatia was unable to help its cause abroad because it didn't have an image-projecting body to combat Serbia's sophisticated propaganda apparatus.

At the onset of hostilities in Croatia, the few foreign journalists who had gone to Zagreb found Croatian sources uncooperative. Zagreb had no viable press bureau to liaison with the foreign press. Croatian government officials were neither readily accessible, nor politically equipped to handle questions. The fact that Western journalists were viewed with suspicion as a carry over from the Bolshevist days didn't help matters. Croatia had and continues to have little understanding of the direct relationship between media reportage and political actions. The only bright spot in the media's coverage in Croatia came after the establishment of the Foreign Press Bureau (FPB).

Before the birth of the FPB most news coverage about Croatia originated from Belgrade or TANJUG (the official Yugoslav news organization) press releases. Without exception, the media reported whatever the Serbs wanted to project. HINA, the official Croatian news organ, was looked upon by the world's reporters as self-serving and lacking in credibility. For some strange reason, TANJUG remained above reproach.

George Bush's nominee for the post of Ambassador to Croatia, Mara Letica, and a few other Croatian-Americans helped found the Croatian American Association (CAA). The CAA became the only viable organization that represented Croatian-American interests in Washington, D.C. Acutely aware of the problems the media faced in Croatia, Letica was instrumental in establishing the FPB to help get objective facts from Croatia to the press. Recommended by Ramsey Clark, she hired J. P. "Pat" Mackley, who had, among his other diverse talents, a solid background in journalism; and sent him to Zagreb. His expertise in military strategy (which he had learned in Vietnam and the Gulf War) and his deftness in dealing with often belligerent Croatian government officials uniquely qualified him to direct the FPB. While he ran the FPB, the Croatian military used another of Mackley's multi-talents; as a master marksman he taught a cadre of Croats to become skilled snipers. Their newly learned expertise played a major role defending Vukovar.

After observing Mackley over the years, I believe that his true forte was political analysis. For example, in a Washington Post Op-Ed piece *The Balkan Quagmire Myth*, on March 7, 1993, Mackley persuasively refuted every one of the American military's arguments against using strategic air strikes and logically showed why unmanned aircraft, like missiles, were better suited. He not only predicted what NATO would do in 1995, once it got its act together, he also named the exact strategic targets. When NATO destroyed those important targets with missiles, it led to the Dayton Accords. The *Post* article was the only one of entire conflict that described the true status of the Serb forces. Alone among other writers, Mackley destroyed the myth of the Serbs' fighting ability.

Mackley molded a cadre of more than 70 dedicated volunteers, mostly second and third generation Croatian youths from the United States, Canada, and Australia, but also a number of native Croats, into a force that earned respect from even the most jaded members of the world's media.

The Bureau opened in August, 1991, and set about presenting the situation in Croatia, warts and all, to the international press. The elusive trait of credibility became the hallmark of the FPB. Reporters turned more and more to the FPB to gain access to Croatian governmental sources. Although doing so placed its volunteers in great peril, the FPB proudly escorted reporters to the front lines. Pulitzer Prize winning reporter Roy Gutman praised the young men and women of the FPB for their indispensable help in getting the true story out. He said, "They are the real heroes."

The FPB played a decisive role in dispelling a number of media preconceptions. For example, the media had been under the impression that the JNA was serving a peacekeeping role in Croatia. This faulty notion disappeared when the FPB took reporters to see the JNA carnage and destruction firsthand. Journalists soon came to depend on the FPB for hard information.

The success of the FPB made many officials in the Croatian government uncomfortable because the FPB staff's Western habit of expressing free thinking and self-initiative threatened the existing order. Although the Croatian government was democratically elected, many officials still thought like Communists, or more specifically, Bolshevists. Many couldn't relate to the new system and were intolerant of any criticism no matter how well intentioned. Despite animosity expressed by some in the Croatian government, Minister of Information Branko Salaj, head of *Hrvatska Matica Iseljenika* (Croatian Heritage Foundation) Ante Beljo, and Minister of Defense Gojko Susak cooperated and backed any decisions regarding the FPB. These three new leaders had lived in exile for over 75 years collectively. Only after Croatia declared independence were they able return home and assume positions in the government. In sharp contrast to many of their colleagues, they were well aware of the value of truth in the media and democracy.

As the FPB increasingly discredited information coming from Belgrade, the Serbs began targeting members of the press for acts of violence. During this relatively short war, more reporters have been killed than had been during both the Vietnam and Salvadoran wars. According to the Committee to Protect Journalists, 44 journalists were killed in the Balkans between the onset of hostilities in 1991 and September, 1994. Another 12 credible reports remain unconfirmed.

The Committee's executive director William A. Orme Jr. asserted that many of the journalists were victims of deliberate targeting.

Once its initial funding dried up, the undercapitalized FPB became a shadow of its former self. Although expatriate Croatian organizations in the United States had allotted funds for the FPB, the organizations found a variety of excuses to avoid dispensing the promised money. For example, the Los Angeles-based Croatian National Foundation withheld funds that were budgeted for the FPB because of personality clashes some of its board members had with certain members of the Croatian American Association. Los Angeles-based Croatian-American activist Mike Volaric explained the situation with convoluted logic: "Our organization rescinded its decision to give money to help the Foreign Press Bureau because they were appalled that the Croatian president, Franjo Tudjman, had squandered other donated funds on an airplane for his personal use."

But the seminal reason why Croatian-American organizations pulled the rug out from under the FPB was because certain Croatian officials in the United States were sabotaging the FPB. The Croatian diplomats felt threatened by the FPB on two scores. They believed that the success of the FPB stole their thunder and, more importantly, that the FPB and they were competing for the same donor pool. Without financing, the FPB collapsed.

The failure of the FPB may sound like an isolated example of squabbling among immigrant Croatian groups. But unfortunately, within Croatian communities this type of conflict is typical. Unlike Serbian immigrants in the U.S. and Canada, Croatian immigrants are deeply divided. A large number of Croatian immigrants who had embraced the Yugoslav concept have clashed with those Croats who rejected it. Among the Serbs, Yugoslavism was never seriously considered. They have considered themselves Serbs first and foremost and therefore remained united.

Los Angeles is home to a sizable number Yugoslav immigrants. Until recently they remained aloof to the internecine squabbles that pervaded their homeland. But as battle lines were drawn between Serbs, Croats, and Muslims in former Yugoslavia, the immigrant communities of Los Angeles developed similar divisions, shattering a long-lived symbiosis. So far Balkan inter-ethnic violence hasn't spread to North America, even though almost every American with Croatian or Bosnian roots has been touched by personal tragedy.

Yet Yugoslav politics have caused a number of criminal acts in the Los Angeles area Croatian community. Most of the acts predated the present conflict by decades. Such incidents have included a car bombing that killed two men and the concurrent bombing of several businesses, including a renowned restaurant. Police disarmed six sticks of dynamite found by a Los Angeles city official, the target, seconds before the dynamite would have detonated. In other cases through the years, arsonists torched social clubs; the most recent was an arson attempt on the Croatian Hall soon after Croatia became independent. Despite substantial rewards offered, none of the perpetrators of any of these crimes was ever caught.

The victims of these assaults were ethnic Croats. But the city official and restaurant owner proudly proclaimed themselves to be Yugoslavs instead of Croats.

These intra-ethnic conflicts occurred in the Los Angeles port of San Pedro, an enclave that is home to the highest per capita percentage of Croats outside of Croatia. The split among the Croats hasn't been limited to my San Pedro, but has been typical in most Croatian immigrant communities. I've talked with Croatian-American leaders from Cleveland, Chicago, Detroit, Dallas, and New York City. They all suggested that whether a person considers himself a Croat or a Yugoslav tends to depend on whether he immigrated to the United States before or after World War II. Suspicion, mistrust, and hatred defined by this divide has even permeated some Croatian-American families.

UDBA (Yugoslav secret police), which infiltrated all émigré groups, played a major role in sowing intra-ethnic dissension. Once Croatia became independent, archives long held secret by UDBA, were opened. In San Pedro's Croatian community rumors circulated that between 32 and 51 individuals had operated as UDBA agents locally. I asked Franjo Golem, Croatia's Plenipotentiary representative to the United States: "Now that the archives are open, which can identify the agents that had worked in San Pedro, when will the names be made public?" His tongue in cheek reply: "In order to prevent retribution or not to create chaos in the immigrant community, the Croatian government will not make public the names at this time," was followed with a wink. Since there haven't been any discernible changes in the community's make up, I suspect that the Croatian government are now using some of them as their own resources.

In an incident that required police intervention, the Croatian-American father of Los Angeles City Councilman Rudy Svorinich was attacked verbally by a member of the Croatian community who accused him of being a Communist. The assailant was a member of the Croatian Club who couldn't comprehend that in the United States political affiliation is a matter of choice. A March, 1994, *LA Weekly* article reported that after the attack Councilman Svorinich allegedly characterized the Croatian Club members as radical, nationalistic, Nazis in disguise—on whose arms, if you rolled up their sleeves, you'd find swastikas. Svorinich didn't deny the allegation that his father was a Communist, and the Croatian-American Club members didn't demand an apology for the councilman's insults.

The pre-World War II Croatian immigrants came to Los Angeles in three waves: from a Croatia under Austrian domination, from a Serbian-ruled kingdom, and from a Yugoslavia that imposed draconian measures on non-Serbs. They were, at best, semi-literate, patriarchal, politically naive, and provincial. These hardworking, honest to a fault, immigrants settled mostly in San Pedro. They remembered the old country as an idyllic fantasy. Tied to the once flourishing fishing industry, the community prospered, adjusted to American mores, and, for the most part, lost its ethnic identity.

Aside from teaching the faith, the Catholic Church in Croatia has perpetuated cultural values. Because the Croatian immigrants in San Pedro were unable to receive the Church's teachings in their first language, they maintained neither faith nor culture. In addition, because many of the males were commercial fishermen who were out at sea for months at a time, the community became matriarchal within a single generation.

Official Yugoslav sources supplied most of the news from the homeland to the San Pedro community. With rare exceptions, the pre-World War II Croats of San Pedro were ignorant of the fact that the Serbs ruled all political and economic infrastructures of Yugoslavia. Similar ignorance existed wherever Croats had settled. A majority of the Yugoslav diplomatic corps were made up of Serbs who eagerly provided official, Serbian-slanted news to the local immigrant communities.

Consequently, the mostly uneducated Croatian émigrés learned "their" history from the Serbian viewpoint. The Serbian propagandists effectively brainwashed the non-Serbs émigrés to look upon the noun Croatian with abhorrence and to call themselves Slavs; a term no Serbian nor anyone used in Yugoslavia. Nonetheless, many émigrés proudly embraced the new term. With the emergent post-war Yugoslavia, under communism, most of the Slavs readily identified with the new regime, heart and soul, since many pre-war émigrés had communist leanings anyway. They embraced Yugoslavia's agenda to an extent that San Pedro's Yugoslav Club was labeled a subversive organization up to the early 1960s. The subversion label preceded Macarthyism.

Unlike the Croatian Club members, the pre-war Slavs had to assimilate into American society. Prior to World War II America percolated with fears of "the red menace" and economic chaos. Anyone with funny sounding names was looked upon disparagingly. The "greenhorns" had to adjust to survive; so they became as "American" as possible, and thrived. The Slavic community emerged from the 1930s' depression without any member having resorted to welfare. Many became lawyers, teachers, judges, or captains of industry. Their sons had fought with valor for America.

Martin Bogdanovich's small fish packing plant became the biggest employer in San Pedro and ultimately the largest cannery in the world—Star Kist. But an obituary upon his daughter's death in early 1994 epitomized the prevailing attitude of Slavs. The article proudly proclaimed that she, a Croat, had been the confidante of Tito, the Communist dictator, and that her father was a supporter of the

Serbian king, both of whom were great enemies of the Croatian people.

The end of World War II ushered in an era when ethnicity was non-stigmatizing. As a result, newly arrived Croats weren't pressured to adjust to American mores and therefore made no effort to identify with American society. The Croatian Club and most of its members avoided involvement in American civic affairs and institutions. In contrast, the Yugoslav Club members actively supported service clubs and charities such as the Boys Club, Lions, or Kiwanis.

The way Yugoslav and Croatian Clubs reflected political party lines of former Yugoslavia and newly independent Croatia are remarkably similar. Any Yugoslav Club member that acknowledged himself as a Croatian (despite 95% of its members were de facto Croatian) or criticized communist Yugoslavia was ostracized. On the other hand, before independence, anyone proclaiming himself a Croatian was welcome at any Croatian Club.

During Croatia's self-determination effort there was a proliferation of new political parties. Astutely, the only Croatian political party which actively courted émigrés world wide was the Croatian Democratic Union (HDZ). Consequently, most of the émigrés, committed themselves to the HDZ party. In attempting to consolidate the party's position, the leaders made certain that any émigré who was not for the HDZ felt uncomfortable in the Croatian Club.

To the detriment of the Croatian community, both locally and in Croatia, the émigré hierarchy, rather than devoting themselves to helping Croatia in a generic sense, spent their energies consolidating personal power and ingratiating themselves with the Zagreb government. To this end they resorted to backbiting and character assassination against non-HDZ members or those that stepped out guidelines they'd instituted. Besides being counterproductive, it caused a great deal of dissension.

Because most post World War II immigrant Croats made little effort to assimilate into American society they never became part of the American mainstream. Although the isolation was self imposed, many developed a lower self-esteem. But the independence of Croatia gave émigrés a cause. For example, a physician with marginal healing skills and who has never formulated an original thought, suddenly found direction when he was appointed a position in the HDZ organization in the United States.

Pedigrees, genetic and political, have become the prevailing criteria for legitimacy in all the republics of former Yugoslavia. Following the breakup of Yugoslavia, the Yugoslav Club largely ignored the issue of pedigree, but the Croatian Club followed the party line and took it one step further. Their most important criterion for bona fide acceptance was predicated upon whether one became a believer in the Croatian nation before or after independence. Anybody who wanted to join or came to the club for the first time after 1991 was viewed skeptically. The zealots had a favorite refrain: "Where were you before?" Yet the backgrounds of some Croatian Club officers have been questionable. A son of a gendarme (the dreaded enforcers of the Serbian King in Croatia) and a half-Romanian somehow slipped through the cracks to become officers.

Despite their nostalgic feelings for Yugoslavia, the members of the Yugoslav Club viewed themselves as immigrants committed to America. Those Croats opposed to the concept of Yugoslavia felt like exiles and therefore immersed themselves in homeland politics. The infighting among Croats may have been a blessing in disguise for Los Angeles. By focusing their chauvinism on each other, they've avoided aiming their hatred at other ethnic groups.

A healing process may have begun, though. After heated debate, the Yugoslav Club changed its name. A reconciliation banquet spearheaded by Cardinal Mahoney brought all the protagonists, the hierarchies of the Croatian and former Yugoslav Clubs, and Councilman Svorinich, together at the Mary Star of the Sea parish center. With the older, hard-liner Slavs fading out of the picture, and the younger generations feeling indifferent about old country politics, the split among Croats in San Pedro may die a natural death—of course, only if there are no further acts of local violence.

Perhaps not surprisingly the conflict in former Yugoslavia has spilled over onto the basketball courts of the NBA. Star players Vlade Divac of the Los Angeles Lakers and Drazen Petrovic of the New Jersey Nets had been close friends in Yugoslavia when they played together on the Yugoslav National Team that won the silver medal at the 1988 Olympics. Divac is a Serb, and Petrovic a Croat.

Divac was quoted by the Associated Press as saying that he couldn't understand why Petrovic hadn't talked to him since the European Cup championship in 1990. Divac seemed to have forgotten that after the game he had grabbed a Croatian flag from a fan, slammed it to the floor, and trampled it. Shortly thereafter the Serbs initiated hostilities in Croatia. Another Croatian ex-teammate, Stojko Vrankovic of the Boston Celtics, ignored Divac when his team played the Lakers. After Divac tried to rekindle old friendships, Vrankovic said, "I can never forget what you did to my flag." No doubt he couldn't forget recent Serbian atrocities either.

Despite the great differences in attitude among Croatian immigrants, many have backed the fledging Croatian state. In fact, support from overseas Croats allowed Croatia to survive its first year of existence. Aside from the fact that it had no allies, Croatia was virtually bankrupt when it declared independence. Whatever federal funds the republic had before the war were held in Belgrade banks, and therefore, Serbia immediately confiscated them. In order for the country to function fiscally, the government had to rely on overseas Croats for a majority of its financing.

Athletes also helped rescue Croatia fiscally during the first few critical years. Former Yugoslavia had no shortage of talented athletes, particularly in soccer and basketball. Because Europe takes soccer seriously, it didn't hesitate to tap the Croatian pool of players. According to *Soccer*, between 1992 and 1996 Croatia sold an incredible 1,553 player contracts abroad for millions of much needed dollars.

Loath to lose their privileged status, the Serbian minority in Croatia campaigned vigorously to maintain the status quo. The Croatian Democratic Union (HDZ) won the early 1990 elections and then ousted the Serbs who had ruled under the Communist Party. While the HDZ prepared to take over the reins of government, rebel Serbs fought back by orchestrating a number of incidents.

Serbs had either supported the Serbian Democratic Party (SDP) or the Party of Democratic Changes, the rechristened Communist Party. The Serbian parties couldn't accept the fact that they had lost the election. So incited by propaganda, which included the belief that the Croats had already slaughtered thousands of Serbs even before they had taken over the government, the rebel Serbs took to the streets, burning Croatian symbols and flags.

A staged provocation in the small Croatian town of Benkovac ranks with the Polish border guard "attacks" on Germans that "justified" Germany's invasion of Poland prior to World War II. Miroslav Mlinar, the president of the local SDP, was attacked by unknown assailants. He was immediately taken to a hospital in Zadar where his injuries were evaluated as not serious. But Mlinar and his family wouldn't accept the diagnosis of Croatian physicians. So they elected to get a second opinion at the hospital in Knin. Hospital director Milan Babic, a dentist who later became the Serbian rebel leader, declared Mlinar's injuries life threatening and grave.

Believing the attack was genuine, Croats overwhelmingly condemned it and urged the authorities, who at the time were still Communists, to investigate. But Serbs from the whole spectrum of Yugoslavia, including the media, had identified the recently elected "genocidal Croatian entity" as Mlinar's attackers.

Dr. Jovan Raskovic, a psychiatrist and president of the SDP, made a number of pronouncements that concluded Mlinar's attack resulted from Croatian nationalistic forces. His arguments convinced the SDP to boycott the Parliament of the Socialist Republic of Croatia. Consequently, the Serbian population that supported the SDP weren't represented in the parliament.

The newly installed government pursued the Mlinar investigation. A commission made up of Zagreb's medical school professors established that Mlinar's injuries were negligible. Although the commission was made up mostly of ethnic Serbs, the Serbian community gave no credence to the commission's report.

The Serbian media and Belgrade threatened the newly elected government with a variety of reprisals and officially demanded that the election should be annulled and a new government installed in Croatia. The Mlinar affair became a cause celebre. Its rallying cry has become a slogan for the Serbian people: "An attack on every Serb, no matter where, is felt as an attack on the whole Serbian people."

Once the dust settled, the Croats were found innocent of the allegations. But the damage caused by the Mlinar affair had irreversible consequences. The SDP refused to settle differences between the Serbs and Croats in Croatia democratically and demanded autonomy. Although Serbia denied autonomy to the majority Albanians of Kosovo, it demanded autonomy for Serbs in Croatia where they comprised only about ten percent of the population. Despite the Serbs' lack of cooperation, in a conciliatory move, President Tudjman offered Raskovic a cabinet position, but was summarily rebuffed. After the SDP refused to cooperate with Zagreb and flatly rejected all government positions, it set about establishing an independent Serbian state within Croatia, the illegal Serbian Autonomous Region (SAO) of Krajina.

Milan Babic succeeded Raskovic as head of the SDP and was named president of SAO Krajina. The head of Knin's police station, Milan Martic, organized the arming of local Serbs with weapons sent from the Serbian Ministry of Internal Affairs and distributed by the JNA. The commander of the JNA garrison was Ratko Mladic, who later went on to better things. Barricades were set up on highways and railroad lines. These barricades effectively suspended traffic between Zagreb and the coast, severely curtailing the tourist industry, one of Croatia's major sources of foreign currency. Meanwhile, the Serbian parliament in Belgrade pledged support for its brethren in Croatia and requested that the JNA enforce their decision. Martic became president after Babic was ousted for daring to question the authority of Milosevic. Martic was later named a war criminal by an international tribunal for ordering the missile attack on the center of Zagreb in May, 1995. Babic was demoted to the post of mayor in Knin after his attempt to usurp Milosevic's authority failed. Later, he was one of the first to leave Krajina prior to the 1995 Croatian offensive.

The newly elected government in Croatia was at a distinct disadvantage by every measure. Aside from being woefully unprepared to govern and faced with an armed insurrection supported by the federal army, they had to contend with a bureaucracy whose members were vehemently opposed to the new order. Prior to 1990, the criteria for appointment for positions in the hierarchy and middle management, from accountants to zookeepers, had been based on Communist Party affiliation rather than personal qualifications. Since the new order was elected on an anti-Communist platform, formerly entrenched bureaucrats found the new order's agenda threatening.

In all communist countries, vocal opposition, or even suspicious activity, could lead to imprisonment or disappearance. Croats coined a catchy phrase to characterize those whose whereabouts had become unknown: "The night ate them up." And if the "disappeared" resurfaced, it was usually because they had safely escaped to the West.

Following the euphoria and bravado set in motion by the crumbling of communism in Europe, would-be democratic leaders were rudely awakened to the reality of running governments. The virgin administrations contained few individuals with political experience and no cadre to draw upon for support. The new order had no practical knowledge of running anything, let alone countries. Because the old regime's political and economic infrastructures were predicated on Communist Party membership, there were very few non-communists to take over. But in Croatia a pool of highly qualified individuals existed outside of the old establishment.

Yugoslav Communism tacitly allowed the development of a subculture of entrepreneurs who were highly skilled in management. As long as they didn't challenge dogmatic issues, kept a low profile, and most importantly, greased the palms of the officials, they were left alone. Using methods that would make Karl Marx turn over in his grave yet are considered laudable in a capitalistic society, they took advantage of the system. Their skill in exploiting the system allowed Yugoslavia to have the highest standard of living in the communist world.

The new government begged these entrepreneurs to join and fill key posts, but found few takers. The most enduring quality of these individuals was survival. Among many Croats, uncertainty about whether Croatia would remain a viable state and fear that Serbia would eventually crush them influenced their decision making. The fear was so real that many talented Croats fled the country. Others held onto the security of their old positions, hoping they could avoid the almost certain pogroms that would visit the nation if Serbia successfully thwarted Croatia's independence efforts. As a consequence, most government posts were filled by second or third choices, particularly by holdovers from the old regime or people whose only talent was patriotism. Despite the shortcoming of having individuals that lacked qualification who filled important positions, the government is surviving by trial and error.

For example, one individual, after having lived in the United States for several years, but had learned how to exploit the American system, returned to Croatia. Before he left, he incurred huge debts, declared bankruptcy and absconded. Apparently this uneducated, former tradesman had no qualms about jeopardizing his American citizenship since he readily accepted his being "elected" a deputy member of parliament and installed as an assistant director to a ministry that deals with sensitive high finance decisions. His only qualifications were loyalty to Tudjman and that he had personally delivered funds collected by émigrés which Tudjman used in his first election campaign. Apparently this money carried the tide, since no other political party exploited professional public relations in their campaigns.

The predominance of Bolshevistic mentalities remained an enduring problem within Croatia's government and state run enterprises. Such anachronisms weren't unexpected, because many in the new government were former members of the Communist Party who had simply switched party labels. Although many Communist bureaucrats originally lost their positions, they were reinstated to give the new government a semblance of efficiency. Despite its best intentions, the new regime couldn't entirely dispense with the skills and knowledge of the old hands, including members of the security services who had for years busied themselves amassing files on internal opponents and external enemies of the state. As long as they swore allegiance to the new order and had no visible blood on their hands, all were welcomed back. It was a classic Hobson's choice. But mores can't be changed with a stroke of the pen. Suspicion and intolerance permeated the new regime.

When the JNA invaded Slovenia in June, 1991, Croatia's military was limited to a police force. Even after the invasion of Slovenia, most Croatian politicians didn't believe the Serbs would turn on Croatia with such brutal force. Lacking *realpolitik* experience, the Croatian government naively believed the rhetoric of self-determination espoused by the United States and other Western nations. They believed that help, such as the Sixth Fleet, would come to their aid. The survivors of the Tito period had idealized Western democratic principles and beliefs learned from Voice of America. They couldn't comprehend that the West had no intention of helping their fledgling democracy.

PHYSICIANS, LEADERS BY DEFAULT

PHYSICIANS, LEADERS BY DEFAULT

In most countries, an overwhelming majority of legislators and politicians come from the legal profession; former Yugoslavia was no exception. Because Communist Party membership was usually compulsory for politicians in Yugoslavia, the anti-Communist sentiment that pervaded newly independent Croatia resulted in the ouster of a great number of the old guard. Although unprepared for the nuances of politics and governance, physicians filled the political vacuum by replacing the ousted lawyers in the new government. The appearance of physicians in government isn't unusual, but the large percentages that filled Croatia's government offices is unique.

As a group, physicians were viewed with suspicion by the Communist system. Aside from having work habits considered abnormal for a socialistic society, their traits of ethics and humanism weren't part of the Communist lexicon. Physicians were still able to flourish because the practice of medicine was less dependent on politics than professions such as economics, law, or journalism. Without political interference, physicians were able to preserve their own free thoughts and individuality.

When it came time to replace the old regime, the Croatian public readily accepted their physicians as leaders. The public perceived them as intellectuals who possessed the qualities of credibility, dedication, and integrity. Most importantly, many physicians weren't tainted with past Communist Party affiliation. These virtues far surpassed their main liabilities: naiveté and ignorance about the machinations of power and the importance of public relations.

The innocents had been healing the physical needs of society and were now nurturing the new democracy while rapidly adjusting to their new roles. Ministries in the new Croatia, particularly the Foreign Office, resembled medical conventions. The number of physicians holding local political positions was equally impressive. Croatian physicians, perhaps to a greater extent than other professionals, were driven by altruism and a strong sense of patriotism, and put off satisfying careers to help manage the new democracy. Given their professional experiences, the physicians-turned-leaders approached the new nation as they would have an infant with an unpromising prenatal history whose congenital abnormalities were amenable to corrective surgery and rehabilitation.

None of the physicians suggested that they planned to remain in government. The majority of the physicians planned to return to practicing medicine when a cadre of qualified leaders had matured to the point where they could effectively run the government. Most of the physicians participating at the federal level were professors at the medical school. All were specialists in their respective fields of medicine.

For example, the position of Deputy Head of the Office of the President of Croatia was filled admirably by Branimir Jaksic. Prior to the conflict he had been a professor at the medical school and the coordinator of the International Multicentric Research Project on the Clinical Therapy of Chronic Lymphocytic Leukemia and the European Organization for the Research and Therapy of Cancer.

Ambassador for Human Rights and Deputy Prime Minister Ivica Kostovic had been the dean of Zagreb's medical school and a professor of neuroanatomy. He had received postdoctoral training at John Hopkins University and had researched neuroanatomy and neuropathology at Harvard, Yale, and several prestigious institutions in Europe.

Kostovic, who is also the leading investigator of Serbian atrocities, has become the victim of a bitter irony. His daughter was almost killed during a Serbian missile attack on Zagreb in May, 1995, while walking to the children's hospital, which the Serbs had targeted. Cluster bomb projectiles penetrated her chest and abdominal cavities, severely damaging vital organs. Although she survived a number of major surgeries, 18 pieces of shrapnel remain in the tissues and muscles of her back.

Zdenko Skrabalo, who played a key role in the formation of the new Croatian state, was a professor at Zagreb's Medical School and head of the Diabetes and Endocrinology Institute before being named Deputy Foreign Affairs Minister. He briefly served as Minister of Foreign Affairs. He's presently representative to UNESCO and Ambassador to Switzerland. Skrabalo was one of the few Croatian officials to recognize the importance of the media. Addressing the World Congress of Croatian Physicians in 1995, he said, "Croatia has overcome a number of major obstacles since declaring independence. But it has not been able to overcome the most important one—getting the message to the media."

Andrija Hebrang led the exodus of physicians into government. Stumbling to get its sea legs, the newly christened Croatia has been characterized by an extremely high turnover rate in the ministries. Minister of Health Hebrang, probably the most respected and charismatic individual in the government, is one of those rare exceptions who has remained in office since the day Croatia was formed.

Unlike its counterpart in the United States, the health ministry in Croatia isn't merely a symbolic office. Aside from being responsible for the entire country's health needs, it cares for the social welfare of the citizenry. Hebrang's talents haven't been limited to his work in the ministry. Even before Croatia declared independence, he was an insider intimately involved in the political aspects of running the government. To better understand why many Croats, such as Hebrang, welcomed the overthrow of communism, I should mention his family history. The history, an example of how the Communists treated enemies of the state, isn't unique.

His father, Andrija Sr., was one of the founders of the Communist Party in Croatia. While serving as Party Secretary, he'd helped organize the most effective fighting unit of the Partisans during World War II. Despite his power, status, and idealized commitment to communism, he was executed by order of Tito; his sin had been Croatian nationalism. Thereafter the Hebrangs were treated as second class citizens. To punish them further, the authorities imprisoned Andrija Jr.'s mother for many years and forbid her from seeing her son.

Since the family name was considered anathema by the regime, the children were forced to assume pseudonyms. School stipends were closed to them. Family members were harassed frequently and followed sporadically, and when they were suspected of having contact with personages of influence, these measures intensified.

Despite the inordinate amount of pressure placed upon the family, they prospered intellectually. Against all odds, Andrija was accepted into the medical school. He eventually specialized in the field of radiology and became a professor of medicine.

In the months before the Serbian-led Belgrade government attacked Croatia, Hebrang's life was in jeopardy. Although Yugoslavia was less rigid and dogmatic than other Soviet Bloc countries like East Germany, its secret police (UDBA or SUP) were 100% Stalinist and probably the most effective and sophisticated in the Eastern bloc. But by the late 1980s, many in the secret police ranks had either lost faith, were jaded, or didn't care any longer. Had SUP preserved its original zeal, it would've crushed any opposition.

A few committed Stalinists in SUP still relished the special cases assigned to them. As the Hebrang name was an abomination to the Communist Party, surveillance of them was stepped up. SUP sensed that Hebrang was up to something. But despite vigorous surveillance, Hebrang and his medical colleagues, Mate Granic, Ivica Kostovic, and Zdenko Skrabalo, the Big Four, were able to set up an ironclad cell and become the nucleus of the physicians' movement. Anticipating the imminent breakup of Yugoslavia, the Big Four's first priority was to draw up contingency plans to maintain the health needs of Croatia's population. Their calculation of 10,000 dead and 20,000 wounded Croats was remarkably close to the mark.

The Big Four's next step was to select trustworthy individuals to form new cells to implement their plans. This task was formidable because some of their friends and colleagues were members of SUP. At the time, SUP had approximately 22,000 members and countless informers in Croatia.

One of the first acts of the new government was to revamp the secret police into a more open intelligence gathering agency. SUP, the greatest nemesis of the Croatian people, had been a law unto itself. The power it wielded and the fear it evoked had kept the old regime in place. The new order was forced to make compromises with SUP to prevent bloodshed. For other valid political reasons, the new government had to keep some of the ruthless old guard in place. A few were even given positions in the highest levels of the government. The ex-SUP members, regardless of how well they performed, were viewed with suspicion by their new colleagues. Ironically, former suspects, such as Hebrang, found themselves working alongside their former oppressors. But the new government appointed individuals from outside the system to fill the most sensitive positions. For example, Goran Dodig, a psychiatrist, was appointed the top official of Military Counter-Intelligence and Assistant Minister of Defense.

In former Yugoslavia, by design, only 17 of 500 military surgeons were Croatian. Weapons of modern warfare, with their awesome projectiles, inflict wounds that are difficult to repair for even the most sophisticated surgeon. Treatment requires a special expertise other physicians lack. So Hebrang immediately assembled a team of the few experts available in Croatia to write a practical handbook for treating war trauma. Miraculously, the book was delivered in 24 hours. Soon after its circulation morbidity rates fell dramatically.

Immediately preceding the conflict, the Serb-led JNA confiscated most of the supplies and equipment from the military hospitals in Croatia. In contrast to other countries, military hospitals in Croatia weren't limited to military personnel; civilians were admitted as well. Because Croatia lacked even the most fundamental supplies, such as dressings and gauze, the country was ill-equipped to treat the enormous number of casualties, let alone patients with mundane diseases.

Zagreb, the capital of Croatia, gave no hint that the front lines were only 30 miles away. But its hospital wards, filled with civilians without limbs, with gaping visceral wounds, and blinded from shrapnel, painted a different picture—a picture of a medical infrastructure that had been stretched to the breaking point.

Hebrang, as Minister of Health, was confronted with an enormous number of problems that demanded immediate solutions. An escalating war, a shortage of weapons with which to defend themselves, an economy and infrastructure in shambles, no cadre of experienced personnel, and nationwide psychological stress caused by a system in transition from dictatorship to democracy, made Hebrang's job all the more difficult.

From the onset of active fighting, the Serbs targeted medical complexes. So basements, bunkers, and warrens created from destroyed buildings became new medical centers, forcing patients and medical personnel underground. The destruction of ten major hospitals in a country the size of Maryland proved devastating. Osijek's General Hospital, the largest hospital closest to the battle line, was blasted by rockets and heavy artillery, but continued to function inside the remaining 20% of its structure. All medical and surgical care was conducted in a maze of tunnels beneath the hospital.

Meanwhile the director of Osijek's Hospital, radiologist Kresimir Glavina, after having served valorously during the trying days of Osijek's bombardment, was elected to serve as a representative in Croatia's Parliament. Another war hero, Juraj Njavro, who was chief surgeon during the siege of Vukovar, became Minister of Health. After the fall of Vukovar, the Serbs imprisoned Njavro. His experiences and exploits were duly recorded in his book, *Glava Dolje: Ruke Na Ledja* ("Head Down: Hands on the Back in Front").

The Serbian ethnic cleansing program in Croatia resulted in hundreds of thousands of displaced persons and severely strained Croatia's remaining medical facilities. But the enormous influx of refugees from Bosnia-Herzegovina, many suffering from major trauma, further overtaxed the already fragile health care system.

The Health Ministry was responsible for operating the refugee camps. By December, 1992, 663,493 refugees and displaced persons from Bosnia-Herzegovina had found safety in Croatia. Despite adverse conditions, Croatian medical personnel were able to keep the rates of refugee mortality and infection morbidity at almost the same level as the general population. Fortunately there were few epidemics. The statistics reflect good hygienic conditions, nourishment, and selfless medical management. But caring for the refugees placed an enormous strain on the teetering Croatian economy. Croatian citizens bore 70% of the cost of operating the camps; the international community donated the rest.

Slobodan Lang serves as Administrator for the Red Cross and special advisor to the chief of the Croatian Office for Displaced Persons and Refugees. A human rights activist since his student days, Lang's also vice-president of the Croatian Helsinki Watch Committee. Lang is no mere armchair human rights dilettante. At great peril to his life, Lang has run many Serbian blockades to deliver humanitarian aid in Croatia and Bosnia-Herzegovina. He's also an assistant professor at the medical school.

Many physicians in Croatia have become critical of Hebrang. But much of the criticism is self-serving, arising soon after Hebrang abolished the "envelope system." Croatian patients, like patients in many communist countries, bypassed the bureaucratic boondoggle by offering tokens of appreciation to medical personnel. Originally the tokens were commodities, like hams or chickens. As the country became more prosperous, money became the token of choice.

After communism imposed its will in Yugoslavia, the practice became more common. By the mid-1980s the corruption was rampant. The process of seeing specialists after being referred or admitted to hospitals for elective procedures was snail-paced. Producing an envelope had the same magical effect as the words "Open sesame."

Although illegal, the envelope system became the accepted norm. The system's tacit approval was the way the Yugoslav government controlled the medical profession. If a physician was perceived by commissars as deviating from the ideological party line, the government would invoke the law against him. Instead of a receiving a political trial, which would come under the scrutiny of international human rights groups, the physician would be tried in civil court. Before the breakup of Yugoslavia, Human Rights groups had cited Yugoslavia as having one of the worst records of abuses.

Because the envelope system provided physicians with a large share of their incomes, Hebrang's ban seemed draconian. Yet even his most vocal detractors admit the envelope system had corrupted and compromised the ethics of the profession.

Economics proved to be the main problem for the Health Ministry. Unbelievable as it may seem, the medical system in Croatia had been operating without a budget for years, with absolutely no form of accountability. "Cost containment" was an expression unknown in the Croatian medical vocabulary. To make the system function effectively, revolutionary changes were necessary. The expectations of the medical personnel and patients had to be altered.

The delivery of health care in Croatia was a true miracle. Although the Health Ministry had 70% less money in its budget during the war than it had in 1990, Croatia's morbidity and mortality rates remained almost constant through 1994. The statistics were much better than those from all other formerly communist countries. The Croatian statistics seem more impressive when taking into account the fact that none of those other countries was at war, or taking care of refugees and displaced persons. The credit belongs to the cost containment programs instituted by the Health Ministry and the cooperation of most of Croatia's physicians.

Several other individuals from the health field participated in Croatia's government. Josip Juras and Ivan Majdak are veterinarians. Juras became Minister of Labor, Social Welfare and Family; previously he was chairman of the Executive Council of the city of Sibenik. Majdak, besides being a veterinarian, is also a medical doctor. He became Minister without Portfolio as Advisor for Economic and Regional Development Questions for the President's Office.

Ivica Kracun, head of the Laboratory of Neurochemistry, Chemistry and Biochemistry, at the Zagreb School of Medicine, also serves as Deputy Minister of Science. Drago Stambuk, an internist, unable to tolerate the system in Yugoslavia, chose exile in England over ten years ago. He became renowned in the clinical aspects of HIV positive patients. By avocation a writer and poet, he is well regarded in literary circles in London. Long before the onset of hostilities in former Yugoslavia he took up the gauntlet to combat the misinformation that was so prevalent in the British media regarding Croatian affairs. His commentaries had a strong influence on Margaret Thatcher. Once

Croatia was independent he abandoned his brilliant medical career to serve Croatia's diplomatic needs. After a stint in London, he was appointed ambassador to India.

Croats at large should also be proud of another achievement. At a time when Serbs controlled over 25% of Croatian territory, the Croats were taking care of refugees whose numbers equaled over 25% of the indigenous population. The Croats accomplished this feat with an economic output that was less than 50% of pre-war production.

By relating these stories about physicians now in government, I don't mean to detract from the exemplary work of the physicians who continued to practice their art under unimaginably adverse conditions. I simply mean to illustrate how individuals from that most honored of professions unhesitatingly changed roles to assist Croatia during its birth as an independent nation.

Although a few physicians serving in the government have proved to be inept administrators, all have been sincere in their patriotism. A surgeon with golden hands, Franjo Golem, put his medical career on hold when he was named the first Foreign Minister of Croatia. But his forte wasn't diplomacy, and so he was removed from his post. To honor his loyalty to the cause, Franjo Tudjman ignored objections from the cabinet and appointed Golem the first Plenipotentiary of the Republic of Croatia to the United States. Golem's performance in Washington D.C. was viewed by many as less than satisfactory.

Mate Granic, an internist, professor at the medical school, and deputy director of the Vuk Vrhovac Institute who had done postgraduate studies for several years at prestigious institutions including Harvard, exceeded all expectations when he blossomed into a world caliber diplomat as Minister of Foreign Affairs and Vice Prime Minister of Croatia. Aside from his diplomatic ability, Granic's moderate philosophy tempers, somewhat, the HDZ's hierarchy hard-liners, who are in the majority.

Bosnian Foreign Minister Irfan Ljubijankic was also a physician. Ljubijankic was elected to parliament in 1990, and the Bosnian government hierarchy soon realized that his inherent political talents surpassed his formidable medical skills. So Ljubijankic was appointed President of the Bihac district. In April, 1992, Bihac became a major target for Serbian bombardment. While the Serbian attacks intensified, and Bihac's civilian population suffered huge numbers of casualties, Ljubijankic divided his energies between the healing art of surgery at Bihac's hospital and service in the political realm. He reluctantly agreed to serve as Bosnia's Foreign Minister, in October, 1993. Unfortunately, he didn't live to see the seeds of his peace negotiations bear fruit because he was killed when his helicopter was shot down by Serbian artillery in May, 1995.

By a remarkable coincidence, individuals from the medical professions seem to be the main actors in the tragedy being played out in other parts of former Yugoslavia. Although contrary to naturalization laws, the United States government allowed a naturalized American citizen, Milan Panich, to serve as Prime Minister of Yugoslavia. Panich is the owner and founder of ICN Pharmaceuticals, one of America's largest drug firms.

Milan Babic, the Serbian rebel leader in Croatia, is a dentist. The Bosnian-Serb leader, Radovan Karadzic, is a psychiatrist who did post-graduate training in the United States. Another psychiatrist, academician, and professor, Jovan Raskovic, was president of the Serbian Democratic Party. British peace negotiator Lord David Owen is also a physician. Given their performances in the conflict, it seems to me that Doctors Owen and Karadzic either kept their fingers crossed or were absent when they were supposed to take the Hippocratic Oath.

CONFLICTS OF INTEREST

CONFLICTS OF INTEREST

Between the time Lawrence Eagleburger left the State Department in 1982 after having served as Ambassador to Yugoslavia, and his 1988 appointment as Deputy Secretary of State, he worked for several Yugoslav government institutions and banks. Another veteran Yugoslav hand, Lieutenant General Brent Scowcroft, who previously had served as military attaché in Belgrade and later at the Pentagon, joined his colleague Eagleburger in the private sector.

According to *The New York Times* (February 10, 1982), while serving as U.S. Ambassador, Eagleburger had pressured U.S. banks to advance credits to bail out Communist Yugoslavia despite the practice being contrary to American policy. He personally summoned executives from nine major banks to Washington, D.C. and coerced them to keep lending money to Yugoslavia. Despite objections by Defense Secretary Casper Weinberger and Treasury Secretary Donald T. Regan, Eagleburger's campaign was successful. Weinberger and Regan felt that the U.S. government had no business intervening in the deteriorating financial situation in Yugoslavia and that this sort of aid was the responsibility of the Treasury, not the State Department. The only time the government openly questioned the ethics of Eagleburger's close affiliation with Yugoslav financial interests was during his confirmation hearings before the Committee on Foreign Relations in the U.S. Senate.

When Eagleburger retired from the State Department in 1982, Yugoslavia rewarded him with an appointment as president of the

Ljubljanska Banka (LBS), in New York. LBS and Yugoslavia had benefited from the loans he orchestrated. Scowcroft was named vice-chairman of LBS.

On August 25, 1982, The *Wall Street Journal* announced that former Secretary of State Henry Kissinger had opened a consulting firm, Kissinger and Associates (K&A), "to help make strategic decisions at the highest level." One of his associates was former British Foreign Secretary Lord Peter Carrington, who later played a nefarious role during the conflict in former Yugoslavia. Eagleburger, Scowcroft, and Carrington became principals and directors of K&A. K&A epitomized influence peddling by exploiting its directors' governmental connections.

According to an article by columnist Eric Margolis, K&A "channeled hundreds of millions of dollars in private investments into Yugoslavia. By *sheer coincidence*, most of it was invested after Eagleburger served as American Ambassador to Belgrade."

While conducting an investigation of the Bank Nazionale di Lavoro (BNL), House Banking Committee chairman Henry Gonzalez uncovered a link between BNL and LBS. Congressman Gonzalez revealed that Eagleburger played a major role in setting up the LBS, a subsidiary of Global Motors/Yugo of America. BNL allegedly channeled billions of dollars in illegal loans to Iraq. The investigation also revealed that Eagleburger and Scowcroft's protégé, Slobodan Milosevic, whom they had nurtured while stationed in Belgrade, had been appointed president of a related bank in Belgrade.

Apparently old diplomats from Belgrade don't retire and fade away, they end up working for Yugoslav owned companies. Former Ambassador to Yugoslavia John Scanlon is now on the Board at ICN Pharmaceuticals, a company whose president is Milan Panich. When Panich served as Prime Minister of Yugoslavia, Scanlon was Panich's security advisor in Belgrade.

The graduates of the Kissinger school did well for themselves. The only fly in the ointment was "Operation Flying Kite," a U.S. Customs sting operation directed against LBS. The bank was apparently involved in an organized crime money laundering operation. LBS intended to use the funds to export highly restricted technology and implements of war. Eagleburger didn't resign from his position at the bank until five weeks after indictment, when his nomination as Deputy Secretary of State was assured. Among the others indicted was a Yugoslav Consul General in Chicago. Although Eagleburger was exonerated, the taint persisted. Eagleburger eventually became Secretary of State, and Scowcroft, National Security Advisor to President Bush. Carrington eventually became U.N. peace negotiator for Yugoslavia.

Although Eagleburger, Scowcroft, and Carrington may be honorable men, their financial interests cast doubt on their ability to give objective and unbiased advice about Yugoslavia.

When I learned about the Yugoslav cabal in the Bush administration I notified California Congressman Dana Rohrabacher. Although Rohrabacher felt there was "no reason to believe that any government official committed a crime, [he would] have preferred if the officials had left policy to others who had not had Yugoslav business dealings."

Eagleburger was also president of Global Motors, a subsidiary of Yugoslav arms producer Zavodi Crvena Zastava whose clients have included Iraq and Libya. The Bush administration supplied a great deal of financial aid to the Iraqi regime prior to the Persian Gulf War. Most of that aid was spent in Yugoslavia on arms. These same arms were eventually used against American soldiers and increased the profits of K&A. The role played by Kissinger and his ex-associates in the Bush administration is analogous to how United Fruit Company manipulated our Central American policy to enhance its commercial position during the 1950s.

Eagleburger's federally required financial statement showed that he received pay from his directorship of LBS. Although he wasn't directly compensated by Global Motors, Global Motors was a client of K&A and Kent Associates—firms for which Eagleburger worked. Notwithstanding Warren Zimmermann's, Eagleburger's apologist, statement that Eagleburger's "remuneration was next to nothing," when he returned to the State Department Eagleburger received $1.1 million in bonuses and severance pay from K&A. Kent Associates paid him $453,872. Additionally, Zimmermann trivialized Eagleburger's connections with Yugoslav firms as merely wanting to help modernize Yugoslavia's economy and introduce Western business practices.

In the February 24, 1992, issue of *The New Republic*, Patrick Glynn reported that questions of conflict of interest and ethics had been raised about Eagleburger and his financial dealings with Yugoslavia, but were dropped after Eagleburger took advantage of a loophole in the law. Ethics regulations apply only to dealings with firms, not (as in the Yugoslav case) to governments that may own those firms.

The 1991 Dun's Consultant Directory listed Eagleburger and Scowcroft as principals of K&A. Yet when Scowcroft disclosed his financial statement, he didn't list his affiliation with K&A. An April 30, 1989 *New York Times* article noted that only after a reporter inquired about the connection did Scowcroft acknowledge that he served as vice-chairman. The next day Scowcroft filed an amendment to his statement.

Exploiting his position as Under Secretary for Policy early in the Reagan administration, Eagleburger frequently overrode objections from the Pentagon and other executive branch agencies when he promoted expanded trade and the advancement of credits to Yugoslavia. He also clashed with Secretary of Defense Casper Weinburger on the same issues. As a man who was never soft on communism, Weinburger objected to Yugoslavia's record of technological espionage on behalf of the Soviet Union.

When Eagleburger was elevated to Deputy Secretary of State, he became the principal policy-maker and public spokesman regarding Yugoslavia. He pontificated on television talk shows and to legislators that nothing could be done in Yugoslavia to prevent a civil war based on deep ethnic hatreds. The war would end only when all the sides got tired of killing one another. Parroting the Serbian position, he claimed that the only key to peace and stability in the area was an indivisible Yugoslavia.

The pro-Belgrade cabal in Bush's administration consistently blocked any action directed against Yugoslavia. They maintained that the non-Serbs were only getting the treatment they deserved. The cabal managed to delay recognition of the breakaway republics and sidelined congressional demands for action against Serbian human rights violations. Yugoslavia's break up imperiled Kissinger-directed investments. So the longer the delay, the more likely K&A investments could be salvaged.

Eagleburger's tentacles extended into the U.S. Embassy in Belgrade as well. Ambassador Zimmermann toed Eagleburger's line in toto even though Eagleburger's positions contradicted intelligence sources and the arguments of the embassy's political analysts.

From their positions of public trust, the cabal effectively sabotaged any suggestions and measures that could have undermined Serbian authority in Yugoslavia. A May 20, 1995, article in *The Guardian* detailed U.S. intelligence reports and their suppression by the Bush administration. In May of 1992, the CIA and the National Security Agency briefed the State Department on Serbian artillery, and only one diplomat attended. During the briefing, intelligence experts produced aerial photos showing unprotected guns sitting in fields and parked beside roads around Sarajevo. The experts predicted that 95% of the Serbian artillery could be eliminated in a single day. The sole diplomat who attended the briefing wrote a memo to the Assistant Secretary for European affairs, an Eagleburger protégé, who later reproached the diplomat for having written without clearance. Weeks later, the CIA erroneously told the Senate Foreign Relations Committee that air strikes against the Serbs would be impossible because Serbian artillery was hidden by dense forest.

In the fall of 1990, the CIA predicted the imminent and violent break-up of Yugoslavia. In January 1991 the State Department received intelligence that the JNA was about to attack the republics. Soon after, a representative of Milosevic told Eagleburger, "There's going to be war in Bosnia." By December of 1991, four months before the war, the CIA informed the State Department that the JNA was digging trenches around Sarajevo.

"We wanted to hold Yugoslavia together. The analysis was that there would be war if it broke up, so, wrongly, we clung on," Zimmermann has explained. "The Serbs were reading us well. They were prepared to push as far as they could, until someone pushed them back."

In the final weeks of the Bush presidency, interventionists from the State Department came up with a counter-policy for defeating and containing the Serbs. But Eagleburger's office greeted the memo with the usual run-around and comparisons to the Vietnam quagmire.

A fact finding group of senators that included Bob Dole, Alfonse D'Amato, and Don Nickles visited Yugoslavia in August, 1990. They witnessed Serbian police brutality on ethnic Albanians while touring Kosovo. Because they didn't have the power to rein in Serbian abuses, they introduced legislation upon their return that would withhold aid to the Yugoslav federal government and redirect the funds to republics that held free elections and maintained clean human rights records.

To head off the so called Nickles Amendment, Eagleburger called on Helen Delich Bentley, a Maryland representative with Serbian roots. Although she wasn't on the appropriate committee, Bentley vigorously campaigned to block the measure. Her efforts caused a six month delay that bought time for Serbia and Eagleburger. She unabashedly admitted receiving a great deal of money from the Serbian lobby. When Bentley next ran for reelection she lost. Some political thinkers believe she lost because of the Serbian money issue.

Although the Amendment ultimately passed, Eagleburger had one more ace up his sleeve. He had his hatchet man, Secretary of State Baker, invoke the State Department's discretionary authority to prevent the Amendment from taking effect.

When credible reports surfaced regarding genocide in Bosnia, Eagleburger publicly raised doubts about their authenticity. Although long aware of the existence and conditions of Serbian-run concentration camps in Bosnia, Western governments remained silent until Roy Gutman broke the story in an August, 1992, *Newsday* article. The State Department knew about the camps as early as April, 1992. But the day after Gutman's story broke, Assistant Secretary of State Thomas Niles testified on Capitol Hill, under oath, that evidence concerning the camps was inconclusive.

Another Glynn article in *The New Republic* pointed to Eagleburger's continued policy sabotage. Glynn wrote that George E. Kenney, acting head of the Yugoslav desk at the State Department, said a "night note" he composed on Serbian concentration camps for President Bush's reading was altered by Eagleburger's office to make the note incorrectly appear to say that all three sides were equally engaged in operating camps. Other former officials cited a similar pattern of evasion and distortion.

After pictures of the inmates from concentration camps appeared in the media, the shocked public urged their government to react. Despite Eagleburger and others of his ilk downplaying the issue, the public outcry couldn't be denied. But Western leaders responded with just some hand wringing. The only world leader with the intestinal fortitude to speak out was Margaret Thatcher. "Ethnic cleansing," she proclaimed, "combines the barbarities of Hitler's and Stalin's policy toward other nations."

Prime Minister John Major staged a bizarre international peace conference in London that only resulted in further fighting. The conference passed a no fly zone resolution without the slightest intention of enforcing it and imposed sanctions nobody believed in. Eagleburger continued to seed disinformation at the conference. In his keynote address, Eagleburger attempted to dilute Serbian responsibility in the conflict. He stressed that Serbia and the United States had a special historical relationship and that the conflict was irresolvable because of ancient and complicated roots. The "special relationship" between the U.S. and Serbia remained nebulous. Eagleburger's pronouncements passed for indisputable truths to an uninformed public. His speech never mentioned Bosnia.

As a result of the conference, Cyrus Vance and Lord David Owen were appointed peace negotiators. Vance, the United Nations special envoy to the Balkans, had been Secretary of State during the Carter administration. According to the *Wall Street Journal* (January 13, 1993), he had been the central player in some of the most demoralizing episodes in recent American history—whenever he had a direct role in foreign policy the result had been lost influence and moral authority for the U.S. During his tenure at the State Department there was an enormous expansion in Russia's nuclear and conventional warfare capabilities and adventurism—which culminated in the invasion of Afghanistan. If his statement, "Leonid Brezhnev (the Soviet leader at the time) is a man that shares our dreams and aspirations," expresses his true feelings, it's no wonder that Russia was so successful during Vance's mandate. He resigned in the midst of the Iran hostage crisis, which was resolved only one minute before Ronald Reagan was inaugurated as president. This "walking embodiment of the Vietnam syndrome" was expected to resolve the first European war since World War II.

Behaving typically hypocritical, Vance and Owen attempted to placate the rebel Serbs by arbitrarily dividing Bosnia-Herzegovina into ten semiautonomous cantons without input from the Bosnian government. Although the Serbs didn't accept the plan, Vance and Owen believed drawing crazy quilt patterns on a map could herd the non-Serbs—most of whom had been robbed of their families and property, and wounded or raped by rampaging soldiers—into widely separated ghettos. The Vance-Owen plan destroyed all illusions that the West considered Bosnia a sovereign state.

Despite attempts by the English, French, and American governments to divert attention away from Serbian atrocities, NGOs and human rights organizations helped keep the public aware. Armed intervention wasn't an option, so governments with a conscience pressured the great powers to at least impose economic sanctions on Yugoslavia, hoping that sanctions might convince the Serbs to more amicably negotiate a peaceful resolution.

But Carrington persistently sabotaged efforts to impose sanction deadlines. He seemed to have borrowed his negotiating strategies from the theater of the absurd. Carrington reworded ultimatums to accommodate Milosevic's wishes, but Milosevic always returned with counter-proposals. The Serbs reneged on every Carrington-brokered cease-fire.

The American Enterprise Institute's resident scholar, Patrick Glynn, interviewed a number of current and former officials involved in the Bosnian situation. Many suggested that both the Bush and Clinton administrations made conscious decisions to deliberately distort the picture of events in order to defuse and reduce public pressure for decisive American involvement. Their collective statements aren't surprising because this sort of duplicity occurred at the international level. According to C. Michael McAdams, in the June, 1995, issue of the *American Croatian Review*: "U. N. Officials have been ordered to find or manufacture crimes by Croatians and Muslims to balance the thousands of charges against Serbs."

By imposing sanctions on Yugoslavia, the United States tried to show the American public that its government was finally doing something constructive. But of the three sanction levels the U.S. might have imposed on Yugoslavia, the U.S. chose to impose the least severe, level one. The Office of Asset Control prevented Serbian products from entering the United States and banned direct money flow from the U.S. to Yugoslavia. The sanctions neither blocked money flowing from Cyprus or Switzerland to Belgrade, nor froze Yugoslav property in the U.S. In a similar vein, the Bush administration turned a blind eye and never attempted to stop the oil flow from Russia, Rumania, or Greece. After all, politics is politics, but business is business.

Due to the State Department's fondness for Serbia, a naturalized American citizen, Milan Panich, was granted dispensation to serve as Prime Minister of Yugoslavia despite stipulations for naturalization that include the swearing of allegiance only to America and the forfeiture of the right to serve a foreign state.

In regard to the government's special treatment of Panich, the U.S. may be guilty of harboring a war criminal. According to the Hague tribunal's charter on war crimes, a superior officer or government official is responsible for war crimes if he "knew or had reason to know the subordinate was about to commit such acts or had done so, and the superior failed to take the necessary and reasonable measures to prevent such acts." Clearly, when Steve Coll quoted the tribunal's chief prosecutor Richard Goldstone in a September 25, 1994, *Washington Post Magazine* article: "It does seem to imply that any political leader who possessed power during the course of a series of atrocities and who failed reasonably to intervene and prevent (them) is criminally responsible," he had Panich in mind. During Panich's tenure the ethnic cleansing and concentration camp operations continued without abatement. He now lives comfortably in the U.S.

Despite the State Department's sad record in the Balkans, the department did employ some honorable men. More career foreign service officers resigned because of conscience over our policy in former Yugoslavia than resigned over the war in Vietnam. Under Secretary of State for Political Affairs Peter Tarnoff was one of eleven (including the entire Yugoslav desk) that formally protested U.S. Bosnian policy to Secretary of State Warren Christopher. At the time the Serbs were committing their worse atrocities, the greatest censure Christopher could come up with to label their actions was to say that they were "misbehaving" and "mischievous."

In December, 1992, preceding the Foggy Bottom palace upheaval, German cabinet minister Christian Schwarz-Schilling resigned because he felt ashamed to belong to a government whose indecisiveness kept it from participating in keeping the peace in Bosnia. He was soon followed by George E. Kenney, the first career diplomat to resign from the U.S. State Department, who departed for similar reasons. Kenney said credible CIA and INR (the State Department intelligence bureau) reports placed the blame squarely on the Serbs. Yet Eagleburger's State Department contradicted the reports and suppressed the appalling information on Serbian atrocities. The State Department was in the middle of a moral struggle between working-level officials and the higher echelons. The former tried to make public the evidence of Serbian atrocities, while the latter thwarted their attempts.

Bosnia desk officer Marshall Freeman Harris (another official who resigned in protest) said Eagleburger's assessment of blame was calculatedly ambiguous and clearly at variance with what the State Department and intelligence agencies knew at the time. "It was cynical, disingenuous, whatever you want to call it."

When I studied in Zagreb in the 1960s, the Voice of America (VOA) broadcasts to Yugoslavia were the most widely listened to radio program in Croatia (and probably in all the Eastern bloc nations). The Croats, including Communist Party members, considered the VOA their best source of information. The short-lived Croatian Spring of 1971 was encouraged by VOA news. But during Eagleburger's tenure, the VOA became infiltrated by Serbs or those sympathetic to Serbian ideals. VOA South European division deputy chief Veljko Rasevic hired Zlatica Hoke as the Croatian services supervisor with the full knowledge that she was married to Srdjan Trifkovic, advisor to and spokesman for Bosnian-Serb leader Radovan Karadzic. Despite the conflict of interest, she also served as translator for President Clinton, Vice President Gore, and other administration officials in delicate negotiations with the Croatian president. If this wasn't a classic case of having the proverbial fox in the henhouse, I don't know what is.

After Bush lost the election and had nothing more to lose, he made a sudden departure from his previous policy and sent Eagleburger to Europe to argue for lifting the arms embargo. But Eagleburger knew the Europeans would be unmoved if he delivered the message unenthusiastically. He was right.

The U.N. has proven to be even more devious than the United States. Every U.N. action since the onset of hostilities has abetted the Serbian agenda. When the JNA supposedly withdrew from Bosnia in May, 1992, it left most of its equipment and 85% of its troops behind. JNA soldiers simply changed uniforms and became the Bosnian paramilitary force. The U.N. smugly accepted this gesture as proof of adherence to their negotiated terms.

The British government has done the most to help further Serbian goals. Foreign Secretary Douglas Hurd used all methods at his disposal to sabotage efforts to recognize Croatia and Slovenia despite the fact that Yugoslavia had died without hope of resuscitation. But Hurd thought Serbia to be the natural successor to Yugoslavia and a counterweight to Germany's influence in the area. So as to prevent the upstart republics from seceding, he penalized their self-determination efforts. The British government encouraged the Security Council to impose an arms embargo that perversely penalized the non-Serbs.

The arms embargo was one of the most perverse policies perpetrated. Before the conflict erupted, Yugoslavia had the third largest standing army in Europe and was among the leading arms producers of the world. The Serbs had insured that key Bosnia-based arms manufacturing plants were under their control. Two years before the war started, the Bosnians naively allowed themselves to be disarmed by the Serbian-controlled JNA. The JNA held all the military weapons in Croatia, after they had seized the armories. With former Yugoslavia's military power in Serbian hands, the arms embargo hardly inconvenienced them, but markedly penalized the Croats and Muslims. In a British initiated debate before the U.N. Security Council considering an arms embargo on Serbia, Yugoslav Representative to the U.N. Budimir Loncar made a compelling appeal that was subsequently implemented: "a general and complete embargo on all deliveries of weapons and military equipment to *all* [my emphasis added] parties in Yugoslavia." U.N. Resolution 713 placed the victims at a distinct disadvantage. The international media largely ignored the resolution's passage despite its tremendous ramifications.In the summer of 1991, when the effort still could have been meaningful, Hurd vehemently opposed the European Community initiative to send a peacekeeping force to Croatia. A few days after Hurd's protest, the Serbs unleashed their juggernaut on Croatia's towns and cities.

All Croatians and Bosnians pleas to lift the arms embargo were never given serious consideration. Bush and Clinton all but ignored the issue (except for Clinton raising a hullabaloo during his campaign). The lifting of the arms embargo on the Bosnian-Muslims and Croats would've enabled them to defend themselves against the aggressor without requiring the help of any outside ground troops.

The West consistently responded to the Serbian carnage in ways acceptable to the Serbs. The U.N. ignored Resolution 836 that reaffirms full sovereignty, recognizes territorial integrity within recognized, preexisting borders, and mandates that those displaced be returned to their homes in peace.

Russia openly flaunted U.N. sanctions imposed on Yugoslavia. *James Defence Weekly* reported that Russia exported four billion dollars worth of military ordnance to Yugoslavia in 1992. In January, 1993, Russia agreed to sell Serbia T55 tanks, anti-aircraft missiles, and anti-missile missiles that have the capability of destroying targets 375 miles away. After the Russians forced themselves into a peacekeeping role in Croatia, they shamelessly armed those they were supposed to disarm.

Russia's peacekeeping role in Croatia has been particularly scandalous. On January 12, 1993, some media accounts reported that the Serbs had taken to wearing Russian U.N. uniforms in some of their attacks. From privates to generals, the main function of Russian troops were smuggling and black marketing. Trafficking of U.N. gasoline was their number one priority. Fearful of alienating Russia, the U.N. turned a blind eye to the indiscretions. But the U.N. couldn't cover up complaints from the Belgian forces.

The Russian commander in Eastern Croatia, Major General Aleksandr Perelyakin, countermanded Belgian orders and permitted Serbian soldiers and military ordnance to enter Serbian-held Croatia. On April 13, 1995, *The New York Times* reported that the U.N. dismissed Perelyakin for this incident as well as a series of smuggling activities. Unfortunately, corruption wasn't limited to the Russians. Many of the U.N. forces exploited their assignments in the Balkans as an opportunity for personal enrichment.

A March 20, 1993, article in *The Guardian* accused Denmark, the holder of the EC presidency at the time, of clearly violating the economic sanctions. The Danish Statistics Service published an official report that revealed that Danish exports to Yugoslavia had risen to almost half of the pre-U.N. blockade level. Exports from Yugoslavia to Denmark, predominantly agricultural products, came from the fertile areas that the Serbs had conquered in Bosnia. The U.S. government confirmed that a number of Greek vessels delivered enormous quantities of oil to Yugoslavia. None of these blatant breaches of sanctions was protested.

As the master of flexibly in interpreting deadlines, the U.N. always gave the benefit of the doubt to the Serbs who in turn showed nothing but contempt for U.N. Security Council resolutions, NATO intervention, and world opinion. The Serbs ignored every accord because negligible Western responses indicated that the Serbs would suffer no consequences.

In the last days of Bush's administration, U.N. envoy and peace negotiator Vance personally called Secretary of State Eagleburger and members of the Clinton transition team and secured a promise from them not to let Bosnian President Alija Izetbegovic meet with the

Bush administration to present his case. Only after their gentlemen's agreement became known publicly did Eagleburger allow the meeting to take place. So much for men of honor.

General MacKenzie, while serving as the highest ranking U.N. officer in Bosnia, vehemently opposed flying humanitarian aid into Sarajevo and opposed President Francois Mitterand's visit to the Bosnian capital. His favorite thesis was that all sides were morally equal. But his assessment contradicted a U.N. investigative commission report which concluded: "There is no factual basis for arguing that there is a 'moral equivalence' between the warring factions." MacKenzie consistently berated the Muslims for defending themselves and for wanting to take back their homes. He was later accused by the Bosnian government of sexually exploiting Muslim women prisoners brought to his quarters.

Although MacKenzie is a general, he's no historian. To perpetuate the mythology about Serbian fighting prowess and make the Serbs appear larger than life, MacKenzie pointed out that 37 German divisions couldn't defeat the Serbs during World War II. Either he purposely lied or didn't know that the Germans had only a few divisions in Yugoslavia during the war. The Serbs had hardly dented Germany's war machine.

MacKenzie accused the Muslims of shelling their own people to get media attention. Even the most naive had a hard time believing his often repeated remark: "The vast majority of cease-fire violations were committed by Muslims." He perversely refused to acknowledge the malignant nature of ethnic cleansing, labeling the genocide a benign "population redistribution" instead.

A June 22, 1993 *Newsday* article pointed out that while MacKenzie espoused opinions to the U.S. Congress, international media, and think tanks, he disingenuously failed to mention that he was on the payroll of SerbNet, a Serbian lobbying firm. His duplicity caused great harm because many senior level American officers based later policy decisions on information received from MacKenzie's briefings. His colleagues didn't challenge his credibility because of his distinguished military background. Former Bosnian Ambassador to the

U.N. and present Foreign Minister Muhamed Sacirbey wondered whether MacKenzie "was bought and paid from the beginning."

The U.N. has consistently downplayed the plight of Muslim civilians even when faced with the most glaring evidence of atrocities. The U.N.'s response to the Serbian siege on the town Zepa is a striking example.

In the spring of 1993, the Bosnian government sent numerous communiqués to the U.N. voicing the government's concern for Zepa's inhabitants. But the complaints were summarily dismissed by U.N. military commanders. The U.N. steadfastly characterized the town as free of imminent danger and decided that the communiqués were merely part of a Bosnian disinformation campaign to provoke Western intervention. A few days after the U.N. received the communiqués, troops who secured the town reported finding only 50 survivors from a pre-siege population of 10,000.

As reported in *The Times* (May 11, 1993), U.N. spokesman John McMillan reacted to the slaughter by saying: "It is obvious from the report that there was something to the Bosnian government's statements." His casual indifference reflected a larger U.N. pattern. Other examples of the U.N. suppression of Serbian violations occurred in 1994 when the safe areas of Gorazde and Bihac were devastated.

When the initial French contingency of troops arrived in Sarajevo they were fired upon. The French commander immediately blamed the Muslims for the attack without a scintilla of evidence. Later investigation revealed that the Serbs were the real culprits. But the French never retracted the accusation.

Bosnian Deputy Premier Hakija Turajlic was brutally murdered by the Serbs while sitting in a clearly marked U.N. vehicle in a U.N. protected zone. The French commander responsible for protecting Turajlic subsequently received the Legion of Honor. The list of U.N.-Serbian agenda cooperation is endless. During the height of ethnic cleansing, Head Liaison Officer for U.N. Refugees Jean-Claude Concoloto said, "The U.N. were not only creating refugees but becoming a partner in Serbia's ethnic cleansing."

The contents of Henry Wynaents book, *L'Engrenage* (The Wringer), most likely haunts those diplomats with consciences who were involved in the Yugoslav fiasco. He explicitly indicts the Serbian expansion program that was abetted by feckless European policies. He chastises the U.N.'s colossal ineptitude and Vance's smug folly. And Wynaents specifically holds the European governments, the U.N., and Vance responsible for the bloodshed that has taken place. Wynaents is a Dutch diplomat who knows the subject intimately. He spent a year working with Carrington as a mediator in Croatia.

Owen and Vance fueled the Bosnian conflict when they introduced the concept of the three warring factions. The negotiators thereby elevated and equated rebel Serbian and Croatian forces with the legitimate Bosnian government. Then Owen and Vance provoked the rift between the Croats and Muslims with a Machiavellian stroke by bypassing Stjepan Kljuic, an elected Bosnian Croat who espoused an indivisible Bosnia, and dealing instead with Mate Boban, an illegitimate politician who advocated a Bosnian-Croat merger with Croatia.

Following the slaughter of 69 civilians in a Sarajevo marketplace, the U.N. placed a great deal of credence in Serbian allegations that the Muslims had planted the explosives themselves to gain sympathy and show the Serbs in a bad light.

Nevertheless, the U.N. imposed a no weapons zone around Sarajevo. In one of many similar instances, Canadian U.N. troops found Serbian tanks and military ordnance within the 20 kilometer zone. According to the *New York Herald Tribune* (March 22, 1994), the U.N. would not condemn the Serbs. Lieutenant General Michael Rose must have given great comfort to the Sarajevans when he explained the reason: "The guns were not aimed at Sarajevo." The U.N. went on a self aggrandizement binge in the media while the Serbs redeployed their ordnance to other besieged areas of Bosnia.

The Serbs shelled the U.N. designated safe haven of Gorazde with tanks and artillery for 10 days preceding their massive assault on the city. Lieutenant General Rose labeled the Serbian attack "tactical" and "not serious." The U.N. showed no reluctance to sacrifice the 65,000 Muslims of Gorazde in order to insure the safety of fewer than 200 U.N. peacekeepers held hostage by the Serbs. In the eyes of the U.N.

the trade was more than equitable. Rose had the audacity to accuse the Muslims of abandoning their defensive positions and criticized them for not fighting the Serbian onslaught. "They think we should be fighting their war for them. One bloke with a crowbar would have stopped [the Serb tank assault]." Bosnian resistance would've been suicidal because most of the Muslim weapons were, in fact, no better than crowbars. B. Djurdjevic reported in *The Arizona Republic* that Rose claimed only a broom was required to restore the ruined Gorazde hospital's operational capacities. After having blocked every attempt to stop the inhumane carnage, Rose felt disappointed that Gorazde didn't fall. He accused the Bosnians of exaggerating their own casualty figures and chasing 12,500 Serbs from the town. Gorazde's pre-war Serbian population was about 5,000. The Serbian population was negligible at the time of the assault because most had been safely evacuated prior to the shelling. Apparently every U.N. official had the task of propagating disinformation about the status of Bosnia and Croatia.

The U.N. was reluctant to use NATO to help carry out its mandates. When the U.N. did authorize NATO air strikes, most of bombs were duds. Prior to September, 1995, the only purpose of the air strikes was to provide practice for NATO pilots because the bombing didn't intimidate the Serbs. In an act of obvious collusion, Yasuski Akashi, the highest ranking U.N. official in Bosnia, tried to alert the Serbs to move their guns prior to one such strike.

Akashi persistently trumpeted unsubstantiated allegations of Bosnian atrocities committed against Serbian civilians, yet he remained mute about verified Serbian massacres of Muslims near Srebrenica and Zepa. The West's attitude was tantamount to complicity in the mass murders that took place. For the sake of political expediency and in order not to jeopardize the peace discussions at Dayton, the U.S. chose to ignore the evidence their intelligence services had gathered that indicated that the Serbs had indeed been guilty of atrocities. The collective inaction of Western leaders makes them as morally culpable as those officials in World War II who saw lines of Jews outside of gas chambers and did nothing.

The scenario played at Srebrenica epitomizes the U.N.'s inept handling of the Balkan crisis. The Muslims of Srebrenica were subjected to increasingly intensive Serbian shelling while living under intolerable conditions and without adequate food supplies. As the town was on the verge of collapse, the U.N. could no longer stomach the mayhem and promptly declared Srebrenica a safe area. The Serbs accepted the concept out of political expediency, but only under the condition that the Muslims would avail themselves of their few weapons.

The citizens of Srebrenica were living as if in a concentration camp. All human needs were supplied from the outside by either legitimate agencies or the black market. More often than not, the latter source commingled with the former. The Ukrainian U.N. troops were especially involved in guarding the legitimate food source convoys and selling whatever they got their hands on to the black market.

In 1995, the Bosnian-Croatian allied counter-offensives resoundingly smashed the Serbian military and retook captured territory. So rather than re-deploy forces from the Eastern front, the Serbs went for easy pickings in the so-called safe areas. Although U.N. forces from the Netherlands had replaced the ever cooperative and pliable Canadian force at Srebrenica, the Dutch were just as ineffective, and the city soon became history. At least the Dutch, unlike the Canadians, didn't hesitate to bear witness against the Serbs. But all requests for air support by Dutch commanders on the ground were stonewalled at headquarters despite a Security Council resolution to use all means to protect the safe areas. Usually Akashi called off the air strikes. The Keystone Kops couldn't have protected Srebrenica any less competently.

On July 21, 1995, the *Los Angeles Times* reported that the U.N. had supplied the Serbs with U.N. uniforms, blue helmets, and white jeeps, that the Serbs then used to lure 91 Muslims, including women and children, from a forest where they had hidden after escaping from Srebrenica. All 91 were summarily murdered. Kris Janowski, an official with the U.N. High Commissioner for Refugees, learned the details of this incident from survivors of the Srebrenica evacuation.

Fleeing refugees who didn't make it to Tuzla, another safe area, fell into Serbian hands. According to eyewitnesses, at least 5,200 Muslims were confined in a football stadium in Bratunac and executed. Several weeks after the Serbian takeover of Muslim Srebrenica, United States satellite photographs clearly indicated evidence of approximately half-a-dozen fresh mass grave sites. The photographs supported credible eyewitness accounts that described large-scale brutal and inhumane treatment by the Serbs after they captured Srebrenica on July 11. The United States government inexplicably withheld announcing the findings for four weeks. The Clinton administration had been in delicate negotiations with Milosevic and was in the process of rehabilitating his image, so it didn't wish to confront him about the atrocities. The U.S. also withheld intelligence reports from the International Criminal Tribunal investigating the atrocities for national "security reasons"—Nixon's catchall phrase during the Watergate investigation.

Akashi made no comment and ignored credible witnesses, including his own U.N. troops, and CIA reconnaissance photos showing the mass graves. Instead, he inveighed against unsubstantiated Croatian misdeeds directed against the Serbs during Croatia's successful counteroffensive in Western Slavonia's and the Krajina.

Akashi and other high ranking U.N. officials chose to ignore numerous reports, including their own military intelligence, that confirmed the appearance throughout Bosnia-Herzegovina of Serbian supplied SA-2, SA-3 and SA-6 surface-to-air missile batteries. Serbia clearly violated the terms of sanctions by supplying aid to rebel Serbs in Croatia who had in turn overtly collaborated with the Bosnian-Serbs' siege on Bihac. Milosevic's borders were sealed like a sieve. Fuel tankers and military supplies regularly crossed borders monitored by U.N. observers. Yet the hierarchy of the U.N. refused to chastise Serbia. Contact Group member Russia even had the temerity to demand that the U.N. Security Council lift all sanctions on Yugoslavia, arguing that Milosevic was doing everything possible to bring about peace. How did the U.N. respond? It eased the sanctions and criticized Croats and Muslims for their efforts to regain their own territory.

Whenever NATO decided to use its air power Akashi counter-manded the orders. So when Clinton finally acquiesced and allowed NATO to bomb Serbian positions in September, 1995, Akashi was taken out of the loop.

With its patience regarding Clinton's inertia wearing thin, the U.S. Congress passed a resolution to unilaterally lift the arms embargo. But Secretary of State Warren Christopher, thumbing his nose at Congress, reassured and promised the allies that the U.S. wouldn't break the arms embargo. In November, 1994, the Associated Press reported that the Clinton administration withdrew its three ships from the international maritime blockade charged with enforcing the arms embargo in the Adriatic in order to placate Congress. Clinton's gesture was mostly symbolic because our presence there had little effect anyway. During the 17 months the blockade was in force, 19 NATO ships found only three vessels carrying arms among 42,000 challenged.

In late 1994, the Contact Group gave up all pretense of honoring the legal and moral obligations that arose from recognizing the sovereignty of Bosnia-Herzegovina. So the group gave the Vance-Owen plan a new twist. French Foreign Minister Alain Juppe clearly articulated the Contact Group's agenda in *Le Figaro* (October 17, 1994). The Contact Group wanted to merge the territory seized by the Serbs in Croatia and Bosnia into a contiguous entity with Serbia and place Sarajevo and Mostar under U.N. control. Aside from rewarding Serbia, the Contact Group was pressing Croatia to give Serbia access to the Adriatic through territory the Serbs were unable to conquer. Once realized, the new plan would have fulfilled all provisions enunciated in the *SANU Memorandum*. Three of the countries in the group, France, Britain, and Russia, had asked the fourth one, the United States, for the tools to stop the fascist juggernaut during World War II, but failed to make the same request for Bosnia. Instead, the Contact Group eased sanctions on Serbia at a time when the Serbs were escalating their ethnic cleansing operations.

In late 1994, the Contact Group grew angry when the Muslims went on their counter-offensive and took back territory held by the

Serbs. Aggression was acceptable as long as the causalities and refugees were limited to non-Serbs. But once the Serbs became part of the statistics, Lieutenant General Michael Rose threatened real air strikes against the Muslims.

In keeping with the disinformation campaign and his personal financial interests, Kissinger glibly spouted half-truths and historical revisions in a televised interview with Charley Rose in September, 1995. He echoed the quagmire theory that would necessitate putting 100,000 American troops in harm's way. He falsely glorified Serbian might by claiming that Yugoslav forces had tied up 17 German divisions during World War II. And Kissinger didn't forget to say that all sides were equally guilty. He claimed that the Muslims and Serbs had committed an equal number of atrocities. Whereas the Serbs did their acts under the media's noses, the Muslims had hidden their nefarious deeds in the countryside away from the media's notice. The Croatian ethnic cleansing, the expulsion of 150,000 Serbs in the Krajina area, was just as immoral as what the Serbs had done in Croatia. When I heard Kissinger's statements I wasn't sure where he was coming from. He must have been trying to protect his K&A investments in Yugoslavia; as a historian he would have known that he was twisting the facts. All objective evidence indicates that the Serbs committed their atrocities as a matter of state policy. Whenever the Muslims or the Croats were involved in inhumane acts, those acts were spontaneous events.

Members of the hierarchy of the so-called Knin government led by Rajko Lezajic, who found refuge in Serbia after the Croatian military success, said in a press conference in Belgrade on August 23, 1995, that the exodus of ethnic Serbs from the Krajina area of Croatia had been ordered and signed on August 4, 1995, by the President of the self-proclaimed Republic of Serbian Krajina, Milan Martic. That entire weekend radio announcements cried, "Run away. Escape. The Ustashe will kill you." Those Serbs that desired to stay were coerced and pressured into leaving by their neighbors. But the exodus was orderly. In contrast to the Croatian and Muslim refugees who were haggard, beaten, and unable to carry anything more than the shirts on their backs, the Serbs left with their vehicles loaded with goods.

CROATIA'S GROWING PAINS

CROATIA'S GROWING PAINS

After U.N. special envoys Carrington and Vance brokered over 50 separate peace agreements in Croatia that the Serbs quickly rescinded, Serbian leader Milosevic tenuously agreed to one more proposal. The media made Milosevic's consent appear as a magnanimous gesture. But Milosevic, ever the fox, knew that because his forces weren't strong enough to capture more Croatian territory and couldn't consolidate the gains they had already made, this last agreement would allow the U.N. forces to consolidate the gains for him.

By the time Milosevic had accepted Vance's plan for 14,000 U.N. peacekeepers to maintain the status quo, Croatia had begun to develop a more structured army and acquire some weapons despite the arms embargo. The United Nations Protective Forces (UNPROFOR) presence helped consolidate the territory the Serbs had conquered. But for the Croats, UNPROFOR bought time to train Croatia's fledgling army and amass more weapons, which proved so effective in the August 1995 counter-offensive. The backbone of the Croatian tank corps were tanks reconstructed from cannibalized parts taken from damaged JNA tanks.

After three years of inertia, UNPROFOR failed to implement even one major provision of the Vance plan, which had called for the return of displaced persons to their homes, the disarming of the Serbian paramilitary, and the return of Croatia's sovereignty over its territory.

When Milosevic agreed to the terms of Vance's plan, the JNA redeployed its heavy weapons and tanks to Bosnia-Herzegovina to block Bosnia's self-determination efforts and to further the goal of a Greater Serbia. The same cast of characters—General Ratko Mladic, Vojislav Seselj, and Zeljko "Arkan" Raznjatovic—all of whom had terrorized innocent civilians and wrecked havoc in Croatia, found no shortage of victims in Bosnia. The JNA, had UNPROFOR to patrol the borders along one-third of Croatia that the Serbs occupied.

When hostilities broke out in Bosnia, the media focused all its attention there and all but ignored the fact that the supposed peace in Croatia was being punctuated by death and daily Serbian shelling of Croatian towns and cities. Serbian ethnic cleansing in Croatia continued unabated under the watchful eyes of UNPROFOR.

Although the Serbs had committed grotesque atrocities in Croatia, nobody had anticipated the horrors they would commit in Bosnia. The Bush administration was unmoved by the human suffering. Democratic presidential candidate Clinton exploited the issue and made it a major point in his presidential campaign. Despite the Bush's administration seemingly resolute inactivity, the Croatians and Muslims expected the United States to reassert its world leadership role and come up with a solution.

President Bush, however, was firmly committed to maintaining the status quo and letting the crises play itself out. Whatever could be said about Bush's policy, at least it was consistent and never disillusioned the victims.

After the election, once Clinton took over the reigns of government his schizophrenic policy became an emotional roller coaster for the non-Serbs. In addition to increasing death and destruction, the Serbian psychological warfare experts couldn't have better orchestrated the results caused by Clinton's vacillating. If his "policy" was, indeed, a conscious effort and not due to ineptness, then Clinton is in a moral equivalent with the Serbs.

He sent Secretary of State Warren Christopher to Europe in May, 1993, to unsuccessfully argue for the "lift and strike" option. Only after U.S. government archives are opened to future historians will we know whether Clinton ordered Christopher to deliberately present an unenthusiastic case or whether Christopher did so on his own initiative. Christopher's efforts failed, and thereafter the administration claimed that it wished to act in Bosnia but was prevented from doing so by the stubbornness of its European allies.

The Clinton administration, like the Bush administration before it, has engaged in its own transparent brand of revisionism. Patrick Glynn of the American Enterprise Institute has said that Secretary of State Warren Christopher's clumsy efforts to distribute blame for the war equally ("There are atrocities on all sides.") lacked the subtlety shown by his predecessor, Eagleburger, yet was equally inaccurate. Christopher's Balkan policy even provoked an angry memo from a State Department analyst. The memo, which was leaked to *The New York Times*, pointed out the blatant inaccuracy of the secretary's assessment.

The lack of principle in the State Department has moved a number of career officers to resign. Marshall Harris was the desk officer for Bosnia at the State Department. After serving for eight years, he became particularly disillusioned over Christopher's disastrous European fiasco. In fact, more State Department officials have resigned over Bush and Clinton's policies in former Yugoslavia than resigned over the Vietnam War under Kennedy, Johnson, and Nixon combined.

As late as November, 1994, the West was pressuring the Bosnian government to surrender, while ignoring Serbian crimes against humanity. The West produced a variety of peace plans that, in essence, legitimized Serbian rebel gains. In August, 1992, and January, 1993, after the Croats dared to take back some of their territory, the West threatened Croatia with sanctions if it didn't withdraw to its prior positions.

Croatian President Tudjman was faced with tremendous pressure from the members of his own constituency who opposed continuing the status quo. During the UNPROFOR mandate, the Croatian casualty and body count continued to mount. But Tudjman's greatest pressures came from the increasingly vocal hawks in his own government who were angered by U.N. Secretary General Boutrous Boutrous-Ghali's early 1995 admission to the Security Council that

UNPROFOR wasn't in a position to discharge its responsibility in Croatia and that its continued presence contributed to the stalemate. Croatia's economy was in a shambles. Because of the arms embargo, Croatia had to buy weapons on the black market and pay two to three times the going rate. Aside from the financial drain of caring for its own enormous displaced population, Croatia had to bear the cost of supporting a flood of Bosnian refugees.

After Croatia announced that it wouldn't renew the UNPROFOR mandate on January 12, 1995, Secretary of State Christopher directed more criticism at Croatia than he'd directed at the Serbs during their four years of rampage. In the words of that great American philosopher Yogi Berra, it was "deja vu all over again." Christopher was reviving his predecessor's technique of blaming the victims. He couldn't quite pull it off, though, because he lacked Eagleburger's deviousness. Christopher, who'd previously labeled the grossest Serbian genocidal acts "naughty," sharply rebuked Tudjman and warned him that he'd be sorry.

The State Department orchestrated media frenzy regarding Croatia's refusal to renew the mandate failed to bring to light the fact that UNPROFOR's seminal mission in Croatia was to implement the Vance peace plan—a mission it had failed to accomplish. Additionally, Croatia had already renewed UNPROFOR's mandate eight times, and eight times the West had miserably failed to fulfill its end of the bargain. The media shrilly castigated Croatia for upsetting the peace. Just whose peace they were talking about was unclear. Certainly the peace didn't belong to the Croats, who were subjected to almost daily shelling from Serbian artillery. Zagreb, Croatia's capital, lay a mere 30 miles from the front lines.

The only ones enjoying peace were the Serbian separatists who occupied one-third of Croatian territory. Prior to the Croatian offensive in July, 1995, the Serbs in Croatia hadn't been part of the war's statistics. Rather than printing stories about Croatian victims who desired to return to homes that the Serbs had confiscated, the media lamented how the Serbs would be inconvenienced if the Croats attempted to take back their territory.

Until the 1995 Croatian offensive, the Serbs in Croatia were crossing the borders of Bosnia with impunity to fight in Bihac. The Bosnian Serbs were especially interested in taking Bihac because with the city under their control they realized their ambition to join a Greater Serbia. Contrary to Strobe Talbott's statement that the United States wouldn't accept the concept of Greater Serbia, the United Nations Contact Group (which included the U. S.) had already de facto recognized Greater Serbia as a *fait accompli*.

Despite objecting to UNPROFOR's continuing presence in Croatia, Tudjman bowed to American pressure less then 24 hours before the deadline was to take effect and rescinded his order not to renew the mandate. Having studied the State Department's psychological profile of Tudjman, Vice President Al Gore and Secretary Christopher knew exactly which buttons to push to change his mind.

Tudjman agreed to extend the U.N. mandate on the condition that UNPROFOR would patrol Croatia's borders between Bosnia and Serbia. But the condition was nebulous because its implementation was predicated upon the goodwill of the Serbs to allow it. By forcing him to change his mind, the United States had placed Tudjman in a precarious position. He had to justify his waffling to a parliament that wasn't noted for agreeing about anything—except, of course, his original decision not to renew the mandate.

When the West's provision proved impossible to implement, even the most naive diplomat realized that Tudjman wouldn't allow the U.N. another chance to extend the mandate. So the West came up with the so-called Z-4 Plan. The plan's signatories, the United States, Russia, the European Union, and the United Nations, hailed it as the ultimate compromise for restoring peace in Croatia. But a cursory examination of the document revealed that, in effect, it set up a state within a state. The plan rewarded the perpetrators of genocide and abusers of human rights with the right to institute their own judiciary, currency, taxation, police force, and to control natural resources and tourism in Serbian-held Croatia. The Z-4 Plan not only envisioned setting up a Little Serbia in Croatia, it also demanded that Croatia amend its constitution and laws to adhere to the Z-4 proposal. The plan hypocritically demanded Serbian autonomy in Croatia, but ignored ethnic Albanian demands for the return of their lost autonomy in Serbian-controlled Kosovo, despite the fact that Albanians comprise over 90% of that region's population.

During the time the Contact Group was urging Croatia to accept the Z-4 proposal, the Serbs had intensified their siege on all the designated safe areas within Bosnia. The attacks on the enclaves of Srebrenica and Zepa came to their predictable bloody conclusions. Despite U.N. protection, Bihac's population of 135,000 was quickly starving to death. With each passing hour it looked as if the city would meet the same fate as Srebrenica and Zepa. The U.N. openly tolerated a massive rebel Serbian military build up and allowed Serbian forces to stage attacks on Bosnian and Croatian towns from areas under U.N. control. Milosevic sent a huge contingency of Serbian officers, including Yugoslavia's top general, Mile Mrksic, and troops to assist in the attacks. Mrksic had commanded a JNA brigade during the destruction of Vukovar; in April, 1994, he was active in the assault on Gorazde, a Bosnian Muslim enclave. Western intelligence sources confirm that over 300 officers in Serbian units operating in the Western Slavonian region of Croatia were being paid directly by Belgrade. When the Croatian forces liberated Okucani in Western Slavonia in 1995, they found records of the names, units, and payroll records of at least 6 colonels, 7 lieutenant colonels, 8 majors, 13 captains, 9 lieutenants, and non-commissioned officers of the Yugoslav Army that directly linked them to the Belgrade government. Despite irrefutable evidence, including reports from U.N. observers, that Serbia had sent over 5,000 soldiers, 25 tanks, and 10 PACs to the Serbian occupied territories of Croatia in clear violation of Resolution 988, the U.N. took no action. The U.N. ignored intelligence reports and objective evidence, as well as letters sent to Boutros Boutros-Ghali and Yasushi Akashi from a number of Croatian officials. They gave Milosevic the benefit of the doubt when he maintained that no JNA forces were stationed outside Serbia.

The Western powers even ignored statements by Milan Martic, the former president of the so-called Serbian Republic of Krajina, who publicly acknowledged Belgrade's involvement and influence in Serb-held Croatia. ". . .FRY (Serbia and Montenegro) paid all the officers (including General Mile Mrksic) that it sent to Krajina. . . .No one in Krajina undertook any moves, even of the smallest nature, without informing or consulting Milosevic. . . .I ordered the withdrawal of civilians into the depth of Krajina," Martic confessed. These revelations (although they were widely known by anyone with a scintilla of background about the situation) came at a time when the Clinton administration was in the process of whitewashing Milosevic and talking about easing sanctions on Serbia.

In late July, 1995, a host of Western leaders stated that the Serbs had won, implying that the Bosnian government, which the West had recognized as a legitimate and sovereign state, had no choice but to take whatever peace proposal was offered. Defense Secretary William Perry said, "Serbs have occupied 70% (of Bosnia). There is no prospect, as I see it, of the Muslims winning it back." A few weeks earlier, British Under Secretary for Foreign Affairs Douglas Hogg urged the Bosnians to "acknowledge military defeat when it stares them in the face." The West's failure to support Bosnia's sovereignty tacitly reminded the Croatian leadership of its own precarious situation.

If the neighboring Bosnian city of Bihac had fallen to the Serbs, Croatia's security and territorial integrity would've been seriously jeopardized. Serbs from the Krajina area in Croatia had been pouring into Bosnia and joining their Bosnian-Serb counterparts in attacking Bihac. Recognizing that the Z-4 Plan would have only aided Serbian goals, Tudjman took matters into his own hands. In a lightning-like move, Croatian armed forces liberated Croatian territory (except for a small portion that abuts Serbia on its western border with Croatia) that had been under Serbian control since 1990. Unexpectedly, Croatia retook the Krajina with minimal resistance and causalities. Prior to the Croatian army's move into the area, the overwhelming majority of Serbs, both civilians and military, had evacuated. In contrast to the Krajina campaign, fighting was furious in the Petrinja and Glina, areas where the Serbian military put up a great deal of resistance. But the relative ease with which the "weekend warrior" Croats soundly routed the professional Serbs in the Krajina must have embarrassed the Western military experts who had championed Serbian fighting prowess.

The Croatian victory unequivocally changed the balance of power in the Balkan conflict. The victory relieved the imminent siege of Bihac and ultimately saved Western Bosnia. When Croatian troops joined efforts with Bosnia's legitimate army, the combined forces were able to recover 20% of Bosnia's territory from the Serbs.

Contrary to the shrill insistence of Western leaders that Croatian forces never should've crossed into Bosnia, the Croatian army's presence on Bosnian territory was legitimate because the Croats came at the request of the sovereign Bosnian government. Although the Croatia-Bosnia coalition had been brokered by Washington, the Croatian military's unexpected successes in Bosnia weren't acceptable to the British and French. As Croat-Muslim forces were taking back territory and rapidly closing in on Banja Luka, fear apparently rose among the British and French that the coalition forces might liberate territory that they had already committed to the Serbs. Western leaders turned a blind eye and probably encouraged the Bosnian-Serbs to use air power to redress the military imbalance. In an obvious attempt to salvage as much territory as they could for the Serbs, the British and French placed enormous diplomatic pressure on Croatia to disengage. A Serbian defeat wasn't acceptable. After all, why would they have allowed the Serbs to kill 250,000 souls only to have the conquerors' territory taken away?

The shift in the balance of power was decisive. NATO and U.N. military commanders expressed surprise at how rapidly Serbian defenses had collapsed. The Serbian defeat must have shattered the commanders' belief in Serbian invincibility and their notions that the Serbs somehow ranked as the greatest guerrilla fighters in history. Whether the Western military experts had based their pre-Croatian offensive assessments of Serbian fighting strength on faulty judgments or, had instead deliberately bent the truth to feed their political masters has yet to be determined. Why European and Pentagon officials, spearheaded by Colin Powell, told the public that fighting the

Serbs would take 500,000 NATO soldiers is an important question to ask.

The myth of Serbian military strength, largely created in the Western military experts imaginations, has only prolonged the conflict. Most Western governments (especially Great Britain) condemned the successful Croatian offensive and expressed indignation because Croatia's success contradicted the mythology that had become sacred to those who advocated non-intervention and preservation of the arms embargo. In keeping with a British tradition of sabotaging any positive Croatian effort, British intelligence officers provided information to Croatian officials before their action in the Krajina indicating that the Serbian rebels were stronger than previously thought. At the same time, Canadian peacekeepers were providing information on Croatian troop movements to the Serbian rebels in Knin.

The Croatian success in the Krajina couldn't have come at a better time for the Clinton administration. The President's vacillating policy over Bosnia had angered Congress to such a degree that it overwhelmingly voted to unilaterally lift the arms embargo on Bosnia. The House vote of 244-178 clearly transcended party lines: 117 yes votes came from Democrats. Clinton vetoed the bill and then tried everything in his political repertoire to keep Congress from overriding it. Fortunately for Clinton, the Croatian offensive dissipated the showdown and alleviated Congress' political pressure.

While Congress and the Clinton administration were wasting energy on their confrontation over the arms embargo, the President had already given his secret blessing authorizing covert arms smuggling operations to the region. He wasn't simply ignoring arms shipments, as he would later claim when the information became public in April 1996, because his administration inspected the shipments in great detail, ostensibly looking for atomic, biological, or chemical weapons. Most likely, the true purpose of these searches was to do an inventory.

While arms were making their way toward Bosnia, Clinton's relationship to Congress resembled a philanderer's to a cuckold. And like a cuckold, Congress was the last to know about an affair that seemingly involved half the world. Although Iran was singled out, such diverse countries as Hungary, Brunei, Pakistan, Malaysia, Saudi Arabia, and Argentina were also supplying arms to Bosnia through Turkey. The Clinton administration didn't object to the shipments despite the fact that the transfers were in violation of the U.N. arms embargo. Regardless of how the Bosnian weapons trade will affect Clinton's future political position, the shipments ultimately benefited the non-Serbs. The arms flow helped create conditions that relieved the Bihac siege and accomplished what diplomats had previously failed to negotiate.

The spin doctors in Clinton's administration worked over-time to exploit the Croatian success. From the moment of the initial JNA attack on Slovenia to the very eve of the Croatian liberation of the Krajina, both the Bush and Clinton administrations had cast Croatia in the same light as Serbia. Suddenly, like St. Paul's revelation on the road to Damascus, the Clinton administration did a 180 degree about face. Although Defense Secretary William Perry initially denied that the U.S. had given the Croats a green light for their offensive, he later—when he saw political advantage in doing so —suggested that the administration had at least given an amber light. The Clinton administration also failed to discourage unsubstantiated speculation that the American military played a major role in helping liberate Croatian territory.

Before the war, 120,000 Serbs and 102,000 Croats lived in the area called the Krajina. After Serbian ethnic cleansing, only 279 Croats remained in the same area. These statistics were never mentioned by the media when they complained about the Serbian retreat. Yet the Serbian exodus was voluntary, orderly, and preceded the Croats entrance to the Krajina. When the Serbs had deported Croats on a massive scale in 1991, the Croats had no choice. They had to leave all their possessions behind. The lucky ones were allowed to take only what could be bundled and carried. None were allowed to take their cars or tractors. During the Serbian occupation of the Krajina, 94% of the region's 158 Roman Catholic churches were destroyed or damaged. Out of the 122 Serbian Orthodox churches, 17 were damaged, but only one was completely destroyed. According to a September, 1995, communiqué from the Permanent Mission of Croatia to the U.N., most of the damage to the Orthodox churches occurred prior to the Serbian retreat.

The Serbs who left Krajina were neither victims of Croatian ethnic cleansing, as the media purported, nor refugees. Rather, they left of their own volition or under the direct orders and urging of the Serbian leadership. People who move voluntarily aren't considered refugees under international law. The organized manner of the exodus, which was conducted under the protection of armed Serbian military forces and confirmed in documents and supporting statements from top Serbian leadership in Belgrade press conferences, offers de facto evidence that the Croats played no role in the migration. In late August, 1995, members of the Knin leadership published documents in the Serbian daily *Politka* that revealed orders by Milan Martic, quasi-president of the Krajina Serbs, to evacuate. Another document, signed by General Mile Mrksic, called for the Serbs to leave the area before the Croatian forces' arrival.

Many of the Serbs had ample reasons to leave. Some had come from Serbia proper and moved into Croatian homes whose previous owners had been killed or purged in 1991. Another large number of indigenous Serbs fled because they had participated in atrocities committed against their Croatian neighbors. As most of the atrocities were committed in front of surviving Croats (a tactic used to scare the remaining Croats into leaving and accelerate ethnic cleansing), the witnesses were sure to return to their homeland and exact revenge. But the majority of Serbs left because of coercion from fleeing neighbors.

In typical fashion, the U.N. later wildly exaggerated the number of Krajina evacuees and incidents of supposed Croatian brutality. The U.N. High Commission for Refugees routinely inflates figures to receive increased funding. But in this case, its numbers game only served to further erode U.N. credibility.

According to a March, 1996, communiqué from the Permanent Mission of Croatia to the U.N., one Geneva based international humanitarian organization has charged that the Krajina Serbs "continue to live in a hostile environment where their physical safety remains precarious." The charges were based on reports from December, 1995, to January, 1996, when the organization "gathered a total of 67 individual allegations of incidents against the integrity and safety of people ranging from looting, harassment and threats of physical assaults and murder." This amounted to 34 incidents per 10,000 persons. Imagine the reaction of those who chastised Croatia for these horrendous statistics if they knew that the statistics for the same crimes were 61 per 10,000 population in New York City, 92 in Washington, D.C., and 143 in Miami. Perhaps the humanitarian group wasn't aware that every country has a natural rate of crime for which no government should be condemned.

BLEEDING BOSNIA

BLEEDING BOSNIA

Bosnia-Herzegovina exemplified the Yugoslav ideal more than any of the former republics. Its government's cabinet reflected the diverse makeup of its citizenry: eight Muslims, six Serbs, and six Croats. The legally elected government was committed to pluralism and the right of all citizens, irrespective of ethnicity, to live where they chose. But an ethnocentric, expansionist, chauvinistic neighbor opposed these concepts with a verve.

Several months before the Croatian election in the early spring of 1990, the Yugoslav Army began quietly arming the Serbian minority in Croatia. When the democratically elected government was installed, the local Serbs, who held all the weapons, initiated hostilities. At the same time these events were taking place in Croatia, Bosnian President Alija Izetbegovic had blindly cooperated with the JNA and ordered weapons held by local territorial defense units to be turned over to the Serbian-controlled Yugoslav Army. But the Croats in Bosnia were acutely aware of the Serbs' true intentions and refused to hand over their arms.

The ethnic makeup of the Yugoslav Army demonstrates how the Serbs dominated Yugoslavia. Out of 16 JNA generals stationed in Bosnia-Herzegovina before the war, 16 were Serbs, one was Muslim, one Montenegrin, and one Croatian.

The Serbs initiated their ethnic cleansing program almost immediately when they rejected the legitimacy of the voting in the same areas of Bosnia where the Chetniks had at the start of World War II.

According to Noel Malcolm, 8.1% of the Bosnian-Muslim population perished during World War II, mostly at the hands of the Chetniks. No other ethnic group in Yugoslavia lost such a high percentage of its people. The disappearance of hundreds of thousands of Muslims from the Foca, Zvornik, and Bijeljina areas received no notice during the World War II and the recent crisis because the ethnic cleansing campaigns occurred out of the media's sight. Even after Serbian paramilitary forces, like the notorious White Eagles, massacred several thousand Muslims in Bijeljina, President Izetbegovic publicly said that he doubted that Serbs were perpetrating such crimes.

The fact that the Roman Catholics in Bosnia fared much worse than the Muslims during the recent conflict has received scant public or media notice. The United States Information Agency reported in December, 1995, that the Bosnian-Croats had suffered the highest rate of injury during the conflict. In fighting across Bosnia-Herzegovina, 42% of Croats received injuries, in contrast to 15% of Bosnian-Muslims and 13% of Bosnian-Serbs. These appalling statistics were calculated prior to a sharp recrudescence of ethnic cleansing in Banja Luka. Despite the report's credible source, the media made no mention of the statistics. According to Cardinal Vinko Puljic, the Archbishop of Sarajevo, half of the 830,000 Croatian Catholics who lived in Bosnia-Herzegovina before the conflict were ethnically cleansed. For example, in the diocese of Banja Luka most of the 120,000 Catholics were purged or killed. The area was home to 47 parishes in 1991; only 3 remain today.

The non-Serbian survivors of ethnic cleansing in the Banja Luka area, as well as those from other areas under Serbian control, suffered in silence without the protection of any Bosnian, Croatian, or international body. Because all medical facilities in Banja Luka were closed to non-Serbs, the only organized institution that could help the survivors was the Catholic church. Catholic relief organization Caritas set up a center that provided health care for anybody in need, regardless of ethnicity. According to the *Croatian Medical Journal,* the center was staffed by 19 physicians, 22 nurses, and 3 other workers. All were volunteers who had been dismissed from state institutions because of their ethnic origins. Because the Serbian authorities didn't provide any assistance, the health center had to rely on donations.

The ethnic cleansing program continued without abatement, but markedly intensified during the first two weeks of May, 1995, when Seselj's Serbian Radical Party (SRA) called upon Serbs to expel Croats and Muslims "immediately and without delay" from Banja Luka. Following Seselj's command, Serbian forces broke into a Roman Catholic church rectory (possibly in retaliation for the Croats' recapture of Western Slavonia). The Serbs murdered a priest and a nun, doused their bodies and the rectory with gasoline, and set them on fire. The Serbs blew up the church next door while the rectory and its inhabitants burned.

Approximately 25 nuns and 25 priests, including Bishop Franjo Komarica of Banja Luka, remain in the Banja Luka diocese. With only three churches left, Bishop Komarica said, "We perhaps fared somewhat better than our neighbor Muslims. Not a single mosque remains in the Banja Luka area." By the same token, not a single Orthodox church has been damaged.

During the early stages of the conflict, I asked Mustafa Ceric, Imam for the Bosnian Islamic community, if genocide was too strong a word to describe the Serbian actions. After a long thoughtful pause he defined genocide: "One group destroying another group's culture, traditions, institutions—but most importantly, their lives. The term genocide is not harsh enough." He coined the term "humanocide" instead because "the Serbs do not differentiate between anyone who stands in the way of their ethnic cleansing program, be they Muslim, Croat or even Serb." "Humanocide" may well become the buzz word that best describes Serbian actions in Croatia and Bosnia-Herzegovina.

Despite highly credible international wire service reports that Serbian paramilitary units had destroyed five Roman Catholic churches, demolished a monastery, expelled nuns from two convents and killed a priest and nun in Banja Luka during a ten day period in May 1995, only one newspaper, *Newsday*, deemed the stories newsworthy enough to publish. According to spokesman for the U.N.

High Commission for Refugees Chris Janewski, the Bosnian-Serb army took over the convents and used the facilities as its headquarters. Most of the media ignored these incidents, yet eagerly reported unsubstantiated allegations made by British U.N. delegates that the Serbs in Western Slavonia had been treated unmercifully by the Croats after they had liberated the area.

To their credit, the media, NGOs, and other international bodies working in the area contradicted the British allegations a few days later when they reported that Croatian treatment of Serbs in Western Slavonia was beyond reproach.

After the Croatian military liberated the Krajina in August, 1995, the Serbs intensified their ethnic cleansing in Bosnia. In less than three days, 15,000 Croatian Catholics were expelled from the Banja Luka area. Although CNN had been in the vanguard of reporting the orderly Serbian exodus from the Krajina, the news service neither mentioned that the mass migration was voluntary, nor covered the plight of Croats from Banja Luka. No news agency bothered to contrast the emaciated Croats who fled from Banja Luka with only the shirts on their backs, with the well nourished Serbs who left the Krajina in cars, trucks, and tractors loaded with goods.

Much as they had in Croatia, the Serbs rationalized their genocidal acts in Bosnia by conjuring up paranoid myths and prejudices. In Croatia, they had claimed to fear the certain return of the World War II era Ustashe puppet state. In Bosnia, they demanded revenge for a Muslim victory over the Serbs that took place 600 years ago.

The Serbs have committed genocide, yet Western governments were reluctant to use the term. Yugoslavia was a signatory to the International Genocide Treaty of 1951 that provides for trying individuals for crimes of genocide within the state they occurred. If a government accused Yugoslavia of genocide, that government would be obliged to indict Yugoslavia. Given the West's complicity with the Belgrade regime, no Western government wanted to utter the term publicly.

The Western governments propagated Serbian paranoia and mythology. But beyond that ideological support, the EC made a major mistake by negotiating with local self-appointed Serbian, Muslim and Croatian renegade leaders instead of the legitimate governments.

The Bosnian government wasn't a faction, but a duly elected government with full rights associated with sovereignty. Those serving in the government were elected by an absolute majority of Bosnian citizens, and although most Bosnian politicians were Muslim, their government was inclusive. The conflict wasn't a civil war, but a war of territorial expansion by another state—Serbia.

The West's see-no-evil, hear-no-evil, speak-no-evil approach to Serbian crimes found a champion in *Los Angeles Times* opinion writer Walter Russell Mead. The Serbs themselves had proudly coined the term "ethnic cleansing," but Mead went to great lengths to downgrade and sanitize their program by calling it "forcible relocation." Mead recklessly suggested that a Bosnian-Muslim surrender would be the best thing that could happen to Bosnia in the long run because prosperity might follow as it had in Germany and Japan after their World War II defeats. His point carefully ignored 250,000 dead, 25,000 rape victims, and countless refugees. In a February 13, 1994, Op-Ed piece, Mead compared ethnic cleansing to a divorce.

In the same article, Mead lauded the Clinton administration for finally agreeing to support the European peace plan it had once condemned and the end of sanctions against Serbia. He cited these changes in policy as a defeat of the "idealistic and fuzzy minded members of Clinton's foreign policy team."

Long aware of the existence and conditions of Serb-run concentration camps in Bosnia, Western governments remained silent until Roy Gutman broke the story in *Newsday*. In the February 28, 1994, issue of *Insight*, R. Rubenstein reported that U.N. officials admitted that they had been aware of the camps at least one month before the story broke, but didn't believe the camps were important enough to warrant publicity. When pictures of the inmates appeared on television, the shocked public, unable to stomach the horrors, rapidly switched TV channels to the safe cocoon of the *Wheel of Fortune*.

At first the Serbs denied the existence of the camps. Later they said the camps were housing prisoners of war. But when representatives from the International Committee of the Red Cross interviewed all 3,640 prisoners at a camp in Manjaca, the ICRC found that only four were soldiers. The remaining 3,636 prisoners were civilians taken from their homes in the ethnically cleansed area of Kozara.

Governments respond to moral dilemmas according to their own national interests. The well-meaning, post-World War II slogan "Never again" has proven to be as empty as George Bush's "new world order." Had the media captured the crimes of Treblinka or Auchswitz on camera, the Western governments of that time would've responded just as they did to ethnic cleansing in Bosnia, with little more than teeth gnashing and hand wringing. The Allies knew of the concentration camps and Jewish deaths in the hundreds of thousands much earlier than the initial *London Times*, *Manchester Guardian*, and *New York Times* reports. Those papers gave exact names and locations of death camps, but the Allies refused to act. Apparently civilian deaths, although regrettable, weren't militarily relevant. The same attitude prevailed regarding Croatia and Bosnia. Although comparing one horror to another is an odious exercise, the similarities between the silences and inaction during World War II and the Balkan crisis is sadly telling.

A religious summit that was chaired by Rabbi Arthur Schneier, whose participants included Serbian Orthodox Patriarch Pavle and the heads of the Muslim and Roman Catholic communities of Bosnia-Herzegovina, concluded that the war's cause wasn't rooted in religious differences and that "crime in the name of religion is the greatest crime against religion." Yet one of Serbia's rationales for the Bosnian conflict was the need to save Europe from Muslim fundamentalism. The Serbs forever quoted out of context from Izetbegovic's 1970 "Islamic Declaration" to prove of his fundamentalist tendencies. "There can be no peace or coexistence between Islamic Faith and non-Islamic social and political institutions; further, the Islamic movement must and can take power as soon as it is morally and numerically strong enough, not only to destroy the existing non-Islamic power but to build up a new Islamic order." Izetbegovic wrote his declaration during one of Tito's intensive anti-religious campaigns. He was jailed for his statements.

No crime has been perpetrated against the Bosnian-Serbs that could justify their rape of Bosnia. President Bush dismissed the crisis in Bosnia as a "mere hiccup" in July, 1992, one month after the UNHCR had said that the conflict had created 2.2 million refugees. Bush's cynical quote ranks with one of Clinton's from early 1993 regarding Bosnia: "I don't have to spend one more minute on that than I have to."

The Western powers sanctimoniously responded to the carnage in Bosnia-Herzegovina by refusing to defend the Muslims or arm them for self-defense. The West banned Serbian air flights over Bosnia, but didn't enforce the ban during crucial moments. The West would neither offer asylum, nor establish safe havens for refugees. The powers placed sanctions on Serbia, yet wouldn't enforce them. The Croats and Muslims did their best not to be mislead by the West's pattern of contradictory measures and actions. They were defending their homes and couldn't afford to be discouraged by inconsistency.

The Croats were initially unable to defend themselves and lost one-third of their country. When the they finally stemmed further Serbian advances, the conflict spilled over into Bosnia-Herzegovina. The Bosnian government rolled over and played dead. Had the Bosnian-Croats not fought back against the Serbs, all of Bosnia, instead of just two-thirds of its land mass, would've ended up in Serbian hands.

The leaders of the Bosnian-Croat communities pleaded with Izetbegovic to take a firm stand against the JNA and Serbian irregular attacks on Croatian towns in the region of Herzegovina. Izetbegovic ignored their pleas and opted, instead, to placate the JNA by dismissing the attacks as isolated examples of Serbian and Croatian extremism. Even after he understood that the Serbs were perpetrating aggressive acts against his constituents, Izetbegovic refused to enter into a loose confederation with Croatia that would've legitimized and facilitated military cooperation against the aggressors. Izetbegovic didn't want to anger the Serbs, so he actively negotiated with the JNA to assume a military role in Bosnia-Herzegovina. When Izetbegovic realized that the JNA's interests lay with Serbia and not with the Bosnian government, he inexplicably appointed high ranking JNA officers to the high command in the Bosnian Army. Naming former JNA officers such as Sefer Hailovic and Refik Lendo, who had committed atrocities against Croats in Vukovar and elsewhere, was an obvious slap in the face to Izetbegovic's Croatian constituency.

Izetbegovic's actions made the Bosnian-Croats feel insecure about their status under his government and suspicious about his intentions. The alliance between the Bosnian-Croats and Muslims had been fragile at best. But all cooperation fell apart when the Vance-Owen proposal to partition Bosnia along ethnic lines was accepted by the Croats. Most Croats had never dreamed that they might receive their own part of Bosnia. So the Croats signed the agreement without hesitation when the U.N. offered them independent territory. The Bosnian-Croats then set about expelling Muslims, often brutally, from villages that were suddenly living on U.N.-mandated Croatian property. Muslims in other parts of Bosnia grew angry and responded by expelling Croats from their regions.

After losing every military encounter with the Serbs, the Bosnian government forces retreated from the battle lines along with great numbers of Muslim refugees. Because his relationship with the Croats had completely broken down, Izetbegovic turned his defeated army toward easier pickings than the Serbs: poorly armed Bosnian-Croat civilians. Izetbegovic had been close to signing the U. N. peace agreements that divided up Bosnia, but once his troops had scored unexpected successes against the Croats, he stonewalled the U.N. proposals. Although both sides had a paucity of weapons, the weapons in government forces' hands far exceeded those in the possession of the Croats. As a consequence, the Muslims captured 3,647 square kilometers of territory previously held by the Bosnian-Croats and wanted more. In another of the dichotomies that characterized this conflict, both Croats and Muslims used Serbian firepower against each other whenever they thought it militarily advantageous. The Serbs' rent-an-artillery did not discriminate and charged either side 2,000 German marks per hour.

The media focused all its attention on the Muslims' plight in Sarajevo, Zepa, Srebrenica, and Gorazde, but rarely mentioned the Bosnian-Croat towns of Konjic, Jablanica, Travnik, Bugojno, and Gornji Vakuf where Bosnian forces had perpetrated the same sort of atrocities that the Muslims had been subjected to by the Serbs. The highest percentage of casualties from fighting in Bosnia-Herzegovina belongs to the Croats. Almost half became refugees or displaced persons. But most of the casualties came after April 16, 1993, when the Muslims launched their attack on the Bosnian-Croats. By November, 1993, the Muslims ethnically cleansed 156 Bosnian-Croat towns and villages. The huge influx of Muslim refugees into what had been predominantly Croatian areas severely changed the demographics. These great shifts of populations have become the seminal cause of animosity between Croats and Muslims, particularly in Mostar.

Although weak at first, the Bosnian government eventually redeemed itself militarily. Their defenses stiffened significantly enough to forestall a complete Serbian takeover. Once their military forces became coordinated and obtained desperately needed weapons, the Bosnian Army retook a great deal of territory. Most of their progress came while allied with the Croatian Army.

When Western realpolitik goals changed from a just settlement to just any settlement, the Bosnian demoralization was complete. The Western powers accepted the concept of partitioning Bosnia-Herzegovina along ethnic lines despite their recognition of Bosnia's sovereignty. The U.N.-created Muslim safe havens in Gorazde, Srebrenica, Zepa, and Bihac weren't safe at all because the cities were completely surrounded by Serbian forces. After the Serbs blockaded the supply routes, the inhabitants of the safe areas began to starve. Despite having created these ghettos, the U.N. felt no moral obligation to protect them and remained inert. The U.S. overruled its allies and unilaterally decided to provide food and medical air drops. But reports from Zepa and Gorazde indicated that most of the parachuted supplies had landed in either the Drina River or Serbian held territory.

Despite Belgrade's shallow pretense to the contrary, the JNA had complete control over the Bosnian-Serb aggression. Only an intact and functioning JNA command structure with its high level of logistic support could've coordinated the Bosnian-Serb artillery and aircraft attacks. The millions of refugees and at least 250,000 dead are testimony to the efficiency of Serbian attacks.

As early as October 28, 1992, U.N. Human Rights Investigator Tadeusz Mazowiecki said, "Serbian ethnic cleansing did not appear to be the consequence of the war but rather its goal, to a large extent already achieved." Mazowiecki's investigations, which most often incriminated the Serbs, were exercises in futility. So when his reports of "horrible crimes and barbarism" committed by Bosnian-Serbs after the fall of Srebrenica and Zepa went for naught, he resigned in protest. Mazowiecki had unimpeachable credentials. But he beat his head against the wall trying to move the U.N. out of its inertia regarding war crimes. His resignation statement best summarized the failed U.N. policy in Bosnia: "I cannot continue to participate in the pretense of the protection of human rights." The Serbs also ethnically cleansed Vojvodina of Hungarians and Kosovo of Albanians with minimum publicity.

The Bosnians gave up waiting for Clinton to fulfill his inaugural promise to use military force in Bosnia when "the will and conscience of the international community is defied." Apparently Clinton didn't consider the Serbian defiance severe enough until 3 1/2 years later when he ordered air attacks on Serbian positions.

According to a March, 1994, UNHCR report, an estimated 4.3 million people throughout former Yugoslavia were in need of relief assistance. Of this total, 3.5 million were classified as refugees or displaced persons: 2.74 million in Bosnia-Herzegovina, 690,000 in Croatia, 406,000 in Serbia, 110,000 in U.N. Protected Areas (UNPA), 62,000 in Montenegro, 30,000 in Slovenia, and 22,000 in Macedonia.

Of the 690,000 displaced persons who found refuge in Croatia, 280,000 were Bosnian-Muslims. U.S. Ambassador to Croatia Peter Galbraith tried to put the amount of Muslim refugees in Croatia into proper perspective in a November 8, 1993, *Matica* interview. He said the situation would be the equivalent of the U.S. taking in 30,000,000 refugees.

To salve its conscience, the U.N. instituted a humanitarian aid program so the Muslims could die with full bellies. This change in policy came relatively late and only in response to NGO pressure. NGOs were the humanitarian organizations that supplied and delivered medicines and food to disaster areas, often at great bodily risk. The U.N. underplayed the plight of the Muslims who had been herded into ghettos and placed almost insurmountable barriers on the NGOs that wanted to provide a modicum of comfort. Because Serbian barricades made bringing supplies by land difficult, the NGOs requested air drops. Their requests fell on deaf ears until their tenaciousness eventually willed out.

Most donations came from individuals or organizations that were moved by the sorry plight of the victims. Reports from the UNHCR clearly revealed that the Muslim ghettos received the least amount of that donated aid. The lion's share had to be given to Serbian forces as tribute for allowing the delivery. Almost from the very onset of humanitarian deliveries to Sarajevo, more than one-half was taken by the Serbs. Even more was stolen through distribution channels. Prior to the Dayton Accords, only about 30% of the aid made it to the Sarajevans. The confiscated food relief was sold on the black market for foreign currency. And almost invariably U.N. forces were involved in this illegal trade.

In what may have simply been a Freudian slip by the humanitarians, or a jaded twist on ethnic cleansing, a relief plane with a cargo hold full of condoms landed at Sarajevo's airport at a time when no bread was available. Many reports complained about medications that were long outdated. Medications in one shipment meant for the mosque in Zagreb had an expiration date of 1947.

Most of the Bosnian aid was delivered to the Serbian-conquered, ethnically cleansed territories. A comparison between the Muslim enclave of Bihac and Serb-controlled Banja Luka typifies the way the U.N. dispensed humanitarian aid. Carole Hodge reported in a January, 1994, *New Republic* article that the UNHCR documented an actual delivery of 2,527 metric tons of food to Banja Luka, a city whose pre-war Muslim population had been ethnically cleansed. But the targeted delivery for Banja Luka had only been 2,075 tons. The protected Muslim enclave of Bihac had received just 126 metric tons out of its 1,936 allotment during the same period.

As part of a major Serbian offensive, planes from the Serb-held Croatian airfield in Udbina struck Bihac. The U.N. acquiesced to international pressure and ordered NATO to launch a massive air attack by 39 aircraft. The West then went on a self-aggrandizement binge. But its euphoria died when the media later reported that the raid only resulted in five, easily repairable craters. Ammunition dumps and fuel stores that the Serbs would continue to use against Bihac were left intact.

When U.N. officials were confronted about why the raid was so indecisive, the officials answered that they had only intended to send a message to the Serbs. Just what message they wished to convey was unclear.

Enes Kisevic's poem, "Hava's Plea," metaphorically epitomizes the abject appeals of the Bosnian nation.

Hava's Plea

That night
when the seven of them
raped me at the camp,
I prayed for you to spit
from my womb the seed of that dog's sort,
why did you not heed my prayers, oh Lord,
when I have done you no wrong?

I prayed to You
to free me, if but an instant,
from the vigil of my captors,
so that with my fingernails
I could scrape out of my womb,

Why did you not heed my prayers, oh Lord,
when I have done you no wrong?
I turned my head from water,
I turned my head from bread,
if only death would heed my prayers,

but how could death take mercy on me
when everything rests in your hand, Almighty.

I begged those who raped me,
the ones who set my house afire,
I swore to them in Your name
that I would forgive them for all they had done
if only they would kill me,
if they would draw and quarter me;

They did not heed my plea, oh Lord,
giving me instead an apple,
feeling day and night
how their brood grew.

That morning,
when the unborn child first kicked inside,
I prayed to You
that my man Alija
not return from the battlefield;

You heeded me not, Oh Lord,
instead You had
the Militia set me free,
instead they took me to the hospital,
where four doctors held me
by my legs and my arms
so that I could not smother this child
with my thighs
whom more than the sun longed to see,
stillborn
or that it should set eyes on its
mother, dead.

Why did You not heed my prayer,
Good Lord,
when this innocent nubbin,
and I,
have done you no wrong?
Give me strength,
oh Dear God,
to raise this male child,
whom no one but You
would spare,
and grace the boy with the mercy
to live among people and with
their truth,
so pleads with You his wretched
mother Hava.

DAYTON: PEACE FOR OUR TIME?

DAYTON: PEACE FOR OUR TIME?

The hand that signed the paper felled a city;
Five sovereign fingers taxed the breath;
Doubled the globe of death and halved a country;
These five kings did a king to death.

. . .

The five kings count the dead but do not soften
The crusted wound nor pat the brow;
A hand rules pity as a hand rules heaven;
Hands have no tears to flow.
The Hand that Signed the Paper Felled a City
———*Dylan Thomas*

Aside from dashing British and French hopes for a Serbian victory, the unexpected Croatian triumph in the Krajina unequivocally changed the military and political equilibrium in Bosnia-Herzegovina. If the Croats hadn't liberated the Krajina, Bihac would have met the same fate as Srebrenica and Zepa.

The Croatian-Bosnian military alliance reclaimed 20% of Bosnian territory from the Serbs that the Western powers had been unable to wrest through diplomatic means. Just as the alliance was at the brink of defeating the Serbs, the Western powers, especially Britian, placed tremendous pressure on Croatia to desist in the Bosnian campaign. Once the Croats had disengaged, the Bosnian army couldn't sustain the momentum alone and suffered defeats.

The Serbs had already seized 70% of Bosnian territory and had no reason to accept the Contact Group's offer of 51%. When the successful Croatian-Bosnian offensive changed the balance of power, the Serbs, fearful that the alliance would retake even more territory, suddenly changed their minds and accepted the offer.

By successfully recovering all but 4.5% of its territory and rescuing Western Bosnia, the Croats had inadvertently influenced politics in the United States. Because Bosnia had disappeared from the front pages, President Clinton could concentrate on policies that helped his 1996 reelection campaign. So Clinton pressured the Bosnian government to join in peace negotiations with Croatian and Serbian leaders at Dayton, Ohio. The West's indifferent reaction to the savage aftermath of Zepa and Srebrenica had a sobering effect on the Bosnian government. Izetbegovic woke up to reality and accepted the fact that the Bosnians had to take whatever peace settlement was offered to them.

In the October 12, 1992, presidential debate, Clinton called for air strikes and an end to the arms embargo. Although Clinton took 3 1/2 years to initiate the first, he effectively sabotaged the second. Bush's policy of inaction had found its rationale in the information he was fed by Belgrade's cabal in the U.S. government. But the reason why Clinton continued Bush's policies remains mysterious. The only gesture the Bush administration made to help non-Serbian victims came when it created a no-fly zone. But that step was simply a reaction to criticism from the Clinton campaign. Once in office, the Clinton administration consistently articulated that it wanted to preserve the integrity of an indivisible Bosnian state, rightly condemning partition as a reward for ethnic cleansing. But at Dayton the administration forced kafkaesque surrender terms on the Bosnian government and therefore actually accepted Serbian gains.

Even though the Dayton Accords are loaded with absurdities that decimate Bosnia's sovereignty, the treaty did stop the rampant slaughter of non-Serbs in Bosnia. The Clinton administration's efforts have put the mayhem temporarily on hold, at least until after the American presidential elections. To this end Clinton sent American troops to Bosnia-Herzegovina. Ostensibly the troops were supposed to be home by Christmas 1996, but given the realities of Dayton they will, most likely, come home when they cross Clinton's metaphorical bridge in the next century. Many have said that sending American troops to Bosnia was a political time bomb for Clinton. But Clinton will reap political rewards as long as there are no body bags. American casualties are unlikely because Clinton placed enormous pressure on all the protagonists to adhere to his game plan. Clinton may be many things, but he's no fool. Although the Dayton Accords don't promise much of a future for Bosnia, they've certainly helped Clinton's political future.

The behavior of Brigadier General Patrick O'Neal and Colonel Gregory Fontenot, as reported in the *Wall Street Journal* (Dec. 12, 1995), may reflect Clinton's true attitude toward Bosnia-Herzegovina and prejudice toward the Croats because O'Neal and Fontenot are products of war colleges, extensive briefings, and Clinton's foreign policies. When O'Neal's troops crossed an international border into Bosnia, a local militiaman had the temerity to ask for passports and blocked their way. The American general pointed at one of his soldiers' M-16 automatic rifles and said, "That's our passport." His next logical statement might have been: "Shoot first and ask questions later." O'Neal's bravado was more appropriate for a successful invasion force than for one engaged in implementing a peace accord.

In the same article, Colonel Fontenot was quoted ordering his troops to adopt a cocky posture during a pre-mission briefing. To illustrate, he had one of his sergeants sling a light machine gun across his chest. "It's the casual, yet 'I'll kick your a__ if you f__ with me' look," the colonel said. He then turned to two African-American soldiers who would be part of his convoy. "It'll be interesting to hear what you two see, because the Croatians are racist," he warned them. "They kill people for the color of their skins."

Since Fontenot most recently taught at the Fort Levenworth School of Advanced Military Studies, the U.S. Army's most elite war college, this prejudicial remark probably reflects current official military doctrine.

The Dayton Accords have essentially partitioned Bosnia along ethnic lines and rewarded Serbia by lifting the sanctions. Instead of condemning the consequences of ethnic cleansing, the accords codify them. The U.S. has rewarded the use of genocide, rape, and mayhem by consolidating Serbian gains and ordering U.S. troops to patrol Greater Serbia's borders.

The accords promise refugees the ability to return to their homes without risk of harassment, intimidation, persecution, or discrimination—particularly in regard to their ethnic origin. But the promises are empty. Even if the refugees are allowed to return, it's highly likely that their former homes which may have survived the battles will be blown up before they have a chance to resettle. But justifiable fear will hold most back. The same Serbian "police" and thugs that ethnically cleansed whole towns and villages will remain in control of those areas. No provision in the accords assures the refugees' safety. Besides, most repatriates would only find heaps of rubble where their homes had once stood. All infrastructure and institutions needed to ensure civility have been destroyed.

With no agricultural production or housing available to them, the refugees will most likely have to be placed in ghettos or, more accurately, concentration camps. Refugee centers typically lack schools, hospitals, or civil administrations and are prey to epidemics. Under such conditions, refugees suffer the humiliation of an aimless existence and total dependence on humanitarian aid. The West shouldn't be surprised when the next Bosnian generation, if there is one, matures into a band of terrorists. The surviving Muslim children won't forget the dead or how those in the West watched while their fathers were wounded or killed, and their mothers and sisters raped. Despite the fact that Bosnians are the most secularized Muslims in the Islamic world, such camps will become fertile breeding grounds for fundamentalism.

Although the Bosnians continue to place trust in the Clinton administration's nebulous gentlemen's agreement to arm and train its army, the accords make absolutely no reference to arming anyone. Given the past performance of these "gentlemen," the Bosnians will be awfully naive if they choose to believe in them now.

The Dayton Accords also call for a general disarmament. The Serbian forces, who had most of the arms anyway, will retain 85% of their pre-Dayton level, while the Bosnian Army will lose 87.5% of its weapons. The Serbs couldn't have received a sweeter deal.

The Dayton Accords seem more and more curious the longer they're analyzed. The agreement may have sounded the death knell for the Bosnian state because when Bosnia accepted Article II, "the rights and freedoms set forth in The European Convention for the Protection of Human Rights and Fundamental Freedoms shall have priority over *all* other laws," it surrendered its sovereignty. The new Bosnian Constitutional Court will have nine justices, two from each ethnic group (Muslim, Croat, and Serb) and three appointed by the European Court of Human Rights. But the foreign judges' authority will supersede that of the local judges. In a March 4, 1996 *Insight* article, Duncan Hunter, chairman of the House National Security Subcommittee on Military Procurement, concluded that the U.N. appointed high representative will be the real government in Bosnia.

All stipulations indicate that Bosnia will be a U.N. Protectorate. A U.N. appointee will monitor the peace settlement, promote compliance by local authorities, and coordinate the activities of all civilian organizations and agencies involved in rebuilding Bosnia. The high representative will give guidance to a U.N. international police task force charged with advising, training, monitoring and inspecting *all* law enforcement activities and facilities, including associated judicial organizations. In the rare instances when the new central Bosnian government arrives at a decision without input from non-Bosnian sources, the government's decision can be vetoed by any of the other parties. This condition isn't very conducive to governance because any law that doesn't accommodate the Serbs will be thrown out.

Although the Dayton Accords granted IFOR (the NATO Implementation Force in Bosnia) virtually complete discretion to take police action, IFOR is neither obliged to do so, nor does it have guidelines to conduct such actions. IFOR has been given the task of creating conditions for free and fair elections, assisting humanitarian organizations, controlling all Bosnian airspace, clearing the roads of mines, and observing and preventing interference with the movement of civilian populations, refugees, and displaced persons. But IFOR has neither the mechanism to implement, nor the means to enforce these mandates. The accords stipulate an international police force, but the force's only real mandate is to train.

Human rights monitors were wrong when they stated that 1992 will go down in history as the year the Muslims of Bosnia were extinguished. Their estimate was premature. Nevertheless, the future looks bleak for the Muslims under the Dayton Accords because the treaty represents a peace only the West can live with.

The Dayton Accords are rife with contradictions. One provision calls for general elections among Bosnian citizens based upon where they had registered in 1991. This provision sounds good because it will allow the people who fled a chance to vote. But Serbian officials are now arguing that voters should be limited to the people presently residing in Bosnia. Adding to the controversy, those responsible for the balloting have sent forms printed in English to the Bosnians. The West's history of pro-Serbian efforts makes this mistake suspicious. Refugees desiring to vote are faced with another dilemma that has far reaching consequences for their well being. If the several hundred thousand Muslim refugees now living in Germany do vote, they may lose their refugee status and be expelled.

The Western nations have failed to understand the importance the Muslims place on pursuing and prosecuting war criminals. For Muslims, justice is the very foundation for reconciliation. Bosnian Ambassador to the United States Sven Alkalij has said to me on a number of occasions, "Justice first, then talk about reconciliation." Unanswered injustices, both real and perceived, may result in future conflicts. For any healing process to occur, those responsible must be tried for their crimes against humanity. Bosnian Ambassador to the U.N. Muhamed Sarcibey said, "[peace] will fail if the war trials tribunal is not supported and does not bring about at least a minimum level of justice."

Bosnian survivors felt encouraged when the U.N. finally set up the International Criminal Tribunal for the Former Yugoslavia in 1993. Although the tribunal has no power to arrest criminals, it offers the prospect of accountability to the perpetrators of murder, rape and havoc. But what the U.N. gives, the U.N. also takes away. In early 1994, the U.N. announced that it would disband the War Crimes Commission, the tribunal evidentiary body, for political expediency. The U.N. most likely emasculated the tribunal in order to avoid complicating the peace process.

The U.N. had intended for the International Criminal Tribunal to remain only symbolic. But the tribunal took on a life of its own under the guidance of its Chief Justice, Richard Goldstone. His tenacity to seek the truth has surprisingly legitimized the judicial body.

While Goldstone's unexpected tough attitude lent a great deal of credibility for the proceedings, the tribunal's numerous breaches has raised a number of questions. Despite voluminous evidence, only three JNA officers were charged for committing war crimes in Croatia and no Bosnian Muslim has been charged for similar acts in the Muslim-Croat fighting.

During the trial of accused Serbian war criminal Dusan Tadic, the tribunal postponed its proceedings for six months because the defense blamed NATO bombing for halting its search for witnesses in Bosnia-Herzegovina. The trial was supposed to have begun in November, 1995, but didn't actually commence until May, 1996.

Since Tadic's arrest, 56 other war criminals have been formally accused. But as usual, the media has used a double standard in its coverage of accused Croats and Serbs. The press has sharply criticized Croatia for not turning over accused Croatian General Tihomir Blaskic to the Hague, but has been loath to criticize and exhort Serbia for not turning over criminal master planners Karadzic and Mladic. What the press apparently failed to understand in the Blaskic case was that legal procedures had to be followed before anyone could be extradited from Croatia. Croatia had no law on its books to implement the Hague's request. Once the legal questions were resolved, Blaskic voluntarily turned himself in.

The U.N. has made a number of colossal errors in judgment since the beginning of the conflict. Under the guidance of Boutros Boutrous-Ghali, the U.N. saw the conflict as a civil war and relegated itself to the role of a supposedly impartial peacekeeper. But the U.N. proved entirely ineffective even in this limited capacity.

Despite the fact that Bosnia-Herzegovina was a duly recognized sovereign nation, the U.N.-imposed arms embargo prevented Bosnia from doing what all states have a legitimate right to do— defend itself against transborder aggression. The arms embargo helped prolong this conflict even more than France and England's tacit complicity with the Serbs or the anemia of the international media. The aggressors had all the weapons of modern warfare at their disposal and the victims had few. But the West's argument, particularly Britain's, that an end to the arms embargo would've increased the violence and caused the Serbs to accelerate their aggression, is only partly valid. Until 1995, the Serbs had held back nothing and yet were relatively free of casualties. The lifting of the arms embargo would've increased the Croats and Bosnians' ability to defend themselves, so any post-embargo increase in violence would've resulted in reduced Croatian and Bosnian casualties and increased Serbian casualties. The effectiveness of the Croatian-Bosnian offensive after the receipt of illicit arms proves the point.

The U.N. was loathe to express any sort of outrage when Serbia clearly attacked another sovereign state across international borders. Britain, France, the United States, and Russia failed to act decisively. In the process, the major powers battered a host of fundamental international agreements including the U.N. Charter, the Geneva Conventions, the Universal Declaration of Human Rights, as well as some basic values like the rule of law, inviolability of borders, and safety of innocent civilians.

According to a CIA report on Bosnia, "More than half of the prewar population of 4,365,000 has either fled the country, been displaced within the country, or been killed." After absorbing 272,000 displaced persons from Serbian- occupied Croatia and 640,000 Bosnian refugees in November, 1992, Croatia informed international bodies that it wouldn't be able to admit more Bosnians. Typically, France and Britain, who had taken 3,000 refugees between them, and the United States, who had magnanimously offered to accept 1,000, sharply criticized the Croatian government for its action. Further illustrating blatant Western hypocrisy, in November, 1993, the *Independent* exposed a secret pact among the European Union member states barring Bosnian refugees.

U.N. peace negotiator and former director of Kissinger and Associates Peter Carrington set a precedent when he all but ignored the only legitimate parties in the war, the governments; and instead negotiated with illegitimate parties, the warring factions. All the Western leaders parroted Serbian propaganda by calling the conflict a civil war between ancient ethnic rivals in which all sides were guilty.

Most perversely, the West blamed the victims. As the Serbians wished, the West didn't take sides and played the role of supposedly impartial peacekeepers. The West preferred Yugoslav unity and made it clear to the Belgrade regime that no Western military would intervene.

The West, the U.S. in particular, must share the blame for allowing the conflict to expand and the slaughter to continue. For example, at the same time American reconnaissance planes were photographing mass graves in Srebrenica, Washington officials were seeking to rehabilitate the image of Serbian President Milosevic.

Whenever the Muslims were victorious against the Serbs, the Western powers protested via the media. More vitriolic threats were lodged by U.N. officials against the Muslims for even the most token advances than were ever made against the Serbs for their overt atrocities. U.N. observers went to great lengths to report that Muslims had mutilated Serbian prisoners, while later reports proved that the incidents never happened.

The West's role ultimately proved either counter-productive or abetted the Serbian position. Any proposal that could've been meaningful came too late.

The breakup of Yugoslavia exposed the fallacy that European security can exist without U.S. leadership and intervention. Due to this conflict, the U.S. has had to bail out the Europeans from their follies for the third time this century.

The West preferred to rely on peace negotiations and peacekeepers to end the conflict rather than allow the non-Serbs to freely defend themselves. Surely the Croats and Muslims would've chosen to defend themselves if they had ever been given the choice.

Europe must now look inward and see that it has a vested interest in helping to rebuild the infrastructure of Croatia and Bosnia-Herzegovina. Europe, particularly Croatia, has been inundated with refugees. As of September, 1992, according to the United Nations High Commissioner for Refugees, Germany has taken 220,000 refugees, Switzerland 70,520, Austria 57,000, Hungary 50,000, and Sweden 47,000.

The Muslims will be the big losers regardless of the final outcome of the Dayton Accords. The only viable option for the Muslims is to put their differences with the Croats aside and cement the historically friendly Muslim-Croat relationship. Such an action would go a long way in helping both groups overcome the harshest vicissitudes they've endured together on bloody Balkan soil.

Instead of cooperating, the Muslims set a dangerous precedent. No sooner was the ink dry on the Dayton Accords, when they began purging Croats from positions of trust in the infrastructure of the military, government, economy, and education. For example, Sarajevo's medical school not only has discontinued to accept Croatian students they have expelled those already enrolled. Consequently, the Croats are now in the process of establishing a medical school in Mostar, which will drive an even deeper wedge between them.

But it isn't only the Croats being discriminated against, Muslims adhering to the pre-war mores of Bosnian society are also being ostracized. Muslim fundamentalism has reared its head in the Bosnian government's hierarchy. Although it isn't as serious as it is in Afghanistan there've been numerous reported incidents of imposing fundamental standards on Bosnian Muslims by coercion.

If the Croats and Muslims don't come to some sort of rapprochement, it's a certainty that as soon as the ground becomes frozen enough so tanks can maneuver the Croats and Muslims will be each others throats, especially in the Mostar area. The Serbs will probably keep out of it, but will occasionally lob a few shells to let them know they're still around. A healthy Muslim-Bosnian-Croat alliance loosely confederated with Croatia would benefit everyone.

The West has been shamelessly reluctant to call ethnic cleansing genocide despite the Serbian actions' fulfillment of the tribunal's definition: acts committed with intent to destroy, in whole or in part, a national, ethnic, racial, or religious group. Instead, the West has elected to treat the genocide of the Muslims with the same blindness it applied for decades to Stalin's murder of over 20 million Russians, Poles, Balts and others. As has happened with Stalin, perhaps some would-be historians will even come to question whether the Muslim genocide really took place. Hitler and Stalin used similar methods, mass murder and concentration camps, but Stalin killed twice as many. Yet Stalin sat at the negotiating table as a man of honor in much the same way that those responsible for similar crimes in Bosnia do now. The end result of the conflict in Bosnia clearly signals the victory of Byzantine deviousness over Western Machiavellianism.

The Balkan conflict between the Orthodox Serbs and Roman Catholic Croats resulted in the Muslims of Bosnia being squeezed out of Europe. A number of commentators and opinion editors have speculated that the reason why the West could stand by and watch the rape of Bosnia without getting emotional was because the victims were Muslims. In his last book, *Beyond Peace*, Richard Nixon argued that if the Bosnians had been Christians or Jews, Europe would've intervened. Instead, during the first half of the 1990s, the European Community was a passive collaborator in the Serbian attempt to purge the last remnants of the Ottoman Empire from Europe.

The crisis in former Yugoslavia was brought on mainly by the West's inability to deal with the collapse of Communism. The masses have suffered the consequences of the West's failure. But even at this late stage, if, by the illumination of the facts, Western humanism can inject a level of justice into this rather hopeless situation then the effort will be worth it. For the West must keep in mind that although the surviving victims of war and injustice suffer, they never suffer from amnesia.